PSI and the
CONSCIOUSNESS EXPLOSION

STUART HOLROYD

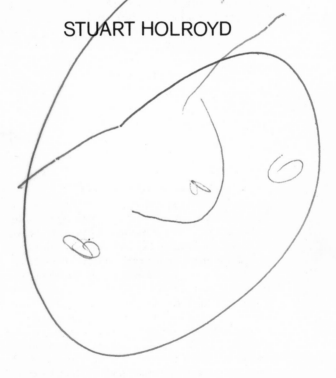

Taplinger Publishing Company | New York

ASBURY PARK PUBLIC LIBRARY
ASBURY PARK, NEW JERSEY

First published in the United States in 1977 by
TAPLINGER PUBLISHING CO., INC.
New York, New York

All rights reserved. Printed in the U.S.A.
Copyright © 1977 by Stuart Holroyd

No part of this book may be reproduced or transmitted in any form or by any
means, electronic or mechanical, including photocopy, recording, or any information storage and retrieval system now known or to be invented, without permission
in writing from the publisher, except by a reviewer who wishes to quote brief
passages for inclusion in a magazine, newspaper, or broadcast.

Library of Congress Cataloging in Publication Data

Holroyd, Stuart.
Psi and the consciousness explosion.

Bibliography: p.   Includes index.
1. Psychical research. I. Title.
BF1031.H648   133.8   76-12188
ISBN 0-8008-6556-1

ACKNOWLEDGMENTS

Reference credits are given in the notes at the end of
the book. My thanks are due to Dr Charles Honorton
of the Division of Parapsychology and Psychophysics of
the Maimonides Medical Center, Brooklyn, for a passing conversational remark which planted the seed that
was to germinate into this book; to Professor John
Hasted of the Department of Physics, Birkbeck
College, London, and Dr John Beloff of the Department of Psychology, University of Edinburgh, for
reading and commenting on the manuscript; and to
Dr Eric Dingwall, the doyen of psychical researchers
and the scourge of parapsychologists, who, although he
declined to read it, is always the impish and sceptical
reader over my shoulder when I write about the
fascinating and treacherous subject of psi.

TO FRED BALL
in appreciation
of his work
his criticism
and his friendship

CONTENTS

INTRODUCTION

The New Gnosis

Introduction
The New Gnosis

Technology has given us two awesome images: the mushroom cloud of the atomic explosion and the slow and graceful lift-off of the space rocket. They're in all our minds, these images of explosion and exploration. Film-makers or advertisers use them to trigger feelings of awe, of terror, of triumph or of doom. Like all potent images they're ambiguous. They symbolise power, transcendence, man's conquest of space and of the forces of nature. Depending on your point of view, they may stand for the height of human achievement or of human folly, the triumph or the nemesis of technology.

In the 1970s these images of explosion and exploration have taken on a significance unforeseen in the '50s and '60s. A 'consciousness explosion' has been taking place in the Western world, and exploration has shifted, in the words of astronaut Edgar Mitchell, 'from outer space to inner space'.[1] It was Mitchell who, in the course of the last moon shot, the Apollo 14 flight of February 1971, conducted an unofficial ESP test, trying to send telepathic messages from the spacecraft to four receivers back on earth. So man's last venture into outer space was remembered by some for one man's effort to probe one remaining area of mystery, the human mind. It was remembered by others for an attempt one of Mitchell's colleagues made to strike a golf-ball across the surface of the moon. The difference between these two unscheduled events nicely reflects the difference between the mentality of the age that was going out and that of the new age that was dawning in the early '70s.

The 'consciousness explosion' has taken the form of a chain-reaction quite as terrifying in some ways as the beautiful and menacing mushroom cloud of the atomic bomb. Wave after wave of occultism and mysticism has swept over Western Europe and America in a tide that shows no signs of abating. The psychic and ideological foundations of Western man and his society have been devastated. There are those who see this as the beginning of the end, who compare this time with the collapse of the Pax Romana in the second and third centuries, when men sought through mysticism, magic and occultism in all its forms to establish an inner world of purpose, power and coherence to compensate for the chaos and desolation of the world around them. Others read the signs more optimistically, speak of the incoming 'Age of Aquarius', of the formation of a new image of man and of society, and contemplate chaos with equanimity, for they see in it the burgeoning seeds of a new order. Who is right? It's impossible to say at this stage, but one certainty is that the hopes of the optimists will not be realised by enthusiasm alone. Reason, intelligence, judgement and sustained thinking may be regarded as attributes of superannuated man, but so to regard them, and consequently to reject them, is a strategy that can lead nowhere but to a disastrous psychosis.

In the new age that our optimists foresee, faculties that have been fettered and inhibited by the rigid orthodoxies of the bourgeois lifestyle and the materialistic values that sustain it will freely flourish. Creativity, mystical experience, telepathic communication, psychic healing—to mention but a few of the boons with which the new man will be endowed—will enrich both the individual life and interpersonal relations. It's an alluring vision, and really not too far-fetched, for after all these things enhance life for many people now and always have done. But the question is, how will these faculties be cultivated? They are faculties of the deepest and richest stratum of man's being, and if they are trivialised, commercialised or sensationalised the new age is going to be a pretty shoddy sort of Utopia. A world in which the high-powered executive can allay existential anxiety and get quick sustenance for the spirit by availing himself of technological or pharmacological short cuts to mysticism is hardly an ideal to live for, let alone die for.

This is a personal opinion. And this is going to be an opinionated book, a survey and a discussion from a personal point of view of the scope and the implications of the consciousness movement, or 'counter culture', which is a social phenomenon of our day, and its allied experimental science, parapsychology, or psi research,* which

---

* The Greek letter *psi* (silent p, long i) is generally used today to designate collectively paranormal events and/or faculties. Used both substantively and adjectivally, it is interchangeable with the older terms 'psychic' and 'psychical' and the more recent 'parapsychological'.

is concerned with the study of non-ordinary states of consciousness and mental faculties and with paranormal interactions between man and his environment. There are, I believe, signs that warrant a cautious optimism. There is a tendency among many people today, particularly the young, to be oriented towards personal growth, interpersonal caring and understanding, non-material satisfactions and harmony with nature and natural processes: an orientation that balances subjective satisfactions with objective responsibilities. This is no new departure for human nature, but the widespread prevalence of such an orientation could herald a new departure for human society. Such a change could hardly have been hoped for in the late 1950s, when in his influential book, *The Lonely Crowd*, the sociologist David Riesmann distinguished between the 'inner directed' and the 'other directed' type of man and demonstrated that the latter was not only the predominant but pretty well the universal type in the society of the day. Then we were all Jonahs, castigating 'Corporation Man' and 'Economic Man' and gloomily predicting that civilisation would die of the inanity and superficiality of its purposes, collapse in ruins owing to the depredations of what Toynbee called the 'inner barbarians'. The foreseen collapse didn't happen, and to his surprise and no doubt bewilderment Economic Man fathered a type that rejected his values, his life-style and loyalties and sought alternatives in a 'counter culture'. This fundamental change, this reorientation of ideals and purposes, is one of the signs that warrants a cautious optimism.

There are other and less encouraging signs, however. I have before me a catalogue that carries some advertising that I find singularly depressing to contemplate.[2] The publishers of a book entitled *Executive ESP* claim that 'research proves' that 'people rise to the top of the business ladder' partly by employing extrasensory perception in decision-making, and add for good measure that *Executive ESP* is 'also a guide-book to letting your own hunches pay off for you in every area of life'. This updated Dale Carnegie programme fills me with horror. The slick salesman or the devious executive with ESP added to his armoury of wiles is surely a type of Future Man that we can do without.

And what about 'Biofeedback is for Everyone' as an advertising slogan? For just $140 you can buy a Biofeedback Monitor 'with brainwave, skin resistance, and heartbeat monitoring capabilities in one package'. This toy will enable you to attend to, and, with training, control internal physiological processes that you are normally unconscious of. If you can learn to produce alpha brain rhythms at will, which an advertiser says takes eight to ten hours in most cases, you may expect 'a sense of relaxed wakefulness, with increased memory ability and dramatically improved concentration'. From the voluntary production of theta brain rhythms you may be rewarded with 'psychic experiences' and the enhancement of creative processes. The message rings out clear: heaven is within, paradise is now (or at the most ten hours away) and for minimal expense and effort anyone can sample the ecstatic transports of the mystic, the poet or the psychic. You don't have to be an old-fashioned elitist to find this kind of trivialisation of the spiritual repugnant. Biofeedback research is exciting. It is an investigative technique, made possible by recent developments in electronics, for amplifying physiological signals and thus enabling a subject to control physiological processes. It has been found that certain of these physiological processes are associated with psychological states, but research into these correspondences is by no means complete and it is certainly premature for biofeedback to come out of the laboratory into the market-place, particularly if fanfared as a nostrum for modern man's psychic malcontent.

I shall have more to say about biofeedback in a later chapter, but to emphasise my warning about its premature commercial exploitation here is Dr Elmer Green, pioneer researcher in the field, addressing a meeting of professional colleagues: 'In each instance the use of the biofeedback instrument is stopped when the method is learned and the practice in self-regulation is continued without it. In other words, the instrument is only a tool to teach the possibility and method of self-regulation; it is not allowed to become a crutch.'[3] No advertiser of biofeedback instruments alludes to the ephemerality of the usefulness of his wares; some even offer two-year warranties. For of course nobody wants to pay $140 or more for a crutch.

Playing around with your brainwaves is a fairly harmless kind of onanism and it is not going to turn anyone blind or mad. But there are more potentially dangerous forms of exploitation of that longing for growth, for expansion of consciousness, for transcendence of mere self, for a sense of 'at-oneness' with others, with nature, with the cosmos and with the divine, which was formerly regarded as a God-given human faculty. 'You are Psychic!' declares an advertiser, and offers for sale a 'Personal Program of Self-Development which enables YOU to learn . . . how to realise and develop your psychic potential . . . in your own home.' Lest he should miss out on a section of the market of malcontent, he goes on: 'Maybe being psychic isn't your first goal. What *do* you want—to lose weight? Quit smoking? Make more money? More friends? Attain greater spiritual enlighten-ment? It's all part of the program. There are no limits to what you can do. Graduates of our Mind Development courses have dis-covered inner creative talents and resources, eliminated bad habits, developed ESP and clairvoyance, gained greater vitality and energy and solved their personal problems by applying techniques that they learned.'

And there's worse. Just below the above-quoted advertisement in *Psi Catalogue* is an announcement that 'You can learn ESP if you use the revolutionary RYZL method'. Milan Ryzl is a distinguished parapsychologist, renowned for his research into the training of psi faculties through hypnosis. When he was still practising in his native Prague in the mid-'6os, before he defected to the United States, parapsychologists from all over the world flew in to test the amazing Pavel Stepanek, card-guesser supreme, who had developed his powers of clairvoyance under Ryzl's tutelage. Over a period of some twenty years before he left Czechoslovakia, Ryzl tried out his psi-training programme on five hundred subjects, and on his own admission just fifty of these showed enhanced ESP ability as a result of it. This ten per cent rate of success was scientifically significant, but I imagine that purchasers of the Ryzl ESP Course would be less willing to dig into their pockets if they knew that they had no more than one chance in ten of success. The advertisement ambiguously states that the 'method was successfully tested on more than five hundred persons,' and 'Now everyone can use it!'

What the Ryzl advertisement doesn't mention is that the method involves hypnosis, which is known to be dangerous when practised by people who are unqualified or inadequately trained. Dr Elmer

Green has warned that as a result of hypnotic programming 'many people are psychically catapulted, so to speak, into existential realms in which they cannot protect themselves from dangers arising either from within their own unconscious, or from psychic manipulation by other persons, or from "extrapersonal" sources (dangers inherent in so-called "astral" dimensions).'[4] And he cites the evidence of a psychiatrist who investigated a group of people who had taken mind-training courses based on hypnosis and found that four people in one group of thirty subsequently became psychotic, two of them so seriously that they had to be hospitalised. So it would seem that a person who takes a commercial psi-training course not only has about ten per cent chance of success but roughly the same chance of going mad. Responsible parapsychologists ought not to be abetting this scandal; they ought, like Dr Green, to be vociferously campaigning against it. The exploration and development of human potentials is work of too great importance for entrepreneurs and charlatans to meddle with.

The case of Dr Ryzl clearly illustrates the relationship that exists between parapsychology and the consciousness movement, and also the anomalous and vulnerable situation of the parapsychologist in the world today. He is working in an area that a vast section of the general public is avid for information about, and, as information is a commodity, the parapsychologist has many opportunities to derive fringe benefits from his work. In these circumstances, he might well be tempted prematurely to 'leak' findings that are not yet conclusive, or even to falsify evidence in order to expedite the 'proving' of a point. Cases of such unprofessional conduct are not unknown, and they have not helped parapsychology to become scientifically respectable. Most parapsychologists would consider themselves to be scientists, but their subject overlaps so many other areas and employs such a variety of investigative methods that many of its critics have considered that it lacks at least two essential characteristics of a science: a clearly defined and delimited area of investigation and a sound, objective and repeatable experimental method. A consequence of this anomalous position of parapsychology among the sciences has been that researchers have tended to separate into two types, those who confine their work to the collection of data capable of statistical analysis and objective assessment according to the principles of probability theory, and those who collect and collate anecdotal material, investigate the powers of psychics and sensitives and all kinds of strange phenomena that fall outside the purview of mainstream science, such as poltergeist activity, hauntings, psychic healing, thought photography, out-of-the-body experiences and reincarnation. The variety of phenomena being investigated illustrates the difficulty of the would-be scientist in the field. These are the stuff of folklore and legend, of literature and ethnology, and to seek a linking principle or a theoretical model that encompasses such a hotch-potch would seem a vain endeavour. So parapsychology occupies a kind of no-man's-land between the sciences and the humanities, an area where scientists dump data they don't want or can't cope with and where writers, philosophers, poets and mystics— not to mention the egregious entrepreneurs and crank religionists— scavenge among the debris for odds and ends that may be of use to them.

The part of parapsychology that is scientific tends to be uninteresting and the part that is interesting is unscientific, at least according to the present consensus meaning of the term among physical scientists, though, as the physicist Henry Morgenau has pointed out, parapsychologists are at liberty to create their own theoretical and methodological constructs and are not obliged to adhere slavishly to those established by any other discipline.[5]

I shall have more to say about psi and science in a later chapter. For the present I just want to point out the ambiguity of the parapsychologist's position as a scientist, and to suggest that this might be a reason why he would be more inclined than colleagues in other areas to go whoring after strange gods. His subject is broad, its pedigree is dubious because the sciences and humanities—those irreconcilable 'two cultures' we heard so much about in the '50s and '60s—are coupled in it, and furthermore it is a subject that interests and concerns the man in the street, that embraces a range of hopes, fears, beliefs, superstitions and aspirations as no other subject of research does. So the parapsychologist has every opportunity to turn guru, circuit lecturer, best-selling author or con man. After decades out in the cold he has suddenly found himself in the hot seat, looked to for guidance, inspiration, empirical evidence to support all kinds of theories of man, nature and society, and for proven techniques for developing psi faculties. Like it or not, he has become a key figure in the consciousness explosion.

For a quarter of a century after J. B. Rhine published his monograph, *Extra-Sensory Perception*, in 1934, most parapsychologists throughout the world followed the pattern he had established, using ESP cards to test subjects for telepathy, clairvoyance or precognition. Precautionary methods were refined, variables brought under control, and the experimental results were subjected to increasingly sophisticated mathematical processing which turned up esoteric phenomena such as 'position effects', 'variance', 'stacking effects' and 'multiple-vote technique'. It certainly looked and sounded impressively scientific, and so far as it went it was, but it didn't go far enough. It got stuck in a rut of stereotyped method. As long ago as 1942 the Cambridge philosopher and parapsychologist Professor Robert Thouless said that enough effort had already been put into proving that ESP occurs and that it was time more attention was given to exploring its properties. But the card-guessing experiments went on, and throughout the '40s and '50s and into the '60s parapsychology remained proof-oriented rather than exploratory. Perhaps the publication of Thomas S. Kuhn's influential book, *The Structure of Scientific Revolutions*, in 1962, awakened some parapsychologists to implications of both their methods and their findings that they had not previously realised. Kuhn pointed out that in science stereotyped methods tend to produce stereotyped results. As he put it, 'The decision to employ a particular piece of apparatus and to use it in a particular way carries an assumption that only certain sorts of circumstances will arise.'[6] Card-guessing experiments had already been found to produce diminishing returns, and Kuhn's analysis suggested that the prevalence of this approach might be preventing other psi phenomena from manifesting themselves. His analysis of how scientific revolutions come about also had important implications for parapsychology. He showed that orthodox science is always conservative. It erects a framework of methodological and conceptual categories and rejects, ignores or discounts anything that cannot be fitted into it. Gradually anomalies accumulate until their combined weight collapses the framework and a scientific revolution takes place. This analysis suggested to some parapsychologists that both the fringe status of their own profession within the scientific community and the anomalous nature of the phenomena they investigated were pointers to a possibility that they might be destined to spearhead a revolution in science.

To what extent Kuhn's book has been responsible for the change in parapsychology during the last decade is impossible to say, but a change there certainly has been, a new bravura both in experimental design and theoretical speculation which would seem to indicate a gain of confidence. Parapsychology's convergence with the counter culture is not adequately explained as a case of two outcasts finding solace in each other's arms. It is a marriage of maturity and out of it could come progeny that, if intelligently and vigilantly brought up, could have a brilliant future.

It will be useful at this point to summarise briefly the points at which the interests of contemporary parapsychology and the counter culture converge to consolidate attitudes and concepts which may constitute a valuable 'new gnosis'. (*Gnosis* was the Greek word for 'knowledge', and is used in the present context with its old religious meaning of 'the knowledge that enables man to develop spiritually and thus confers salvation'.)

1. *Altered states of consciousness.* Most psi research in Europe and America was until recently conducted with subjects in normal, wakeful, states of consciousness. Rhine reported in his first book the effects of mild doses of depressant and stimulant drugs on ESP, but no significant attempts were made to alter states of consciousness in order to improve ESP performance until the late '60s (except in Russia, where officially-sanctioned experiments with hypnosis had been conducted in the '20s and '30s). The use of drugs to alter consciousness was a much-publicised feature of the counter culture of the '60s. Aldous Huxley's account of his own experiments with mescalin and LSD, *The Doors of Perception,* was doubly influential, being interpreted by some as a licence to 'freak out' but also drawing attention to the need for clinical supervision and controlled experimentation with ASCs.* Some parapsychologists conducted such

---

* The abbreviation commonly used for 'altered states of consciousness'.

experiments, but on the whole European and American researchers eschewed the use of hypnosis or drugs, inhibited no doubt by a culturally ingrained respect for the integrity of the person. However, with the development of sophisticated techniques and instruments for monitoring subtle changes in physiological and mental states, controlled experiment became possible with ASCs that do not involve induced violations of normal consciousness. Dreaming, creativity and meditation, for instance, have been intensively studied in recent years and have been found to be psi-conducive states, and at the same time the counter culture has purged some of its more violent and nihilistic impulses and tended to consolidate around a concern for inducing and exploring such mental states.

2. *A positive attitude towards the unconscious.* The Freudian model of the unconscious, with its emphasis on the pathological aspects of sexuality and fantasy and on the psychic conflict resulting from the irreconcilable demands of Superego, Ego and Id, has tremendously influenced Western man, society and arts during the present century. It has been a dubious boon, this undoubted gain in self-knowledge, for it has resulted in the negation, frustration and deformation of human functions that serve no material purpose. Anti-art, anti-religion, anti-sex, anti-play, anti-reverie, Freudian psychology concealed behind its stunning insights into human nature a nineteenth-century materialist and positivist bias. Jung's explorations and theories of the unconscious redressed the balance, related man more positively to subliminal elements of his psyche, but were less widely influential than the Freudian model during the first half of the century. But then the Jungian emphasis was endorsed and complemented by Abraham Maslow (humanistic psychology), Victor Frankl (logotherapy), Frederick Perls (gestalt therapy), Carl Rogers (client-centred therapy), Roberto Assagioli (psychosynthesis), who with others collectively constitute what has been called the 'Third Force' in psychology, and share an orientation towards growth and a concern with harmonising and integrating conscious and unconscious aspects of mind. This Third Force psychology has powerfully influenced the counter culture. Parapsychology, of course, is a field of investigation and not a method of therapy, but its investigations are chiefly of unconscious mental processes and it converges with Third

Force Psychology in adopting a positive attitude towards the unconscious, in seeking to stimulate its activity rather than repress it. Recent investigations (detailed accounts of which will be found in Part One) of dream telepathy and psychic healing, and also developments of 'psychenaut training' programmes, demonstrate that the unconscious is not the unregenerate dark side of the human personality that threatens to destroy the whole if given its head, but has powers of integration and organisation that Freud never credited it with.

3. *Openness to exotic cultural influences.* Recognition of the fact that different cultures establish different 'Reality Principles' (Freud's term) has led parapsychologists in recent years to extend their researches to field studies of alien and primitive cultures. Paranormal events appear to be more common in some cultures than in others, and anthropological evidence suggests that the limits of the possible are largely determined by the conceptual categories that make up the Reality Principle of a society or culture. African witch-doctors, Indian yogis and Brazilian psychic healers, for instance, have, under close observation and sometimes under controlled conditions, produced paranormal effects that are quite inexplicable in terms of Western science. The term 'paranormal', in fact, is not descriptive of events or faculties, but rather of the boundaries that give the Western cultural construct its shape. A dissatisfaction with the limitations imposed by these boundaries has caused many people in the counter culture to look to exotic alien cultures and traditions, to Zen, Tantra, the *I Ching* or the *Kabbalah*, for instance, for guidance and knowledge. The quartet of books in which Carlos Castaneda has given an account of his years of apprenticeship to the Yaqui Indian sorcerer, don Juan, have almost become instant Holy Writ in the counter culture, and at the same time they have profoundly interested parapsychologists, for they offer dramatic experiential evidence for the existence of 'separate realities'.[7]

4. *Body and sensory awareness.* As both psi functions and contemplative or mystical states are related to physiological variables, parapsychology and the counter culture share an interest in techniques for monitoring and controlling these variables, such as biofeedback. They also share an interest in biological rhythms and their

relation to environmental influences, even cosmic and astrological influences. Reports of recent work done in Russia and elsewhere have caused some Western parapsychologists to investigate the existence of occult energy systems in the body, as allegedly proved by the process known as Kirlian photography and by the medical efficacy of acupuncture. Psychic healing of the 'laying on of hands' type has been investigated by several researchers working on the hypothesis that some kind of energy transfer takes place. Techniques employed in consciousness training at such places as the Esalen Institute in California—for example body awareness and sensory awareness training, encounter groups and psychodrama—have been found to produce spontaneous psi experiences as side-effects.

5. *Field theory*. Psi functions such as telepathy, clairvoyance, psychokinesis and healing, suggesting as they do that under certain conditions normal ego boundaries are dissolved or transcended, have led some theorists to postulate a 'psi field' model as a conceptual framework to contain them. Researchers such as Dr Harold Burr of Yale, using highly sensitive instruments, have demonstrated that electromagnetic fields of the body can be detected at a distance of several feet. The recorded field forces are not powerful enough to explain long-distance telepathy or psychokinetic effects with heavy objects in terms of known physical energies within the electromagnetic spectrum, but this does not necessarily invalidate the psi field theory, for weak forces can be amplified under certain conditions and most psi phenomena involve transfer of information, not energy, and a minimum energy output can convey a maximum information content (a glimmering light on a buoy at sea carries as much information as a powerful light). But leaving aside the vexed question whether known physical energies are involved in psi functions, the psi field theory has great appeal as a plausible model, for it rescues the paranormal from the limbo of the paradoxical and links it with what Huxley called the Perennial Philosophy, with the intuitive knowledge of poets and mystics that *all of life is one*, that living organisms throughout the 'Great Chain of Being', from the mollusc to man, are interrelated, interdependent and interresponsive. One of the most controversial subjects in modern research into the paranormal has been Cleve Backster's investigations of 'primary perception' in plants.

Rhine has attacked Backster scathingly and very few parapsychologists have a good word to say either for his methods or his findings, but his claim that plants respond to human emotions and to the sufferings of other living organisms in their vicinity has been more widely publicised by the media than have the better-authenticated findings of researchers in other areas. Why? Because people are excited to have scientific evidence that they are not self-contained biological systems built after a mechanical model, but are intimately connected with all living things at a level that orthodox science cannot probe. A characteristic of the counter culture is a reverence for life at all levels, and its chief criticism of the scientific-industrial societies of the West is that they have blindly and ruthlessly exploited the resources of the planet without regard for the interdependence of living systems. Field theory merges man with his environment and provides a theoretical model for the paranormal phenomena of psi that relates them to the ideological foundations of the counter culture, the socio-political aspect of which is the ecological movement.

The preceding pages summarise in terms of broad generalisations some of the correspondences between psi research and theory and certain aspects of the consciousness explosion. This is a sketchy survey which later chapters will elaborate. To conclude this introductory chapter I propose to discuss the question: to what extent has the consciousness explosion produced a coherent 'new gnosis'?

The chief tenet of the old Gnostic religion which rivalled Christianity during the first three centuries of the Christian era was that man is saved not by virtue of his faith or conduct but by knowledge (*gnosis*).[8] Deriving mainly from Eastern sources, Gnosticism opposed the state Christianity of Rome with a visionary, individualistic and implicitly elitist prescription for salvation, a cosmology that made God unapproachably transcendent and detached from the affairs of the world and stationed a hierarchy of tyrannical and inimical demons between Him and man, a philosophy of dualism that regarded eternal strife as the law of life and of nature, and an image of man that combined grandeur and despair, for it sharply dichotomised his spiritual and physical existence and made him a 'stranger' on the earth. The universe, in the Gnostic view, is a prison, and the earth is its deepest dungeon, and as man is imprisoned in this dungeon so there is imprisoned in the depths of his being a portion of the divine substance, the spirit or 'spark' (*pneuma*), which longs to be reunited with the transcendent Godhead, but is prevented by the Archons, or demons, who are at once in the universe and in man's own soul, in the form of his appetites, passions and attachments to worldly things. The spirit, the divine portion, sleeps in matter, unconscious of itself, and the only worthwhile purpose of life is to awaken and liberate it through knowledge. But the knowledge that awakens and liberates is not rational knowledge attained through processes of argument and cerebration, but the knowledge vouchsafed by secret lore or obtained through mystical illumination. It is knowledge both of the Being of God and of the Way the spirit must travel to escape from the prison of the world, and this practical knowledge of the Way involves immensely detailed knowledge of magical and ceremonial preparations for each stage of the long journey and for combating the powers of the demons.

This religion of *gnosis* was ruthlessly suppressed by state Christianity. The burning of the great library at Alexandria was an attempt to destroy all evidence of the existence of such rivals to the official religion that was becoming the orthodoxy of the Western world. The recent discovery of libraries of sacred texts at Nag Hamadi in Egypt and near the Dead Sea in Israel has given an indication of how widespread Gnostic and other similar sects were in the early Christian centuries. As the secular empire of Rome crumbled, religions that offered the hope of self-realisation and personal salvation prospered. Consciousness turned inward and sought strategies to liberate the spirit from the dross of the world. Gnosticism had its day, but ultimately the ecclesiastical empire of Rome triumphed where the secular empire had failed, the hegemony of Europe under the rule of the Church was established, and the Gnostic religion went underground. It was never completely suppressed, though. Its message and myth were too close to perennial aspects of human experience and aspiration. It survived particularly in Kabbalism, and the *Zohar*, a kabbalist text written in Spain in the thirteenth century, contains many Gnostic elements. It surfaced again in the fifteenth century, when the ancient Hermetic writings, attributed to the legendary Hermes Trismegistus, were rediscovered and translated. The Hermetic tradition, which supplied the philosophical foundation for the work of the alchemists, combined classical Greek and Gnostic influences. The 'Royal Art' of the alchemists, the transmutation of base metal to gold, was an analogue of the Gnostic striving to liberate the divine element imprisoned in matter, a task that could only be accomplished by an initiate possessed of arcane knowledge. In the anonymous but much-prized alchemical text, the *Amor Proximi*, we read: 'Whoever is to work out a thing practically must first have a fundamental knowledge of a thing; in order that man shall macrocosmically and magically work out the image of God, all God's kingdom, in himself, he must have its right knowledge in himself.'[9] The doctrine that the divine element is latent within man and must be worked out by the application of 'right knowledge' is pure Gnosticism. And when orthodox science combined with orthodox religion to discredit and suppress alchemy, the tradition again went underground and survived in secret societies, such as the Rosicrucians and the Freemasons.

Gnosticism in its heyday in the early Christian centuries was strongly opposed by another mystical philosophy, Neoplatonism. The main point of contention between the two was over the question of man's relation to nature and the cosmos. The word 'cosmos' means 'order' and a venerable Greek tradition going back to Pythagoras regarded the universe as a grand ordered design of which man was a part. The Gnostics' contempt for nature and the physical world, and their dualistic philosophy, contradicted the Greek belief in the harmony and unity of everything in the universe, and it drew the fire of the great Neoplatonist Plotinus, who wrote: 'They should desist from the horror-stories of the frightful things which allegedly take place in the cosmic spheres, those spheres which in truth are the givers of everything beneficial. . . . Even the basest men they deem worthy to be called brothers, while with frenzied mouth they declare the sun, the stars in the heavens, and even the world-soul, unworthy to be called by them brothers.'[10] The Neoplatonic belief in the brotherhood of man and stars and man and nature merged in the Hermetic philosophy with the Gnostic belief in the entrapped spirit's aspiration to liberate itself from the flesh. The great mages of the Renaissance, Cornelius Agrippa, Pico della Mirandola and Paracelsus, drew on both ancient traditions, taught the latent divinity of man and the unity of man and nature. But the reconciliation was short-lived. The philosophy that underlay the scientific revolution, and that was formulated at its outset by Bacon and Descartes, brought back dualism with a vengeance, for it was a dualism that annulled the spirit and held no hope of transcendence. Nature (Descartes' *res extensa*) and man (*res cogitans*) were irremediably cut off from each other, locked in an opposition that in the Baconian–Cartesian view could have but one outcome. 'We shall become the masters and possessors of nature,' Descartes wrote. And Bacon said that science would 'endow the life of man with infinite commodities . . . with new powers and works.' The irony of these buoyant seventeenth-century claims in the light of twentieth-century experience surely doesn't need to be emphasised.

This is no thumbnail sketch of Western occult philosophy, but if we are going to talk about a 'new gnosis' I think we must do so against a background of at least a rough idea of what the old gnosis was, how it fared in the world and what ideas opposed it. Also, an historical perspective can be instructive and illuminating with regard to a contemporary situation. Spengler wrote that the early Christian centuries and the twentieth century were 'contemporaneous', meaning that they were identical periods in the context of the history of their respective cultures. And certainly there is something modern and familiar about the Gnostic myth and message: the alien God, the loneliness, homesickness, forlornness of the man in whom the spirit is quickened, the sense of being a stranger in the world, the agonising over attaining freedom and authentic existence, the contempt for the physical and the sense of nausea that man experiences confronted with the immensity, the mindlessness, the proliferation of nature. We have read it all before, in Nietzsche, Kierkegaard, Sartre, Heidegger, Camus. It is pure Existentialism.

Except that what is missing in Existentialism is the doctrine of *gnosis*, of salvation through knowledge. Neither mystical illumination nor hard-won possession of the secrets of arcane lore rescue man from being, as Sartre says, 'a useless passion'. Existentialism is Gnosticism divested of its mysticism and its hope. It is the residue of the old gnosis after it has been ground through the mills of scientific rationalism. When Sartre's Antoine Roquentin in his novel *La*

Nausée contemplates the roots of a chestnut tree and has an over-whelming sensation of nausea and alienation, he is living out the Cartesian dualism, he is *res cogitans* face to face with *res extensa*. He repeats the experience of Pascal, the first man to express the psychic implications of the new science and cosmology. 'When I see the blindness and the wretchedness of man,' Pascal wrote, 'when I regard the whole silent universe, and man without light, left to himself, and, as it were, lost in this corner of the universe, without knowing who has put him there, what he has come to do, what will become of him at death, and incapable of all knowledge, I become terrified, like a man who should be carried in his sleep to a dreadful desert island, and should awake without knowing where he is, and without means of escape.'[11] This, the quintessential Existentialist experience, is much bleaker than the Gnostic view that in many ways it resembles. Not only is the universe Godless and utterly alien to man, it is also totally indifferent. A universe thronged with demonic powers bent on frustrating the efforts of the divine element in man to liberate itself from matter is preferable to a universe of total indifference. Existen-tialist man has no divine spark, no transcendental longing; his wretchedness is not a condition resulting from a state of inertia from which he can escape through effort and knowledge, it is simply his inalienable condition. Authentic existence begins with the recognition of this bleak fact and continues just so long as man continues to hold this recognition foremost in his mind and does not succumb to the 'bad faith' of finding purposes and meanings relevant to human life in a universe that is indifferent and meaningless. Man is, writes Sartre, 'nothing but his own project', and consequently 'all is per-mitted to him'.[12] This is the ultimate ethical implication of the Baconian–Cartesian world-view and programme: a rationale for murder, libertinism and ruthless exploitation of human beings and the natural, physical world. The Gnostics reached a similar conclusion by a different route, arguing that as the spirit is a separate and in-corruptible entity no sins of the flesh or actions performed by man in the physical world can affect it. But for the Gnostics man was 'his own project' only so long as the spirit remained asleep in him. When it was awakened he had a well-defined project: through knowledge and effort to unite the spark of the divine in him with the immortal and transcendent Godhead. It was a project more likely to lead to asceticism than to libertinism or murder, though there were among the second-century Gnostics, as Bishop Irenaeus wrote, those who 'serve intemperately the lusts of the flesh and say you must render the flesh to the flesh and the spirit to the spirit'.

The Existentialist philosophy has both reflected and profoundly influenced the character of social and political life in Western countries in the present century. In wars and revolutions, in industry and social institutions, a pervasive cynicism bred of nihilism has treated human beings and nature's resources as objects or tools, to be manipulated, exploited and ultimately scrapped. Not only has the sense of *cosmos*, of universal order, been lost, but also the sense of a human order and community, of what Ivan Illich calls 'conviviality'. Man has arrogated the right to be 'his own project' regardless of the consequences for others, to endow his life 'with infinite commodities' though they be commodities that he doesn't particularly need and others desperately do, to act on the assumption that 'all is permitted to him'. Criminal acts that carry Existentialist nihilism to its logical conclusion, like the Moors murders in Britain and those of the Manson 'family' in California, get maximum coverage by the media, books written about them by distinguished authors, and are vividly remembered by the general public for a decade and more. It is as if we were fascinated to contemplate, safely objectified, a face we dare not recognise in the mirror, or a picture which, like that of Dorian Gray, bears all the marks of the desolation of the life we have lived, but which we keep locked away in an attic. Wilde's story, in fact, may be read as an allegory of the fate of the man who lives an other-directed life in a society dedicated to the rational goals of progress, industrialism, power, and technological control over all and everything: he keeps a fair face presented to the world while corruption rots him within. Thomas Hobbes was the first philosopher thoroughly to elaborate a mechanistic model of man and society based on the (in his day) new scientific gnosis, and he came to the conclusion that the life of man is 'solitary, poor, nasty, brutish and short'. It is the Existentialist view neatly encapsulated centuries before Existentialism as such was conceived, but springing from the same root in the scientific philosophy that desacralised nature and depersonalised man and has led to the creation of a world based on sound rational principles in which it has become increasingly difficult for human beings to live humanly.

In the mid-'60s young people in increasing numbers and from all social strata started to 'drop out' and seek their own kind of 'authenticity'. For the most part they had no conception of the Sartrean indictment of the type of 'bad faith' that precludes 'authentic living', but they had a very clear conception of the hypocrisy of the preceding generations. In a courageous Commencement address to the Harvard Law School, a young man told the assembled parents and faculty: 'You have told us repeatedly that trust and courage were standards to emulate. You have convinced us that equality and justice were inviolable concepts. You have taught us that authority should be guided by reason and tempered by fairness. *We have taken you seriously.*'[13] He went on passionately to deprecate the authorities that had harassed and persecuted young people who had worked for civil rights, protested against the injustices of the war in Southeast Asia and laboured in rural and urban ghettoes. This was a voice representative of a generation. Others expressed their protest in their life-style, became 'hippies', 'flower children', 'Jesus freaks', lived in communes, smoked pot, spoke their own 'hip' language, ate macrobiotic food, professed universal love and practised free and uninhibited sex. Bizarre though many of its manifestations were, this spontaneous movement of protest, self-indulgence and spiritual quest was the start of the consciousness explosion. It spread rapidly throughout America and Europe, constituting what was at first referred to as a 'sub-culture'. Simon and Trout, two social scientists who studied the phenomenon in 1967, came to the conclusion that 'we may well be in the presence not of just the latest wrinkle in youthful rebellion, but an emergent social movement'.[14] Looking back on that time from the mid-'70s, and bearing in mind the prevailing nihilistic mood of the preceding decades, I think it is no exaggeration to say that we were in the presence not only of an emergent social movement but also of a fundamental change of consciousness, in fact a 'new gnosis'.

In 1970 a *New York Times* survey established that there were more than 2000 communes in thirty-four states. In 1968 a young journalist on a New Jersey newspaper, Robert Houriet, clashed with his employers over the right of one of the reporters to wear long hair. He resigned his post and set out on a personal odyssey, travelling all over the United States in an attempt to find out what the commune phenomenon was all about. 'Almost a year after starting my research,' he wrote in his book, *Getting Back Together*, 'I first realised that the contemporary commune was the outward form of a movement in consciousness.' He summarised his conclusions in two paragraphs which have a relevance to the present discussion that justifies quotation at length:

'At their outset, communes looked as though they were simply repeating the past, returning to the secure, natural comfort of a bygone era, escaping upstream to the clean, clear headwaters of the American pioneer experience. But that was only the first lap in a long journey. Somewhere in the line of history, civilization had made a wrong turn, a detour that had led into a cul-de-sac. The only way, they felt, was to drop out and go all the way back to the beginning, the primal source of consciousness, the true basis of culture: the land. There, they would again move forward, very slowly, careful not to take the wrong turn and keeping to the main road and to the central spirit and consciousness that modern man had lost along the way.

'Re-examining, testing, and adapting, they would evolve a micro culture—a synthesis of forms, ideas, art and technology. They built smaller, more self-sufficient communities in harmony with the earth. They tested broader, more flexible forms of the family and ways of raising children. They started freer, more creative schools and developed home industries and retained the integrity of individual craftsmanship. They established churches, ashrams and lay orders, revived old religions, and created entirely new ones. Above all, they infused their rediscovered awareness of immanent divinity into every action of daily life, seeking rituals and traditions with which to pass on to their children the timeless vision.'[15]

It is the easiest thing in the world to mock, scorn or discredit the commune movement. Any graduate in economics, politics, psychology, ethnology or philosophy could turn out a competent thesis proving that it was all pie in the sky. The communes were economically dependent on the society they supposedly rejected, they channelled off a movement of political protest and made it ineffectual, their anarchic idealism was too simplistic, too self-indulgent, too incoherent. These are all arguable criticisms, but one thing that is not arguable is that the commune movement was a spontaneous expression of a need felt by thousands of young people to live more authentically, spiritually and responsibly. Yes, responsibly, odd though the word may sound if you are entertaining an image of a bunch of unwashed, hirsute, workshy layabouts. These people often acted with a sense of responsibility for the future, for their children, and towards the earth itself that you don't always find among the socially well-adjusted. It was a form of responsibility based on a revival of the Neoplatonic belief in the unity and interdependence of man and nature.

Houriet found daubed in bright orange letters on the cement facing the main building of one of the communes he visited, this quotation from the Book of Proverbs: 'Where there is no vision the people perish.' It could have been adopted as the slogan for the whole movement, with the word 'vision' having the double meaning of awareness of the future and intense experience of illumination. Mystical experience was highly prized and eagerly sought by members of the communes. Many sought it through drugs—LSD, peyotl and marijuana—and others practised techniques of 'mind expansion' derived from Eastern religions.

It is difficult and hazardous to generalise about such an amorphous phenomenon as the commune movement and the consciousness shift that it was symptomatic of and that was happening simultaneously in branches of the orthodox culture such as music and literature. But certain broad features stand out, and to consider them in the light of the old Gnostic religion and in contrast with its modern counterpart, Existentialism, is illuminating.

Houriet speaks of the members of the communes 'seeking rituals and traditions with which to pass on to their children the timeless vision [of immanent divinity].' In the Gnostic philosophy, as we have seen, divinity was not immanent in the sense of pervading all the universe, but was on the one hand transcendent and on the other locked away and generally forgotten in the inmost recesses of the human soul. The modern gnosis is visionary and lays emphasis on the importance of liberating the spirit, but it doesn't go along with the old

Gnostic metaphysics and cosmology. There are no archons or demons in its scheme. The forces that snare and curtail the spirit are psychological and social. It is as concerned with salvation as was the old Gnosticism, but not exclusively with individual salvation. It believes in the saving power of knowledge, and particularly the knowledge of revelation. But where it departs from the old religion most fundamentally and emphatically is in its rejection of dualism. It believes in unity, in community, in the *cosmos*, the universal order. It does not regard man as a stranger on the face of the earth, set apart from the rest of the natural world by his endowment of divinity and transcendental longing, but rather as a creature that belongs to, relates and responds to, is dependent upon and ultimately responsible for the organic whole of which he is a part.

A pendulum or cyclic theory of history may regard contemporary transcendentalism as merely a reaction after a long period when culture and society were dominated by science, materialism and rationalism. And certainly when you take a broad general view of the occult revival of recent years, including the revived interest in witch-craft and the 'black arts', in sorcery, astrology and numerology, in demonology and exorcism, you may well suspect that the West has culturally regressed to the Middle Ages. It depends which set of facts you focus on. These cruder manifestations of occultism do seem to justify a gloomy pessimism, to be symptomatic of a loss of nerve and control and of a desperate repudiation of reason and responsibility. But there are, I believe, facts that justify a more optimistic view, and it is with these that this book is concerned. There is reason to believe that the consciousness shift that is taking place in our day is not just another swing of the pendulum. An image of balance or reconciliation would represent it better. Above all it brings into balance those traditionally opposed truth-seeking functions of man and society: science and religion. Traditionally they came up with different and conflicting 'truths'. With the development of scientific means of exploring those areas of human experience that hitherto some have considered sacrosanct and others irrelevant—psychic experience and mystical vision, for instance—an increasing body of evidence ac-cumulates which not only shows that these subjective experiences are real and measurable, but also that they are relevant; relevant not only to the individual life, but to interpersonal relations, to society and to the world at large. In many areas, the truths established by modern science coincide with or confirm truths expressed long ago by psychics, mystics or poets. We have heard a lot in recent years about ecology—the science that studies the interdependence of living systems—and except for the statistics, the measurements and specific details, it was all in Blake, Wordsworth, Whitman. This is not to claim that poetry and mysticism are superior truth-seeking functions to scientific investigation, but to point out that in many areas today the two are complementary. And these areas are chiefly those that fall under the general heading of parapsychology or psi research.

'Where there is no vision the people perish,' said the prophet. Theodore Roszak wrote, 'The next revolution . . . is the struggle to liberate the visionary powers from the lesser reality in which they have been confined by urban-industrial necessity.'[16] In 1969 U. Thant, then Secretary-General of the United Nations, warned that 'the members of the U.N. have perhaps ten years left in which to subordinate their ancient quarrels and launch a global partnership to curb the arms race, to improve the human environment, to defuse the population explosion, and to supply the required momentum to development efforts'.[17] What the Secretary-General was in fact pleading for was the revolution that Roszak predicted, the liberation of the visionary powers. Roszak believed it was happening. He wrote, 'There is a strange, new radicalism abroad which refuses to respect the conventions of secular thought and value, which insists on making the visionary powers a central point of political reference.' We should hope that his reading of the signs of the times was correct, for at the time I write more than half of the decade that U Thant gave the world to mend its ways has elapsed.

Never has there been such consensus as there is today among informed and thinking people that survival depends upon change. And never has such a majority among those that would agree to this proposition further agreed that the change must be effected at the level of consciousness. Societies have experimented with institutional, ideological and behavioural changes without effecting a corresponding change at the consciousness level, and the problems they set out to combat have not yielded to such approaches. So the crucial question is: how is a change of consciousness to be brought about? The world's religions concur in giving quite a clear and definite answer to this. It is brought about by prayer, meditation and the power of belief. Modern psychological studies provide confirmatory evidence. In studies of learning processes, psychotherapy, athletic coaching methods, the behaviour of prisoners and conquered peoples, to mention but a few areas, behaviour, performance and achievement have been shown to be directly dependent upon self-image and self-expectation. Autosuggestion and hypnotic suggestion have been observed to bring about fundamental personality changes in numerous cases. So the teachings of esoteric religions combine with the findings of modern psychology to show that a change of consciousness can be brought about through a change of image. The importance of psi research is that it turns up well-proven facts that are incompatible with the mechanistic and materialistic image of man that has predominated in our culture for nearly four centuries. It shows that the psychic and spiritual faculties of man have been stunted and repressed in the consciousness produced by this predominant image, and it provides factual and theoretical material to create a new image to supersede the old in which man's psychic and spiritual dimension will be restored. This is why the advocates of consciousness change as the only survival strategy that can work look to the parapsychologist for support.

But hasn't this image-change strategy and transcendentalism been tried before? a sceptic might ask. Weren't there, near the very beginning of the industrial-technological era, men of genius in every country in the West who foresaw the psychic and social dangers inherent in the new developments, and who tried to combat them by creating a rival image of man that emphasised his spiritual dimension, his affinities with nature and his transcendental longings? And what effect did they have? The argument has to be acknowledged and the questions answered. One line of counter-argument is that at the time the Romantics were writing the dangers inherent in the scientific-rational image and ethic were far from the purview of the man in the street or the country mansion, whereas today they are all around us, in the supermarket, on the highway and in our daily newspapers. People today are generally aware that the urban-industrial-scientific-technological experiment has created more problems than it can solve. And the question should not be, What effect did the Romantics have? but, What effect are they having? Roszak, for instance, bases his long critique of the urban-industrial ethos and image, *Where the Wasteland Ends*, on the Blakean vision, and includes chapters on the contemporary relevance of Blake, Wordsworth and Goethe.

A second answer to the sceptic who asks, Haven't we been here before? is a flat denial. The difference between nineteenth-century and contemporary transcendentalism is that today so much that could be dismissed by the nineteenth-century sceptic as hypothesis, idealism or mysticism is demonstrably true. The evidence for this claim will be the subject of later chapters, but we may briefly summarise its import by saying that a view of man, nature and cosmos as subtly interrelated and interdependent is more true, quite objectively and verifiably, than the view of them as having distinct and unrelated characteristics, purposes and functions. When we talk about the necessity for a consciousness shift and an image change we are not proposing a merely pragmatic panacea. We are talking about basing life and society on a deeper and broader truth than they are based on at present. It has become increasingly clear in recent years that most of our problems, personal and social, are attributable to our basing values and priorities on a view of man, nature and cosmos that is partial, uni-dimensional, short-sighted, tendentious, inadequate, and in the last analysis untrue. The consciousness revolution begins with this awareness, and psi research provides it with the support of factual evidence.

At the beginning of this chapter I stressed that parapsychological research and experiment, and such spin-offs as biofeedback and psi-training techniques, should not be trivialised, sensationalised or commercialised. The reason for my vehemence on this point should now be clear. They can be instrumental in effecting a fundamental change that is important to survival, and it is essential that they should not be assimilated into and thus rendered ineffective by the psycho-social orthodoxy that they challenge. The spectre of the slick executive who can smoothly change psychic gear at will still worries me, for such a man would be the possessor of a new technology, not a new gnosis.

PART ONE

From Spiritualism
to Paraphysics

I

The Dream of Reason

The philosopher who gave us the image of Rational Man, who believed that reason could unravel all the secrets of the universe, that all physical processes were mechanical and that nature had no inscrutable mysteries, had his life's work and purpose revealed to him in a paranormal dream. Here is one of the greatest ironies in intellectual history.

René Descartes was in his twenty-third year. He was going through a period of great emotional and intellectual crisis. He had conceived, but not yet got down on paper, an ambitious plan for a unified mathematical science. Some of the problems seemed insurmountable, though, as did some of his personal problems. On the night of November 10, 1619, he had three dreams. The first two were frightening experiences of menace, violence and impotence. He interpreted them as representing the consequences of his sins and faults. The third dream was the one that determined the future course of his life and work. In it he believed that he had been visited by 'the Spirit of Truth which had wanted to open to him the treasures of all the sciences', and that he had received a command from the Almighty to devote his life to the search for truth by application of the mathematical method. Some days later he started writing again, and for the remaining thirty years of his life he pursued the straight and narrow path of intellectual clarity that he believed had been revealed to him in the dream of that November night. And such was the influence of Descartes' life's work that orthodox Western science and philosophy continued on the same path for more than three centuries after his death. Very few men have had dreams that have had so far-reaching an effect.[1]

Rational man, Cartesian man, has little time for dreams, and if he finds a place for them in his philosophical or psychological theories, it is to dismiss them as wish-fulfilments or by-products of physiological processes. Rational man keeps an orderly house, and dreams are embarrassingly untidy, wayward and idiosyncratic; he simply refuses to give them house-room. The same goes for everything else that defies reason and the mechanical cause-effect view of the world. A man has manly work to do ('We shall become the masters and possessors of nature') and has no business wasting time indulging in fantasy and wonder. The sense of wonder, Descartes writes in a passage that is as remarkable for its peculiar physiology as for its dogmatism, 'has so much power in causing the (animal) spirits which are in the cavities of the brain to flow towards the place where the impression of the object of our wonder is located, that sometimes it draws them all there, and causes them to be so completely engaged in conserving this impression that none pass thence into the muscles, and indeed that none depart at all from the tracks they have antecedently been following in the brain. In this way the whole body is caused to stay as immobile as a statue, disabling us from apprehending the object otherwise than as initially presented, and so from acquiring more particular knowledge of it. This is what we commonly entitle being astounded. It is an excess of wonder, and can never be other than harmful.'[2] You can almost hear in this the accents of the stern Victorian father, telling his son that he must stop day-dreaming and put his shoulder to the wheel; or of Dr Freud rescuing one of his patients from infantile fantasising and making him come to terms with his Reality Principle; or, for that matter, of a certain type of modern critic of parapsychology.

One can go along with the argument up to a point, agree that just to gawp in wonder at a phenomenon is not going to get anyone anywhere or contribute a jot to the range of human knowledge. And there are too many books published about parapsychology that adopt a breathless 'Gee whiz!' approach and rest their case on wonder. Rational Man's argument that we should not allow a sense of wonder to corrupt judgement or preclude investigation is tenable. But he goes further than this, and asserts that there is nothing in the universe or in man that will not ultimately prove to be rationally explainable in terms of scientific principles already known. If he comes across something that cannot at present be so explained he ignores it, or pigeon-holes it as something that in the present stage of our theoretical knowledge it is unprofitable to investigate further, confident that a perfectly rational theory will ultimately be found to explain it. He can support this attitude with historical examples. Hypnotism, for instance, was formerly regarded as a paranormal function and, as 'animal magnetism', was thought to be connected with a 'psychic fluid' diffused throughout the universe. The bat's apparently erratic but always unerring flight, and certain birds' ability to migrate across great oceans, were until not very long ago thought to be examples of ESP. But then it was discovered that bats navigate on a principle similar to radar, and that migrating birds use visual clues, such as the positions of the sun, moon and stars. Here are just three examples out of many that could be cited of phenomena that once were thought to have an occult explanation and now have a perfectly rational one. Rational man is convinced that everything else at present labelled paranormal will ultimately yield its mystery to scientific investigation, and that everything that doesn't will be shown to be either delusion or deception. For three and a half centuries this has been the dream of reason, but the residue of irreducible fact still remains substantial, and as scientific knowledge progresses the possibility that it will ever fit into a physical or mechanical framework becomes more and more remote. It has been remarked often enough that scientific investigation has reduced the territory of the paranormal. What hasn't so often been remarked is that it has also cut the ground from under the feet of the critic who bases his antagonism to the psi hypothesis on Cartesian rationalism.

Consider an example to illustrate this last point. The Cartesian argument was put very eloquently and forcefully by Professor Joseph Jastrow in a symposium on 'The Case for and against Psychical Belief' held at Clark University in 1926. In a key passage he deprecated 'the common belief in some form of occultism, that underlies, interpenetrates, accompanies and reconstitutes and gives higher significance to the practical world of occupation; by its dominance it stands as an obstacle to the discovery of material cause and effect in the naturalistic scheme as we moderns know it so familiarly and dominantly. The story of thinking is the story of the long struggle and slow emergence of the single-threaded scientific view of things as they present themselves to an objective observation, detached from a personalised interpretation of the meaning of events and forces.'[3]

This, written three centuries after Descartes, is almost an exact repetition of his argument against 'wonder'. It is a fair indication of how the Cartesian world-view has collapsed in the fifty years since Jastrow wrote that there are no less than three ideas in this short passage that no philosopher of science would endorse today. That 'material cause and effect' is a universal law of nature, that all knowledge can be encompassed in a 'single-threaded scientific view of things', and that purely 'objective observation' is ever possible, are ideas that scientists and philosophers have had to abandon as a result of the discoveries of modern physics. The fact that the concepts and terminology of theoretical physics have become increasingly 'occult' over the last few decades does not in itself validate any of the beliefs of occultists or the theories of parapsychologists, but it does signify that Western man has to awaken from the dream of reason that has preoccupied him these three centuries and more if he wants to learn more about himself and the universe around him.

Science having at the same time reduced the area of the paranormal and taken the wind out of the sails of the rationalist critics of the psi hypothesis, the situation today for the genuine truth-seeker both presents great opportunities and is fraught with great hazards. It presents great opportunities because, as the area of the genuinely paranormal becomes more clearly defined, the possibility of finding principles of coherence in the irreducible residue of well-attested fact proportionately increases. It is a situation fraught with hazards because the lack of a coherent theoretical framework for psi phenomena and of a clear conception of their significance leaves the field open for a host of crank interpretations and abuses—blind alleys down which the truth-seeker can get irretrievably lost.

Bearing in mind both the opportunities and the hazards, I propose in these chapters to take a look at some of the psi research of recent years that seems most promising, convincing and suggestive. But first a brief sketch of the historical background will be necessary to put contemporary research work in perspective.

2

The Slow Fuse

In the mid-nineteenth century there was an occult explosion in Europe and America of comparable dimensions to that which is happening in our own time, but with a different focus of interest. The difference may be expressed by saying that the nineteenth century was preoccupied with the question, Are there aspects of human personality that survive death? whereas today the question of deepest concern is, Are there latent faculties in man that he can develop so as to enrich and enhance his life before death, and whose development might avert the threat of planetary death? They are different questions, but they lead to the same field of investigation: the hidden ('occult') aspects of human personality and mind, aspects which so long as a materialist philosophy prevailed could have no official recognition.

Mid-nineteenth century spiritualism was crude and sensational, thronged with bogus mediums who with a repertoire of a few cheap conjuring tricks were able to bamboozle thousands of people, bring spurious reassurance to the bereaved and provide the sensation-seeker with the thrill of seeing or hearing 'ghosts'. It was, to an age inclined towards sentimentalism, comparable to what brainwave-monitoring is to an age inclined towards vague mysticism: a profitless indulgence of ego-satisfaction divorced from any, except perhaps a superstitious, metaphysic. It is not surprising that intelligent minds and sensitive souls found the whole spiritualistic wave, with its table-rappings, spirit-photography, feverish automatic writing, direct-voice communications and bizarre séance-room materialisations, utterly repugnant. Dickens did, and the philosopher T. H. Huxley, magisterially declining an invitation to investigate spiritualistic phenomena, declared, 'The only good that I can see in a demonstration of the truth of "Spiritualism" is to furnish an additional argument against suicide. Better live a crossing-sweeper than die and be made to talk twaddle by a "medium" hired at a guinea a séance.'[1] But there were men of equal eminence, both in Britain and America, who although they deplored the hysteria and exploitation that went with spiritualism, yet wondered whether there might not be some genuine phenomena among the bogus and some truth in the survival hypothesis. These were men profoundly ill at ease with the prevailing rationalist-materialist philosophy and well aware of its disastrous social consequences.

When Henry Sidgwick was Lecturer in Moral Science at Trinity College, Cambridge, there was among his students a brilliant young man who had already won distinction as a poet and classical scholar, Frederic W. H. Myers. The two men became lifelong friends, though temperamentally they were very different. In Sidgwick's temperament there dominated what he himself called a 'cold corrosive scepticism', that stripped any argument to its bones and laid bare its flaws. His manner was aloof and forbidding. Myers was a man of eager and passionate temperament and poetic sensibility, given to fits of unrestrained enthusiasm and at other times of black depression. His trepidation when he first broached the subject of psychic phenomena with Sidgwick is understandable in view of the older man's reputation and the ill-repute of spiritualism among intellectuals. Myers recalled the occasion years later, when he wrote Sidgwick's obituary: 'In a star-light walk which I shall not forget . . . I asked him, almost with trembling, whether he thought that when Tradition, Intuition, Metaphysic, had failed to solve the riddle of the Universe, there was still a chance that from any actual observable phenomena—ghosts, spirits, whatsoever there might be—some valid knowledge might be drawn as to a World Unseen. Already, it seemed, he had thought that this was possible; steadily, though in no sanguine fashion, he indicated some last grounds of hope; and from that night onwards, I resolved to pursue this quest, if it might be, at his side.'[2] This conversation, and the decision that Myers made as a result of it, led to the formation in 1882 of the Society for Psychical Research and the beginning of systematic investigation of the paranormal.

Most of the early work of S.P.R. was done by Myers and another brilliant Trinity College scholar, Edmund Gurney, who not only had an incisive intellect and literary style, but was also qualified as a doctor and psychologist and was, like Myers, an indefatigable worker.

In 1886 their massive joint effort, *Phantasms of the Living*, was published. In it 702 cases of spontaneous psychic experiences, all of which Gurney or Myers had personally investigated, are reported and discussed. There are also reports of controlled experimental work on thought-transference (telepathy), notably the famous Guthrie experiments in which a series of simple drawings were executed in one room and telepathically 'sent' to a person in another room who attempted to reproduce them. The correspondences between the sets of drawings were remarkable, and as the experiments were carefully controlled and supervised, one series by Gurney and another by the distinguished physicist Oliver Lodge, the results seemed to constitute conclusive proof that telepathy had taken place.

Many of the cases reported in *Phantasms of the Living* were of 'crisis apparitions', visual or auditory experiences of communication from a distant person that were later found to coincide with the time when that person died or underwent some other crisis experience. Gurney planned to follow up this line of investigation, and organised through the S.P.R. a vast 'Census of Hallucinations' which aimed to recruit evidence from 50,000 people, but before the work could be completed he died, in mysterious circumstances which suggested suicide. The work, however, was completed by other members of the S.P.R. Of 17,000 people who were asked if they had ever had a paranormal experience of another's presence, 2272 answered in the affirmative. These cases were investigated more closely and 588 of them were ruled out as attributable to dream or delirium. The most stringent standards were applied in checking the evidence, and in the end the Census Committee was left with 32 cases supported by solid evidence and corroboration, of people who had seen or heard another person within twelve hours either way of the latter's death, which they were unaware of at the time of the 'hallucination'. The possibility of chance coincidence was calculated and found to be 1 in 19,000, so the 32 well-evidenced cases must have consisted of a majority of genuinely paranormal events.[3]

They did not necessarily prove survival, however, which was the question above all others that concerned Myers. He painstakingly collected evidence, which he presented and discussed in his monumental *Human Personality and its Survival of Bodily Death*. Taken together, *Phantasms*, the *Census* and *Human Personality* constitute a body of evidence for psi, establish standards for the assessment of experimental and anecdotal evidence, and discuss the philosophical and psychological implications with a breadth and cogency that have never since been excelled and rarely equalled. If one man were to be nominated the founder of psychical research, it would have to be Myers. Not only did he devote his life to the work, but it would seem, on the basis of the evidence afforded by some very curious automatic scripts produced by three mediums over a period of fifteen years after his death in 1901, that he continued it as a discarnate spirit. Psychical researchers have been puzzling over the 'cross-correspondences' found in the automatic writings of Mrs Verrall, Mrs Holland and Mrs Willett, three mediums who lived respectively in Cambridge, India and New York, for decades without coming up with any explanation less preposterous than that the discarnate Myers devised an ingenious way of proving his own survival. Normally, 'spirit-writing' may be more plausibly explained as originating in the unconscious of the medium, or being picked up telepathically by the medium from the minds of other living persons, than as a communication from the spirit world. But what if a message is communicated fragmentarily, some bits of it through one medium, others through a second, and the key that relates these otherwise meaningless communications is given to a third? This is the scheme that Myers is alleged to have posthumously devised. The fact that the separate scripts contained allusions to classical scholarship that none of the mediums, except possibly Mrs Verrall in Cambridge, could have been acquainted with, gives substantial weight to the hypothesis that the discarnate Myers really did originate these communications.

The survival question, which was of central importance to early psychical researchers in Britain and America, has shifted to a peripheral position in modern parapsychology, though some researchers, notably Dr Ian Stevenson of the University of Virginia, have continued to work on it and have collected some very curious data suggestive of reincarnation.[4] The trend of twentieth-century research has been to concentrate on experimental rather than anecdotal evidence for psi. This has meant that the psi functions that most easily lend themselves to investigation under laboratory

46

conditions—telepathy, clairvoyance, precognition and psychokinesis
—have tended to predominate. A pioneer of this approach was Dr
Charles Richet of the Institut Métapsychique in Paris, who in the
1870s and '80s conducted experiments with playing cards to test
subjects for telepathy and 'lucidity' (clairvoyance) and applied the
calculus of probability to assess the results. Richet put forward the
theory that man possesses a 'sixth sense', which he termed 'crypt-
esthesia', an all-inclusive psychic faculty which is brought into play
through mysterious influences which he called 'vibrations of reality'.
He adopted a firm stand against the survival hypothesis on the grounds
that it was inherently improbable, though he put the full weight of
his considerable authority (he was a Nobel prizewinner in physiology)
behind a claim that most people today would find equally improbable:
that certain mediums are able to materialise living forms. He
admitted that 'to ask a physiologist, a physicist, or a chemist to admit
that a form that has a circulation of blood, warmth, and muscles,
that exhales carbonic acid, has weight, speaks, and thinks, can issue
from a human body is to ask of him an intellectual effort that is really
painful.' Yet he asserted that he had witnessed this phenomenon
often enough under controlled conditions to be confident that it was
'as certainly established as any fact in physics'.[5]

The middle period of psychical research, roughly the first three
decades of the present century, was the one in which the investigation
of physical paranormal phenomena produced by mediums predominated. It is amusing to visualise distinguished and dignified
gentlemen sitting in darkened séance rooms, engaging in a tug-of-war
with a spirit over a wastepaper basket, listening to unearthly hands
rap out a message on a typewriter or splash about in a bucket of
paraffin wax in order to make 'spirit gloves', fending off the attentions
of a materialised hairy ape-like creature with a penchant for licking
everyone, or engaging in a half-hearted sing-song as directed by a
spirit voice. These and numerous other absurdities are to be found
in the records of séances that distinguished men of science held with
the famous physical mediums of the early twentieth century:
Eusapia Palladino, Willi and Rudi Schneider, Franek Klusky, Eva
Carrière, Stella Cranshaw and Anna Rasmussen. Many parapsychologists today write off this entire episode as one in which a

group of exceptionally talented charlatans and conjurers managed consistently to fool assemblies of exceptionally naive and credulous men of science, or alternatively allege complicity between the mediums and the scientists to dupe the public and get publicity. Undoubtedly there was a lot of fraud practised by the mediums, but a thorough study of the records will leave any reader with little doubt that at least some of the effects they produced were genuine psi phenomena. Anna Rasmussen could, in full daylight conditions, make any one of a number of pendulums suspended in a sealed glass case at a distance from her move in any required direction. Stella Cranshaw could produce a similar psychokinetic effect: bring together two electrical contacts to complete a circuit though they were protected from physical interference by a cage, a glass case and a delicate soap bubble which would have been burst if the contact had been effected by normal means. Such evidence of paranormal powers, obtained under strictly controlled conditions in the presence of several observers, cannot easily be dismissed as fraud or delusion. Nor can the fact, automatically recorded by a thermograph during several independent sittings with Stella Cranshaw and Rudi Schneider, that the temperature in the room dropped by as much as 20° and that the sharper drops coincided with the more violent physical manifestations of the séance. When all the fraud, delusion and absurdity of the middle period of psi research is allowed for, there remains a residue of hard paranormal fact which is well-evidenced and cannot be explained away. We do not have to accept the mediums' explanation of it as the result of spirit activity (Anna Rasmussen's pendulums would only move when the instructions were addressed to her 'control', Dr Lasaruz), but may prefer to think that the phenomena suggest that there is a source of psychic energy within man himself which certain people can activate under certain conditions (of which they may not be aware). This is the hypothesis generally held by parapsychologists today to explain the involuntary psychokinetic effects generally but misleadingly known as poltergeist phenomena.

Really thoroughgoing scientific research into psi is generally held to have been initiated by J. B. Rhine when he went to Duke University in North Carolina in 1927. This belief does scant justice to Myers, Gurney, Sidgwick, Richet and many other early researchers who were no less thorough and conscientious than Rhine and in fact developed the experimental methods that he employed, but did not work exclusively with them because they were not primarily concerned, as Rhine was, with proving the reality of ESP to a scientific community that was not only sceptical of the idea but often violently hostile to it. G. N. M. Tyrrell, one of the older generation of psychical researchers, said in his Presidential Address to the Society for Psychical Research in 1945, 'Let us now, before the restricted view of the laboratory worker gains too firm a hold, try to realise how wide our subject is. We should try once more to see it through the eyes of Frederic Myers as a subject which lies at the meeting place of religion, philosophy and science, whose business it is to grasp all that can be grasped of human personality.'[6] Rhine himself can't be accused of taking too restricted a view, in fact he has tried to argue a case for psi proving the existence of God. But his temperament, to judge from his writings, is not religious or philosophical, and his contributions on these levels have none of the trenchancy, sustained logic, passion and style of Gurney or Myers. His achievement has been considerable. He has demonstrated the existence of paranormal faculties in man, using methods of experiment and data-processing that satisfy the standards demanded in the exact sciences. But it has been an achievement gained at the cost of diminishing the psi faculty to a weak and erratic anomaly in the human personality.

Tyrrell foresaw this outcome when he warned of the effect of 'the restricted view of the laboratory worker' and pleaded that the broader philosophical view characteristic of Myers should not be lost. It was lost, however, and inevitably, for the evidence for psi obtained in the card-guessing and dice-throwing experiments conducted at Duke University and elsewhere from the 1930s on was basically uninteresting because it had no obvious relevance to anything outside the experimental situation. That a few people were able consistently to guess over many series of trials an average of about seven correct cards out of a pack of twenty-five consisting of five each of five different symbols, when by the laws of probability they should only be able to average five correct guesses, might be a phenomenon that wouldn't happen purely by chance once in a billion times, but what did it signify? That there were a few people around who were good card-guessers and nobody could explain how they did it? Well, there were greater and more intriguing mysteries than that in nature, and to go to the trouble of proving it by turning tens of thousands of cards would seem to prove more than anything else an inveterate superficiality of mind on the part of the experimenter. Such, at least, was the reaction of many thinking people who were not particularly impressed by the mathematical 'law of great numbers' and who looked to parapsychology for knowledge of the psyche not of the probability calculus.

But scientists and philosophers were impressed, or at least some of them were. They argued that although psi effects produced in the experimental situation may not be so startling as spontaneous ones occurring in life, it is an established principle of science that a small event produced in the laboratory may give us important information about much larger events that take place in the universe. For instance, men did not understand lightning until they discovered that sparks are produced between two electrically charged objects. The value of the card-guessing and dice-throwing (for testing for PK, or psychokinesis) experiments was that they were simple, repeatable and objectively assessable, and even if they only produced minimal psi effects these could be sufficient to enable researchers to learn more about this elusive human faculty. Such an argument makes sense, but the trouble was that the card-guessing technique did not meet the main requirement of the repeatable scientific experiment: that it should produce the same result every time. Some remarkable subjects were discovered, like Hubert Pearce at Duke and Basil Shackleton in London, but such consistently high scorers were few and far between, and after a time even they began to show what Rhine called a 'decline effect', a euphemism for the fact that they became bored with the whole business.

The characteristics of the psi function that emerged from the first phase of the modern period of experiment may be briefly summarised:

1. It is sporadic and ephemeral, even in the best subjects, but nevertheless it is not entirely an involuntary process. Gifted guessers showed the ability to score high or low, directly on the target card or on one of its neighbours, at will.

2. ESP works best when the subject is in a relaxed and unanxious state of mind. Performance is influenced by circumstances and by the relationship of the subject and agent.

3. Depressant drugs can destroy the faculty temporarily and stimulants restore it.

4. Consistent low scoring (technically known as 'psi-missing') produces extra-chance statistics which point to the operation of the psi faculty in a negative way.

5. It was difficult to ascertain in a straightforward card-guessing test precisely what kind of psi ability was being employed. Early experiments assumed that telepathy, mind-to-mind transference of a thought or image, would be the commonest form and the easiest to demonstrate experimentally, but some subjects showed an ability to guess 'down through' a pack of cards even before it had been opened, which suggested clairvoyance, and others revealed a tendency to guess a card which came one or two ahead of the target, which suggested precognition.

These and other characteristics of the psi function that emerged from the early work at Duke gave parapsychologists something to get their teeth into. Rhine established an area and method of research that remained the virtually unquestioned orthodoxy for some thirty years. Their strict demarcation of the research area and expertise with the probability calculus earned the 'psientists' a pat on the head from the establishment in 1969, when the Parapsychology Association was formally affiliated to the America Association for the Advancement of Science.

Some of the most interesting experiments of this phase of laboratory research into psi were carried out by women and showed perhaps a female interest in human personality and relationships in contrast to traditional male concern for logical integrity and mathematical abstraction. Dr Gertrude Schmeidler of City College, New York, conducted thousands of clairvoyance experiments in the '40s and '50s with standard card-guessing techniques, but she introduced a variation by finding out before the trial whether or not each subject believed in the possibility of a paranormal event occurring under the conditions of the experiment. Those who said they believed in the possibility she classified as 'sheep' and the disbelievers as 'goats'. The sheep consistently scored significantly above chance expectation and the goats below it, so here was clear evidence that attitude was a factor that influenced psi functioning and that a positive mental approach would enhance the chances of success. Dr Schmeidler also discovered through experiments in hospitals with patients recovering from concussion and with mothers after childbirth that the passive mind-states attendant upon these experiences favour psi functioning.

Dr Betty Humphrey of Duke had each of her experimental subjects draw something before the psi test. Those who executed bold drawings with strong lines and used all the space on the paper she classified as 'expansive' types, and those who produced small or conventional drawings she classified as 'compressive'. These are standard psychological terms roughly analogous to 'extrovert' and 'introvert'. Dr Humphrey's finding was that expansive types consistently scored well in ESP tests and compressive types below chance expectation.

The classroom situation was used by Drs Margaret Anderson and Rhea White to examine how basic interpersonal relation patterns affected psi. Teachers administered the tests, and the results showed a correspondence between success and failure in the test and the nature of the teacher–pupil relationship. If there was mutual liking the scores were high, and if there was dislike on one side or the other they tended to be low.

Such experiments as these went beyond simply establishing that psi occurs and tried to find out under what conditions it occurs and what factors, psychological and environmental, inhibit it or enhance it. In this they anticipated the trend of parapsychology in the '70s. Addressing the parapsychology seminar at the 1975 annual conference of the AAAS, Dr Charles Honorton, Director of Research at the Division of Parapsychology and Psychophysics at the Maimonides Medical Center, Brooklyn, said, 'We can now produce in the laboratory psi phenomena of much greater magnitude than in the 1930s, when the card-guessing method prevailed.' He was able to claim this on account of some fundamental changes that have taken place in recent years in experimental design, in technological aids to investigating psi functions, and in attitudes to psi research both at the establishment and the popular level, changes which have made possible bolder, more imaginative and searching investigations.

When Myers asked Sidgwick, in fear and trembling, whether he believed that 'from any actual observable phenomena . . . some valid knowledge might be drawn as to a World Unseen,' he lit a slow fuse that was to burn away for nearly a century before it finally exploded the rationalist-materialist view of man and the world that he found so repugnant, depressing and frightening. Though the 'actual observable phenomena' of modern parapsychology—mostly readings on super-sensitive electronic monitoring devices—were not of a kind that he could have imagined, and though the 'World Unseen' of today's investigations is not the spirit world (of which, if the 'cross-correspondences' evidence is what it seems, Myers must now be either a highly honoured or highly disreputable member), I think that if he were an observer of the contemporary scene he would be excited and heartened by the emerging implications of the science that he helped to found. In the Epilogue to his great work, *Human Personality*, he predicted that '. . . in consequence of the new evidence, all reasonable men, a century hence, will believe the Resurrection of Christ. . . . The ground of this forecast is plain enough. Our ever-growing recognition of the continuity, the uni-formity of cosmic law has gradually made of the alleged *uniqueness* of any incident its almost inevitable refutation. Ever more clearly must our age of science realise that any relation between a material and a spiritual world cannot be an ethical or an emotional relation alone; that it must needs be a great structural fact of the Universe, involving laws at least as persistent, and identical from age to age, as our known laws of Energy or of Motion.'[7] He was wrong about the general return of 'reasonable men' to Christian belief, but the rest of this passage is a precise statement of the central concept of the new gnosis, which is today gaining ascendancy over the Cartesian view through the empirical evidence brought to light by both parapsychology and modern physics.

3
Inter-Psychic Communication:
The Evidence for Telepathy

A Peruvian youth, kidnapped by Amazonian Indians, participated with them in a tribal ritual in which an hallucinogenic drink called *ayahuasca* was communally used, and later published a fascinating account of his experience in a book, *Wizard of the Upper Amazon*. He related how he had gone with eleven tribesmen to a secluded glade in the forest where, after some preparatory rituals and chants which established 'an intense feeling of rapport among the group', they each drank first one cup, then another of 'the magic fluid'. When the drug began to take its effect and the hallucinations started, he soon became aware that every member of the group, himself included, was seeing the same visions.

A procession of jungle cats prowled among them. A giant jaguar appeared, and 'a murmur from the assembly indicated recognition'. It 'shuffled along with head hanging down, mouth open and tongue lolling out. Hideous, large teeth filled the open mouth. An instant change of demeanour to vicious alertness caused a tremor to run through the circle of phantom-viewers.'[1]

This vision made him recall an experience from his own past, when on a forest path he had come face to face with a rare black jaguar. No sooner had the experience surfaced in his own memory than a shudder passed through the group and he realised that the terrifying animal he envisaged had entered into their collective vision. There followed other animals, snakes, and birds, scenes of battle with the tribe's enemies, which seemed to be re-enactments of past events. In one of these he recognised the present chief of the tribe as a much younger man and saw him kill another man in violent hand-to-hand fighting. The session concluded with visions of scenes in the new village where the tribe now lived, then, after taking some food to restore their bodily sensations to normal, the group returned to the village. 'Everyone seemed aware of the source of the black jaguar sequence of visions. It left a strong impression on them and resulted in my being given the name Ino Moxo, Black Panther.'

This account would seem to be an authentic example of the occurrence of telepathy at the mental level that Jung called the 'collective unconscious'. To doubt the writer's veracity would be merely captious, particularly as similar tales have been told by other travellers and anthropologists who have lived or worked among so-called 'primitive' people (for example Alexandra David-Neel in her *Mystery and Magic in Tibet* and Ronald Rose in *Living Magic*, an account of experiences with the Australian aborigines). Yet a curious situation exists with regard to the question of telepathy. Of all the psi functions it is the one that otherwise sceptical people find easiest to accept and believe they have personal experience of, but at the same time it is a thing that parapsychologists themselves are not sure ever occurs.

In the June 1974 issue of the *Journal of Parapsychology*, J. B. Rhine published an essay under the title 'Telepathy and other Untestable Hypotheses'. In it he argued that telepathy 'belongs on the list of unsolvable issues in parapsychology', and that time spent trying to prove its occurrence could be much more profitably occupied. At first sight, this is a surprising recommendation from the man who is credited with having demonstrated the reality of ESP to the satisfaction of a sceptical scientific community. However, Rhine is not saying that general extrasensory perception (GESP) does not occur, but only that the kind of ESP known as telepathy, as generally defined and understood, cannot be proved to occur, and that experiments designed to prove telepathy that start from the generally accepted definition are fruitless.

The generally accepted definition is that of Frederic Myers, who coined the term and defined it as 'transmission of thought independently of the recognised channels of sense'. In the nineteenth century the term 'thought-transference' was frequently used as synonymous with telepathy, and the phenomenon investigated was mind-to-mind communication. Experiments were designed in which an agent tried to 'send' a thought or mental image to a subject situated in another room, and results were obtained that appeared to confirm the hypothesis that there existed a parasensory channel of communication between minds which certain particularly gifted people were able to use. The hypothesis also seemed to be confirmed by the vast amount of anecdotal evidence, collected by the S.P.R., of spontaneous thought-transference, particularly in circumstances of crisis. All the evidence seemed to point to the conclusion that by means of deliberate concentration, or in circumstances that spontaneously produce such concentration, the mind can generate a kind of thought-energy that can be picked up by another mind with which it is attuned. This is a view still commonly held, but no parapsychologist accepts it as proven as an explanation of what occurs when the form of paranormal communication that we call telepathy takes place. When the novelist Upton Sinclair published accounts of his remarkably successful telepathy and clairvoyance experiments with his wife, he titled the book *Mental Radio*. It is the assumption that telepathy is a process analogous to radio communication, that *transmission* occurs by means of a *channel* and necessitates the *generation* of some kind of electromagnetic *energy*, that has turned out to be at once an unprovable and improbable hypothesis.

As ESP research became more sophisticated in the 1930s, it became increasingly obvious that the radio analogy was inapt. Early experiments by Rhine and his colleagues at Duke University established that it was not necessary for a 'sender' to be conscious of the target material for a 'percipient' to achieve significant extra-chance scores in card-guessing experiments. Higher scores were often achieved when nobody was aware of the targets until the subject had recorded his guess, which suggested that the psi faculty operating was clairvoyance or precognition.[2]

But if mind-to-mind thought-transmission and the radio communication model constitute an unsatisfactory definition of telepathy, both because they raise the semantic and philosophical problems involved in defining the terms 'mind' and 'thought' and because they assume that some kind of energy exchange takes place, we can still retain the term telepathy if we broaden Myers' definition to 'inter-psychic communication independently of the recognised channels of sense'. This is not mere hair-splitting, for it leaves the possibility open that telepathy may not be exclusively a function of the mind but may involve the whole person. As we shall see, there is now good experimental evidence that telepathy occurs at the physiological level. But before considering the evidence for telepathy that recent laboratory experimentation has turned up, let's look at some of the evidence for its occurrence in everyday situations.

A prominent member of the British S.P.R., Mrs Rosalind Heywood, has written a fascinating and thoughtful analysis of her own psi experience in her own life, *The Infinitive Hive*. As a description of these experiences, she favours the term 'telepathic interaction', which was suggested by Professor C. D. Broad, for she believes that such interaction is much more common than is generally supposed. Telepathic interaction, Mrs Heywood believes, often takes place without being noticed, as when two people have corresponding sensations or thoughts. The correspondence will only be noticed if one of them gives verbal expression to a passing thought or feeling, and this has happened enough in most people's experience to suggest there must have been many times when such a correspondence has gone unremarked. Again, changes of mood or impulses to do something, like telephone someone, might be attributable to telepathic interaction.

Mrs Heywood recalls an occasion when she obeyed an impulse to telephone Victoria station and check the time of a train her husband was arriving on. This was during the war, and he was returning for his first leave since the D-day landings in Normandy. She not only learned that the train would arrive an hour earlier than she expected, but she had a further impulse to go and meet it and to have a porter ready. Her husband was delighted when he stepped off the train. He said that as he had been unable to get into a phone-box at Folkestone he had decided during the journey to try to send her a mental message that he had more luggage than he had anticipated and would need help, and that when he had told her the arrival time he had forgotten the hour's difference between British and Continental time. Mrs Heywood's book[3] is full of incidents like this, sometimes quite trivial ones, some of which might be attributable to chance or to normal but unrecognised cause, but which collectively add up to strong and credible evidence for the operation of telepathy.

Puzzling over the fact that on two occasions when her husband was in mortal danger she had no telepathic impression of the fact, Mrs Heywood considers the conditions under which a coherent content of telepathic interaction gets through to consciousness. 'Quiet and a more or less inactive brain are important,' she writes, 'and *no expectation* on the part of my conscious mind.' On one of the occasions she knew at the time that he was in a dangerous situation, but she had no intimation of it, for 'worry . . . can inhibit the emergence of subconscious material'. On the other occasion, she speculates, she might have happened to be actively engrossed in something else. ESP occurs, it seems, only when the mind is in a passive, relaxed and receptive state. Schmeidler's investigations of hospital patients recovering from concussion or childbirth confirm this, as does research into psi-conducive states currently being done by Charles Honorton and his team at the Maimonides Medical Center.

In 1971 a New Jersey psychiatrist, Dr Berthold Schwarz, completed and published a ten-year study of telepathic interaction within his own family, *Parent-Child Telepathy*. He too comes to the conclusion that telepathic interaction is much more common than people normally suppose and that it often goes unnoticed because the information communicated is not of a dramatic nature. He and his wife paid particular attention to incidents involving their children, Lisa and Eric, and 'became skilled in recognising what really went on in the family in a nonverbal, subliminal, telepathic way'. Here are some examples from his book, which lists and analyses 505 'possible telepathic episodes' out of a total of 1520 that he had recorded by the time Lisa was fourteen and Eric twelve.[4]

'July 21, 1959, Tuesday, 6:00 p.m. I was taking a walk in the backyard with Lisa after dinner. While going down the hill and holding on to her hand, I noticed a few stray leaves on the ground from the pear and apple trees. The thought crossed my mind, "I wonder if the pear tree will die with these leaves coming down?" Lisa then verbally repeated the same words. When I asked her why she thought that, she said, "Mommy said so." I later checked with Ardis, who said she has never commented on the pear tree or any other trees to Lisa. During this walk Lisa was very affectionate.'

'October 31, 1959, 4:00 p.m. While I was reading a magazine

article, my mind tripped on the last words of J. P. Morgan, who died in 1913, "I must go up the hill." I wondered what this enigmatic statement meant to a man who had so influenced the growth of our country. While I was pondering over his last words, Lisa, who was playing at my side with pretzels on the lid of a can, said, "Go up the hill; go up the hill." When asked why she said this, Lisa remained quiet and looked straight ahead. Of course, Lisa was unable to read or write, and she had not said these exact words in the past. In her game and words Lisa faithfully acted out her father's perplexed absorption in a magazine article.'

'December 20, 1961, Wednesday, 3:10 p.m. My intention of writing "First Class Mail" on an important letter that had to go out right away was completely frustrated because there was no red pen on my desk. My search for it was to no avail. My thoughts went, "Oh, I suppose Ardis took it for the Christmas cards and never returned it! That poor blue pen is no good." At that point Eric bounded downstairs and into my office, "Here, Daddy, is the red pen!" This is a characteristic reaction for Eric. He is quick to comply with a wish of his parents, even when he is separated by distance with no known usual method of communication.'

Schwarz does not believe that his children are exceptional. He concedes that some of the possible episodes he has recorded may be due to coincidence or the picking up of subtle sensory clues, but he is convinced that telepathic interaction is normal between people with close emotional bonds, and that if other parents kept systematic records, as he and his wife did, many would come up with equally substantial evidence. He conjectures that we are all 'immersed in a sea of telepathic suggestions. We are tossed and buffeted by the waves, and what we often consider to be solely the products of our own independent judgement and jealous prerogatives can sometimes really be the result of subtly operating telepathic influences that can tie us together in bonds of a complex interdependency.'

To return now to laboratory evidence: a famous experiment devised by E. Douglas Dean of the Newark College of Engineering appears to substantiate Schwarz's hypothesis. Dean used a device called a plethysmograph, which measures fluctuations in blood volume in the fingertip. The index finger of the subject was connected to the device, and in another room an agent was given a list of names and instructed to concentrate on the names one at a time in random order and at the same time visualise the subject and his location. Some of the names were out of a telephone directory, others were of people emotionally connected with the subject. Now when a person receives information that has emotional significance for him certain physiological body changes occur. The plethysmograph registered that significant changes in the subject's blood volume frequently occurred when the agent concentrated on names of people the subject was close to, but when he was thinking about an unfamiliar name there were no such changes. The significant point of this experiment is that the subject was never *consciously* aware of what the agent was thinking. It was not mind-to-mind telepathy; he never said, for instance, 'Now he's thinking of Mary, my wife.' Without the evidence of the plethysmograph, nobody would have known that telepathic interaction was taking place.[5]

Similar experiments demonstrating that telepathic interaction takes place below the level of consciousness and in a manner that would not have been detectable by the card-guessing method of investigation have been reported by Charles Tart of the University of California at Davis, and by Harold Puthoff and Russell Targ of the Stanford Research Institute.

Tart's subject was 'wired up' to physiological recording devices, and was required to guess when electric shocks were administered to a second subject, who was in another room in the laboratory area. The second subject was given shocks at random intervals, and when this happened significant physiological changes in the first subject were registered by the recording devices. His conscious guesses, however, did not correlate with the physiological information.[6]

In Puthoff and Targ's experiment, a stroboscopic light was randomly flashed in the eyes of one subject, and a second, remotely isolated subject was asked to guess at given moments whether the light was on or off. Brainwave activity in both subjects was monitored, for the effect of exposure to stroboscopic light at about fifteen flashes per second is to produce alpha brainwaves. Puthoff and Targ found that although the second subject's guesses as to when the light was on were no better than might be expected on a chance basis, his EEG recorded alpha activity coincident with the first subject's and the shining of the light.[7]

These experiments all suggest that consciousness suppresses or censors telepathic information, and the object of a great deal of research work done in recent years has been to investigate the conditions under which this censoring process is itself suppressed and to incorporate them in the experimental setting.

Borrowing terminology from communications theory, parapsychologists today often refer to information received through ESP and information received through normal sensory channels as 'signal' and 'noise' respectively. To facilitate the emergence of psi information into consciousness the 'noise' produced by incoming information has to be reduced. A proven way of reducing sensory 'noise' is by Eastern techniques of meditation. Gertrude Schmeidler has reported a significant increase in subjects' scores in ESP trials following instruction by an Indian Swami in meditation and breathing exercises. The meditative state is characterised by the production of alpha brainwaves, and a number of researchers in recent years have found a correspondence between successful performance of ESP tasks and high alpha density in the EEG record of brain activity. Biofeedback has proved an invaluable investigative tool in these studies, which are the basis of Charles Honorton's claim that parapsychologists can now produce in the laboratory psi phenomena of much greater magnitude than they could produce in the 1930s. Honorton further believes that psi is not necessarily as elusive and erratic as it has generally been assumed to be, and that with the new techniques for reducing 'noise' and at the same time amplifying the weak ESP 'signal', 'we could achieve the goal of at least limited control of psi in the next decade'.[8]

On a visit to the Maimonides Medical Center in January 1975 I had an opportunity to discuss the research programme with Charles Honorton and to view a film made during a typical experimental session. These experiments, Honorton says, are designed to facilitate 'psi retrieval', i.e. to retrieve information from the subject's subconscious which is presented in visual form to the consciousness of the agent. They are based on three hypotheses: '(1) that conscious sensory isolation increases access to internal mentation processes;

(2) that mentation processes are susceptible to weak influences, including sensorially-noncontingent events in the external environment; and (3) that the correspondence between external event and internal process need not be literal.'[9]

A young woman is put into a state of sensory isolation. All inputs to consciousness through the normal channels of sense are blanked out. She wears a headset which delivers continuous 'white noise'. She reclines at ease in a chair in a shielded, sound-proof room. Halved ping-pong balls are fitted into her eye-sockets to ensure 'a homogeneous visual field'. She is asked to 'think out loud' for a period of thirty minutes, to give a running commentary on the thoughts and images that cross her mind. At some time during that period the agent, in another room, views a series of stereoscopic slides that are thematically related. The object of the experiment is to see whether material from the target slides viewed by the agent will be incorporated in the subject's commentary.

In the experiment featured in the film the target theme was scenes of Las Vegas. During the 'sending' period the young woman reported imagery of neon lights, nightclubs and theatre marquees in Las Vegas.

In a paper prepared for professional colleagues in 1974, Honorton gives verbatim transcripts from subjects' commentaries in other experiments in this series which show striking correspondences with the target material:

Target: U.S. Air Force Academy. Extract from commentary: '. . . An airplane floating over the clouds . . . Planes passing overhead . . . Thunder and angry clouds . . . Airplanes . . . Ultrasound . . . An airplane pointing down . . . A blaze of fire, red flames . . . A five-pointed star . . . A giant bird flying . . . Six stripes on an army uniform, V-shaped . . . Flying through the mountain . . . The sensation of going forward very fast . . . Machine gun. A ladder.'

Target: Rare Coins. Extract from commentary: '. . . now I see circles—an enormous amount of them. Their sizes are not the same . . . some are really large, and others are very tiny—no larger than a penny. They just keep flashing in front of me—all these different sized circles . . . Now I see colours—a complete array of colours. Two . . . in particular, gold and silver, seem to stand out more than all the others. I sense something important. I can't tell what but I get a feeling of importance, respect, value.'[10]

The close correspondences in these examples between the target material and the commentary, and the fact that the commentary including the on-target material occurred simultaneously with the brief 'sending' period within the thirty minutes of the experiment, would seem to constitute fairly sound proof of the occurrence of para-normal cognition. The experiment design has no controls to exclude clairvoyance or precognition, but the simultaneity of the commentary and the viewing does suggest that the agent plays an active part in the situation and therefore that telepathy, in the sense of inter-psychic communication without the mediation of normal sensory channels, takes place. Over a long series of such experiments, Honorton reports, 'the target programs were correctly identified in 43 per cent of the cases, which is significantly above the expected chance level of 25 per cent'. This statistic is based on the fact that a 'hit' is recorded when, at the end of a session, the subject correctly chooses from among four different thematic programmes on slides the one that was 'sent' during the experiment.

In one of the sessions at Maimonides the target pictures were taken from a magazine feature about the secret bombing of Cambodia, and while the agent was viewing these the subject reported images of President Nixon cleaning his nose! Such a symbolic 'hit' may have been coincidence, but on the other hand it may illustrate a significant point about telepathic interaction. Honorton's third working hypo-thesis was that 'the correspondence between external event and internal process need not be literal'. In other words, the conscious mind may sometimes make its own reconstruction of material received telepathically at the subconscious level. This happens in normal sensory perception. Modern physics and sensory physiology have shown clearly that our perception of the external world is a personal symbolic construction, sometimes quite idiosyncratic. If the same applies to extrasensory perception, this would make it extremely difficult to detect, and would also lend support to the theory that telepathic interaction is a normal function that continually takes place without our being aware of it.

The Maimonides Medical Center is no doubt best known for its 'dream telepathy' research, which Dr Montague Ullman initiated in 1964. Over the years many subjects have spent nights at the laboratory wired to electronic devices that record brainwave patterns and the rapid eye movements that signal dream activity. The aim of the experiments has been to incorporate extrasensory stimuli 'sent' by an agent in another room into the dreams of the subject. At the beginning of the session the agent randomly selects an envelope from a pile of them, each of which contains a postcard reproduction of a work of art. He concentrates on the picture throughout the night, and the sleeper is woken up periodically when the REM (rapid eye movement) monitor indicates that he has been dreaming for several minutes and asked to give an account of his dream while it is still vivid to him. In the morning the tapes of the subject's dream reports and the target pictures are given to independent judges who assess them for correspondences.

Here is an example. The target picture was of two boxers, one standing in the ring and the other falling over the ropes into the audience on the right of the picture. Awakened from his first dream, the subject reported: 'Something about posts. Just posts standing up from the ground and nothing else. There is some kind of feeling of movement . . . Ah, something about Madison Square Garden and a boxing fight. An angular shape, an irregular shape coming down from the right. The angular right-hand shape of the picture is connected with a Madison Square boxing fight. I had to go to pick up tickets to a boxing fight . . .'[11] This is clearly a 'hit', incorporating not only the theme of the picture, but at least a partially visualised reconstruction of it, with the 'shape coming down from the right' corresponding to the boxer falling over the ropes on the right of the picture.

Correspondences are not always as close as this, however, and very often are analogous rather than direct. For instance, one target picture was of two dogs standing with bared teeth over a piece of meat, and the subject reported a dream of eating a rib steak at a dinner party and being aware of two greedy friends eyeing her plate to see if she had more meat than they had. It was as if the subject had picked up the emotional rather than the visual content of the picture. In other cases there was evidence of telepathic interference. A young woman dreamed she was involved in a car accident on the Verazzano Bridge and found when she got home the next morning that her boyfriend had had a minor motorcycle accident on the same bridge the previous night. On another occasion the subject's dream report incorporated no details from the target picture viewed by the agent, Van Gogh's *Starry Night*, but had clear correspondences with the stories and pictures in a magazine that the young psychologist monitoring the session was reading, particularly an illustrated feature on topless swimsuits.

The most original and imaginative of the Maimonides team's experiments involved an English sensitive named Malcolm Bessent and crowds of young people at rock concerts. On six different occasions, while Bessent slept at the 'dream laboratory' in Brooklyn, the 2000 agents 45 miles away viewed a target picture projected on a screen and were told to try to 'send' it mentally to him. One evening the target was a picture of a man practising meditation. He was seated in a lotus position and the seven 'chakras'—the energy centres of the body believed in Indian 'occult anatomy' to be centred on the spinal column—were colourfully marked. In his account of his first dream, Bessent incorporated both the idea of energy and the image of the spinal column: 'I was very interested in using natural energy . . . I was talking to this guy who said he'd invented a way of using solar energy and he showed me this box . . . to catch the light from the sun which was all we needed to generate and store the energy . . . I was discussing with this guy a number of other areas of communication and we were exchanging ideas on the whole thing. He was suspended in mid-air or something . . . I was thinking about rocket ships . . . I'm remembering a dream that I had about an energy box and . . . a spinal column.'[12]

All the evidence of modern studies of telepathy points to the conclusion that information is conveyed in bits, not in coherent wholes directly corresponding to the original stimulus, and that these bits are interwoven with the contents of the subject's own subconscious memories or preoccupations. Professor Gardner Murphy, the Harvard psychologist who has been President of both the British and the American Societies for Psychical Research, has some suggestive thoughts on this subject: 'There seems to be something about the very nature of the process which involves a breaking up and a repetitiousness. It may be due to the fact that, after all, we have to live our lives in terms of the Darwinian principle of the struggle for existence, and it may be that there is much about the telepathic process which would interfere with everyday living. . . . One often gets the impression that . . . there is something deep within us that is reaching out and does want to make the contact, but really cannot bear the full impact of it, and so fragments it; then, in a moving tide, it tries to duplicate it and support it. Not able to do this, it finally flounders in the accretion of detail which can never assume the meaningful form of the totality.'[13]

The idea that a kind of biological censorship of psi experience operates has often been expressed, and we shall come across further evidence for it in later chapters. The psi faculty is not essential to survival or to the provision of primary needs, and indeed it may even put these in jeopardy for it is less focused and purposeful than the mental and sensory faculties we employ to sustain our biological existence. Modern parapsychological research has demonstrated that telepathic interaction is a much more common and continuous feature of life than we normally suppose, and if it is true that it is censored at a subconscious level and rarely allowed to impinge upon the conscious mental processes that we depend on for order and control, then we ought to ask whether biological survival and the maintenance of order and control are our sole needs. They may be primary in the sense that they have to be satisfied before any other needs can be, but they are not primary in the sense of being top of the list of our priorities of *values*. The biological censor is clearly a kind of motor mechanism serving the needs of an organism existing within an environment, but when those needs are satisfied the censor goes on operating just the same, cutting out experiences and information that serve what Abraham Maslow called man's 'meta-needs', i.e. needs that have life-enhancement value rather than life-sustaining value. We are not obliged to tolerate this situation, but in order to combat the tyranny of subconscious censorship we have to be aware that it is happening. Modern parapsychology has both made us aware of it and suggested methods of combating it. It is not surprising that the consciousness movement has shown interest.

4
The 'Psychic Eye':
The Evidence for Clairvoyance

Of all the ways a man can discover his vocation and peculiar talent, falling off a ladder must qualify as one of the most original. One day in 1943 a Dutch housepainter named Peter Hurkos fell thirty feet and landed on his head. For three days he was in a coma and his life was in the balance, but then he recovered consciousness, and shortly after he discovered a curious thing. He had become clairvoyant. In his book, *Psychic*, he relates how it happened:

'I did not know what it was at first, but I knew that suddenly I had a strange insight into the affairs of other people.

'I first became aware of this fact when, after the nurse had gone, I noticed another man in the bed next to mine. I had never seen this man before, but suddenly I knew a great deal about him.

'"You're a bad man," I blurted out.

'He looked at me, startled, not knowing whether to be annoyed or amused at a poor joke.

'"Why?" he asked.

'"Because when your father died, he left you a large gold watch— he died only a short time ago, and you have already sold the watch."

'The man in the next bed was dumbfounded.

'"How did you know that?" he asked, turning toward me.

'I felt my head. How had I known it? I was as dumbfounded as he was.'[1]

A short while later, Hurkos found himself suddenly moved to tell a nurse to be careful or she would lose a suitcase belonging to someone else on a train, which amazed the girl because she had done just that on a train from Amsterdam that morning. Then he had a sudden insight about a patient who was leaving the hospital, and told nurses and a doctor that the man was a British agent and that unless they stopped him leaving he would be shot by the Germans in a certain street in The Hague in a few days' time. Of course, nobody took any action. They later heard that the man had died in the manner and place that Hurkos had foretold.

Strictly speaking, clairvoyance is the ability to obtain extrasensory information about an object or event which is not known to any other person at the time. Many of Hurkos's feats could be put down to telepathy, but those he is best known for, namely his achievements as a psychic sleuth, if they have been truly reported, would constitute good evidence of clairvoyance. Hurkos claims to have helped police in many countries by clairvoyantly locating killers and murder weapons, and his name has been associated with the Boston Strangler investigations and the recovery of the Stone of Scone after it had been stolen from Westminster Abbey in 1950, but police departments have generally been cagey about corroborating his claims. Sounder evidence of his abilities has been furnished by the neurologist-parapsychologist Andrija Puharich, who between 1956 and 1959 spent a lot of time investigating Hurkos.

The form of clairvoyance that the Dutchman is reputedly most skilled at is that known as psychometry, or object-reading. He would hold an object, or a package containing one, in his hands, and give a spoken commentary on the associations that came to his mind in connection with it. In one carefully controlled test, Professor C. J. Ducasse of Brown University supplied an object in a sealed cardboard package for Hurkos to 'read'. Ducasse was not himself present during the experiment, and only after Hurkos had recorded his impressions did he send Puharich a letter giving information about the object. It was a small pottery jar which had been given to him thirty-six years ago by a friend who was now dead, and which had come from the ruins of Pompeii, the Roman city that had been buried in an avalanche of lava from an eruption of Vesuvius in A.D. 79. Hurkos's commentary when he handled the sealed package, which was tape-recorded and given before several witnesses, went: 'This object blew up—an explosion. There was an explosion—a long time ago. I hear a strange language. It is very old. It had to do also with water. I don't know what it is. I see a dark colour. It is not straight, not regular. It is very jagged, sharp points. It belonged to three people. I am sure of this. Dr Ducasse didn't buy this. It was given to him, and it was repaired. A souvenir. I am sure that the owner of the cylinder is dead. I do not mean Dr Ducasse, he is well.'[2] Though he did not specifically identify the object as a jar, Hurkos was clearly correct in most of his associations. Dr Ducasse's letter, which was written after the 'reading' took place, also confirmed that the jar had once been broken and repaired.

Puharich believes that when Hurkos gives a psychometric 'reading' the object serves as a kind of relay station which enables him to tune in telepathically to the consciousness of the person who has the relevant information, in this case Professor Ducasse. But he gives some further accounts of Hurkos's work which do not support this theory, for on several occasions the psychic gave correct information about future events connected with the object or its owner which could not have been in anyone's mind at the time. And sometimes he gave apparently wrong information which was subsequently found to be correct. For example, there was an occasion when Julian Huxley visited Puharich's laboratory and put Hurkos's abilities to an informal test. He produced a sealed envelope, which was then held by another person at the opposite side of the room from Hurkos. Hurkos gave a detailed description of the life and looks of a certain blonde woman. When he had finished Huxley said he was completely wrong, for the envelope contained a photograph of his son. Hurkos was puzzled, for the impressions he had been getting were quite definite. He suggested to Huxley that they must have come from a photograph that had lain next to that of his son in his wallet, and when Huxley looked in his wallet he found a photograph of a woman who answered to the description Hurkos had given, and he was able to confirm that the information about her was correct. He had not been thinking about this person or the picture of her in his wallet when Hurkos had been giving his 'reading', so the possibility that Hurkos obtained his information telepathically is diminished, though it cannot be entirely ruled out, for the information was in Huxley's mind even though he wasn't at the time consciously entertaining it.[3]

When telepathy can be definitely ruled out as an explanation of psychometry we are left with no alternative but to contemplate the phenomenon of the transfer of information from matter to mind.

This implies that matter has a memory, or at least some way of retaining traces of information which can be picked up by a sensitive, and this idea is so intrinsically improbable that many people prefer to believe that all the alleged evidence constitutes a massive fraud that psychics and parapsychologists have colluded in. Collusive fraud is not unknown in parapsychology, but when many different investigators of unimpugnable integrity report similar findings fraud is as improbable for any reasonable man as the infringement of the known laws of physics is for any intransigent sceptic. It may therefore be relevant to give another example of psychometry, which could in no way be put down to telepathy, and in which both the experimenter and the sensitive were people with long experience in the field and whose integrity had never been called in question.

The most respected medium of modern times was Eileen Garrett, who in her long life (1893–1970) worked unstintingly with parapsychologists who wished to investigate the psychic faculties that she possessed to an extraordinary degree. In her last years she co-operated with Lawrence LeShan, a psychologist who after completing a fifteen-year research project on psychosomatic medicine was led to pursue his investigations into the area of the paranormal. In his important book, *The Medium, the Mystic and the Physicist*, LeShan gives an account of some of his work with Mrs Garrett. One of the most convincing demonstrations he had of her abilities was the totally unexpected result of an experiment in psychometry.

LeShan was in New York and Mrs Garrett was 1500 miles away in Florida when he decided to conduct the experiment and made his preparations for it. He was going to see her the following day, and he assembled in his office a number of small objects, including an old Greek coin, a tiny fossil fish, a bit of stone from Mount Vesuvius, a piece of used bandage from a hospital and an ancient Babylonian clay tablet with an inscription. Each object was wrapped in tissue, sealed in a box and put into an envelope which was given a code number. To make doubly sure that no one knew what was in each envelope, another person, working alone, put the envelopes inside larger ones, which were also coded, and he alone was to retain a record of the double code numbers until the experiment was completed. This 'double blind' procedure ensured that the experimenter could neither practise fraud nor unwittingly leak information either telepathically or by means of sensory cues he might involuntarily give in the course of the 'reading'.

When the objects were being packed, LeShan found that he was one box short, so he went into a neighbouring office and asked a secretary if she had a suitable one. The secretary returned with him to his office to see what kind of box he needed, and happened to notice the clay tablet, which she picked up and examined. They talked about it briefly, then she went to look for a box, but while she was gone LeShan found one of his own and used it to pack the clay tablet in.

It was two weeks after this trivial incident before LeShan was able to conduct his psychometry experiment with Mrs Garrett. An assistant took notes, a tape-recorder was switched on, and Mrs Garrett picked up one of the envelopes, read the code number written on it and began to give the impressions she received from the object it contained. 'There is a woman associated with it,' she said, and went on to describe the secretary from the office next to LeShan's in New York, whom she had never met and could have had no knowledge of by normal means. She not only described her physical appearance in correct detail, even down to two scars on her body which subsequent checking showed to be exactly where she said, but also gave accurate information about her job history and her relationship with her daughter. When in due course Mrs Garrett's psychometric 'readings' were matched with the code numbers on the envelopes, it was found that the envelope she had handled when she gave this commentary contained the clay tablet that the secretary had picked up in LeShan's office two weeks before.[4]

This would appear to be a good example of pure clairvoyance, for the information Mrs Garrett obtained when she handled the envelope was unknown to anyone at the time, except of course to the secretary in New York, who did not know that the experiment was taking place. Was the clay tablet somehow charged with information by the last person who had handled it before it was packed, or did it function as a link or relay station for telepathic communication between the sensitive and the secretary? Both explanations are equally unacceptable to reason and science, and neither of them offers any clue as to why the sensitive picked up the particular information that she did, which had only a superficial and tenuous relation to the history and nature of the clay tablet. Conjecture can run wild confronted with such a mind-boggling phenomenon, can invent multiple universes, psychic networks, theories of mind imprinting memory traces on matter or matter possessing some of the properties of mind, but as such speculations can neither be proved nor disproved most parapsychologists have chosen to pursue their research and eschew conjecture, observing Wittgenstein's cautionary dictum, 'Whereof we cannot speak, thereof we should remain silent.'[5]

Pursuing a line of research suggested by the work of the Russian parapsychologist Leonid Vasiliev, Andrija Puharich conducted some experiments with Mrs Garrett in the 1960s. The object was to study the relation between electrical field forces and psi functions. Vasiliev's work had suggested that people in electrically charged environments would show enhanced psi ability, and this appeared to be independently confirmed by reports that men working with low-frequency electrical equipment had sometimes suddenly and quite unexpectedly found themselves susceptible to telepathic impressions. For the purpose of his experiments, Puharich had Mrs Garrett sit in a seven-foot-square Faraday cage. This is a metal box lined with copper which when the door is shut constitutes an electrical vacuum, for no electromagnetic waves from the outside world can penetrate it. The electrical field environment within the cage can be controlled and varied by electrically charging the walls of the cage. Using this equipment, Puharich was able to test whether Mrs Garrett could detect changes in the electrical field surrounding her, and also whether variations in this environment would enhance or diminish her psi faculties. Both hypotheses were positively and quite dramatically confirmed in the course of the series of experiments.

An automatic random-switching generator supplied the charge, and Mrs Garrett's task in the first experiments was to call out when she felt that a charge was present on the walls of the cage. Charges were randomly spaced between 30 seconds and 12 minutes apart and their occurrence was automatically recorded. Mrs Garrett's reactions to the changed electrical conditions corresponded with the record 86 times out of 91, which demonstrated quite clearly that she was able to sense these subtle changes. Placed near her in the cage was a highly sensitive microphone which picked up changes in Mrs Garrett's breathing also corresponding with the occurrence of the charges, an effect for which there was no known precedent with other subjects. The effect was a very slight inspiratory gasp, which Puharich conjectures was due to a disturbance of the charged ions within the cage. Ions are clusters of molecules present in the atmosphere which may have either positive or negative charges, and it is a well-established fact that variations in ion-density have effects on both physiological and mental processes. In later experiments Puharich found that under ion-deficient conditions subjects could not exceed better than chance scores in ESP tests, whereas in ion-enriched conditions they consistently scored significantly above chance and moreover did not exhibit the usual tendency of ESP subjects to produce diminishing returns as the experimental series progressed.[6]

Mrs Garrett having demonstrated that she could detect subtle electrical field changes on the outer walls of the cage, two further control experiments were conducted to ascertain whether this was a case of paranormal cognition. The first was designed to check that the cage was completely impermeable to electromagnetic radiation of the frequencies used in the experiments, and the second to find out whether it was possible that the sensitive's body was acting as a detector for these frequencies. Both tests produced negative results, which clearly lent support to the paranormal hypothesis. The next stage was to compare the results obtained when the sensitive was given an ESP task while sitting in a charged cage with those obtained when she sat in an uncharged cage.

The target in this case was situated 0.3 miles from the sensitive, and was a crystal device designed to detect large showers of cosmic rays from the ionosphere, several miles above the earth. Its output was recorded on a moving paper graph, and Mrs Garrett's task was to guess when particularly intense bursts of cosmic rays were recorded on the device. As cosmic ray showers are totally random events and the target device was completely automated, this was an experiment in which any extra-chance results could only be attributable to Mrs Garrett's clairvoyant powers. The periods for which the cage was to be electrically charged or left uncharged were determined by reference to a table of random numbers. When the results were analysed they yielded clear proof of an interaction between an electrical field and the process of paranormal cognition. During the periods when the cage was uncharged Mrs Garrett's guesses corresponded with the markings on the graph paper with no greater frequency than might be expected, but when the cage was charged the correspondences were of a frequency that gave extra-chance odds of a million to one. And this wasn't all. Mrs Garrett's clairvoyance was so enhanced in the charged ambience that she was able to say what people were doing in other parts of the building. She identified a researcher in a neighbouring laboratory and said that he was at that moment putting a cylinder into a boxlike machine, which Puharich immediately checked and found to be true. On another occasion she said that an engineer in the control room was at that moment writing the figures 0, 2, 3 and 5. Later checking revealed that the engineer had written the figure 23:50 some three-and-a-half minutes after Mrs Garrett had said he was doing so, which would appear clearly to demonstrate that under favourable conditions her clairvoyance could reach into the future.

The stupendous problem that confronts parapsychologists investigating clairvoyance is to find an approach, theoretical or methodological, that will enable them to get their research off the ground. The phenomenon is so complex and erratic, it functions so differently with different people and under different conditions, that there are an infinite number of variables to be distinguished and brought under control before anything can be said about it with any degree of confidence. Puharich's work is an example of good parapsychological research guided by intelligent conjecture and making use of modern technological expertise. It does not unravel the mystery of clairvoyance, but it contributes a significant gain in knowledge of the conditions under which it best functions. And even those who hold that psi faculties are a vestigial phenomenon biologically and socially useless to modern man surely cannot deny that evidence of subtle interaction between human mental processes and environmental influences constitutes an advance in knowledge that is both valuable in itself and of potential practical use.

In her state of heightened mental acuity Mrs Garrett often experienced what she called 'travelling clairvoyance'. By this, Puharich says, 'she meant that she had the distinct impression of literally looking in upon friends in New York City, Washington, D.C., London, and Southern France'. In one observed long-distance experiment, she is said to have 'travelled' from New York to Reykjavik in Iceland and correctly described the appearance, activities and surroundings of a certain Dr Svenson. The subject of travelling clairvoyance is a dicey one for parapsychologists to tangle with, for it leads them into the thickets of the occult where they have to rub shoulders with survivalists and believers in astral projection and the existence of the etheric body. But out-of-the-body experiences have been recorded in all cultures throughout history, and reports from widely different and unconnected sources have so many similarities that the phenomenon cannot be lightly dismissed as superstition or hysteria. One of the most sceptical psychical researchers of the middle period, Hereward Carrington, who specialised in exposing fraudulent mediums, co-operated with a young psychic named Sylvan Muldoon in writing a book, *The Projection of the Astral Body* (1929), in which many examples were given of Muldoon's having obtained correct information about distant events allegedly by travelling out of his physical body. More recently Professor Charles Tart of the University of California has conducted some controlled experiments with subjects who claim to be able to practise out-of-the-body projection. His first subject was a young woman who told him that since childhood she had quite regularly woken up briefly in the night and felt that she was floating near the ceiling of her bedroom and could look down on her body lying in the bed. It had never occurred to her to ask whether the experience was a dreamlike hallucination or a genuine projection of a part of her consciousness, so Tart suggested a simple home experiment, which she proceeded to carry out according to his instructions. She wrote the numbers 1–10 on slips of paper, scrambled them in a box and after she went to bed at night blindly picked one out at random and placed it on her bedside table in a position where she could not see it from the bed. If she had an out-of-the-body experience during the night she should be able to look down on the number from her position near the ceiling, make a mental note of it and check its accuracy the following morning. The young woman tried the experiment on seven nights, she told Tart when they met some weeks later, and each time she got the number right. Of course, this couldn't count as proof of anything, but it was clearly a claim that invited further investigation.

Miss Z, as Tart called her in his paper describing his experiments, slept under observation in a psychophysiological laboratory on four different occasions. Her brainwaves, eye movements, bloodpressure and the electrical resistance of her skin were monitored by means of tiny electrodes attached to her skull and body, and when she was settled in bed and wired to the recording machines Tart retired into a nearby office and wrote a five-digit random number on a large white card which was then placed on a shelf near the ceiling. There was an observation window overlooking the place where Miss Z slept, and anyway she could not stand up without disrupting the operation of the recording machines in the neighbouring room, so if she correctly reported the target number she could not have obtained the information by normal means. On all four nights Miss Z said that she had had out-of-the-body experiences, but only on one occasion did she feel that her second body had floated to a position from which she could observe the target number, which she said was 25132. This was a correct answer which could be obtained by chance only once in 100,000 attempts. [7]

Similar experiments were carried out by the American Society for Psychical Research in 1973 with the New York psychic Ingo Swann. Swann said that when he was in his second body his vision was not acute enough to distinguish figures, so in these experiments the targets were randomly selected objects which were placed in an open-topped box suspended from the ceiling. Swann either gave a verbal description or made a drawing of the object in the box. A series of eight such experiments was completed, then an independent judge was given the task of matching Swann's drawings and descriptions with the actual target objects. He made a correct match each time. Swann's explanation of how he acquired the information was that he felt his spirit leave his body, rise to the ceiling, look into the box and then return to his body. The ASPR researchers devised some ingenious experiments to test this explanation. They created target material in the box that would look different from different points of observation, so that if Swann were identifying the targets by ESP from his seated position his description would differ from the one he would give if he were really looking down into the box. For example, two flickering slides of a horse were projected on to a screen in the box so that, viewed by normal vision from the ceiling directly above, the horse would appear to run to the left. And this is what Swann in fact saw. Tart writes, 'All the initial data from studies of Swann . . . seem to fit the hypothesis that he has something analogous to an eye located at the OOBE [out-of-the-body experience] location, rather than using ESP from the position of his physical body.'[8] If this were conclusively demonstrated, it would certainly be a fact to delight the survivalists and believers in the etheric body.

Despite this evidence most parapsychologists today think it is very much a moot question whether clairvoyance is in any way analogous to physical vision. To invoke one unknown and unprovable factor to explain another is neither sound science nor sound philosophy, and though clairvoyants may feel that they occupy a location removed from their physical body, and account for the feeling in terms of an astral or etheric body or a third eye, there is not a vestige of convincing evidence for the existence of any such entity. And the logical difficulties in the way of accepting its existence are immense. It would have to be a non-physical entity, or, if physical, composed of matter so subtle and diffused as to be undetectable by the most sensitive instruments, and yet it would have to be able to travel in physical space and to interact with matter. Normal sense perception is a physical interaction involving an object, light rays emanating from it and electrochemical activity in the eye and the brain of the percipient. This interaction is what we refer to when we speak of 'seeing' something, and unless the postulated third eye or etheric body can be shown to have nerve cells to receive the visual image and brain cells to interpret it, to speak of it 'seeing' is not only imprecise but misleading and meaningless. Furthermore, even the correspondence between the end results of the processes of normal vision and clairvoyance—the fact that a certain scene looks the same viewed normally or clairvoyantly—is difficult to explain if we hold to a theory that sense perception and clairvoyance work analogously. For modern studies of vision have shown that the human eye is a very imperfect

77

optical instrument, that the image projected on the retina is extremely blurred and distorted and that in the act of perception the brain corrects these faults and composes a correct image of the external world. As the image of an object perceived clairvoyantly corresponds with the image formed by sense perception, an analogy between the two functions implies that a similar process of distortion and correction, involving electrochemical activity in brain cells, takes place in paranormal perception. Tart's hypothesis that a psychic like Swann has 'something analogous to an eye located at the OOBE location' seems very dubious in the light of these considerations, for it would necessitate the existence of a separately located brain as well as an eye. The dilemma might be skirted by postulating that the remotely located psychic 'eye' somehow transmits impulses that activate the percipient's visual cortex, but it is a poor theory that has to resort to the word 'somehow', and in discussing psi phenomena we ought to observe Occam's law in favour of parsimony in baseless speculation. The present brief discussion is not intended to lead to any conclusion as to how clairvoyance works, but simply to draw attention to the kind of problems that arise with the adoption of a perceptual model of its operation. The point needs to be emphasised because the very terms 'clairvoyance' and 'extrasensory perception' imply such a model.

To name a phenomenon is to circumscribe it, to adopt a conceptual model is to delimit the area of the possible, and consequently terminological and conceptual innovations can open up new vistas of possibility and fields of investigation. Broad's term 'telepathic interaction' is, as we have seen, both more definitive and more suggestive than the word 'telepathy', and perhaps we need a similar neologism for clairvoyance, a term that does not imply a perceptual function and which allows that the phenomenon may not be a freak occurrence but an ability quite common among human beings and possibly animals, which is generally unnoticed, undeveloped and neglected. The parapsychologist Rex Stanford has suggested the term 'psi-mediated instrumental response'; it may not be very felicitous even when reduced (as parapsychologists maddeningly reduce everything) to its initials, PMIR, but the idea behind the formulation does for clairvoyance what Broad's term does for telepathy: expands the range of its influence to everyday behaviour and situations. The basic idea is that organisms, human and animal, commonly make use of clairvoyance to enable them to make responses that are instrumental in fulfilling their needs. PMIR can occur, Stanford writes, '(a) without a conscious effort to use psi, (b) without a conscious effort to fulfil the need subserved by PMIR, (c) without prior sensory knowledge that the need-relevant circumstance even exists and (d) without the development of conscious perceptions (e.g. mental images) or ideas concerning this circumstance.'[9] The fact that clairvoyance occurs has been demonstrated by hundreds of experiments, and surely, Stanford argues, it does not exist only for the purpose of enabling people to call cards in the parapsychological laboratory. It must serve some purpose in everyday life, and to assume that it does would be to give a new direction and impetus to research.

That ordinary people who would not consider themselves at all psychic can develop and exhibit clairvoyance is a possibility that has been explored by a number of researchers using hypnosis. This is by no means a new departure, for Mesmer and his followers recorded many incidents in which people in a condition of what was in the nineteenth century known as mesmeric sleep gave descriptions of contemporary distant scenes or happenings which were later verified. Hypnotism, however, was not much used for the purpose of psi research in Western countries—though it was in Russia—until quite recent years, and the man who has been chiefly responsible for making it an investigatory tool is Dr Milan Ryzl, whose 1966 paper in the *International Journal of Parapsychology* under the title *A Method of Training in ESP* stimulated a great deal of interest and further research. We have had occasion to refer earlier to some unfortunate developments of Ryzl's work, but although his one in ten success in developing psychic ability in unselected volunteer subjects may dampen the hopes of would-be psychics who purchase the 'revolutionary Ryzl method', from a parapsychological point of view it is a highly significant success rate.

The Ryzl technique takes trainee psychics through five stages. The first is a psychological preparation designed to instil confidence, get rid of any fears and give the subject an understanding of the procedures of hypnosis. In the second stage the subject is trained to

79

enter hypnotic trance easily and quickly and to experience visual, auditory and tactile hallucinations. He must quite clearly and distinctly see objects, shapes, colours, hear music or bells, feel warm or cold breezes. With eyes closed, and in deep trance, he learns to observe himself as from a distance, to check the time on his watch, to visualise details of his surroundings. This stage of training continues until the hallucinatory world is as real to him as the world of waking consciousness. Then comes the crucial step, the crossing of the frontier into the area of the paranormal. The subject who has learned to visualise vividly commonplace objects and scenes is now required to see equally vividly things he has never experienced before, such as a green flower on a blue stem. He has to mentally travel into a neighbouring room where he has never been and describe the surroundings. He has to describe what an object placed where he cannot see it looks and feels like. This normally takes a great deal of time and effort, and many subjects never succeed, but those who do discover in themselves a latent psi ability which is further developed in stage four of the process. At this stage the clairvoyant learns to identify increasingly difficult and distant targets, to 'travel' clairvoyantly, drop in on friends or relatives and report what they are doing, and even to predict future events. Then comes stage five, when the fully-fledged psychic learns to function independently of the hypnotist, autonomously to enter and emerge from deep trance, and generally to bring his developed psi faculty under control.

If Ryzl is right and one person in ten is capable of developing paranormal abilities by his method, prevailing ideas of human nature and potentials clearly stand in need of revision. In recent years a number of investigators have achieved results that suggest that he is right.

In 1970 Dr Burton S. Glick, chief of psychiatric research at Mount Sinai Hospital, New York, read in a professional journal about some of the work being done in a 'dream laboratory' at the Maimonides Medical Center. He was sceptical, but interested enough to wish to attempt to replicate the work himself. However, he lacked the necessary monitoring equipment to work with subjects in dream states, so he decided to see if similar results could be obtained with hypnosis, which he frequently used in his clinical work. He obtained the cooperation of a twenty-year-old nurse named Beth, a girl who had never had any paranormal experiences but who believed in the possibility of their occurrence. When Beth was in a deep hypnotic trance, Glick crossed the room to a large box which contained a number of envelopes and picked one out at random. The envelope contained two others, which ensured that the target, an art print sealed in the inner one, could not be seen by normal vision even in the brightest light. It was only after the experiment that Glick himself knew what the target picture was. It was a print of a painting entitled *The Gulf Stream*, which depicted a man standing on a boat, an agonised expression on his face as he struggles to prevent it sinking.

Glick placed the envelope on Beth's lap and told her, 'You will concentrate so hard on the picture that it will seem as though you are walking right into it. You will participate in whatever action is depicted. You will see everything very clearly because you will be part of it. When I count to three, you will start telling me of your thoughts, fantasies, visions, associations, feelings and moods concerning the picture.' Here, transcribed verbatim from the tape-recording made at the time, is Beth's account of what she clairvoyantly saw:

'There's a figure—the figure in the foreground—a figure that's suffering—more than suffering—the figure is in great pain.

'It's a beautiful scene, though: the scene in the background is beautiful and the figure doesn't belong in that scene. Trees, and the colours—beautiful colours. The figure can't move; the figure can't see, can't see the—everything around him he can't see. It's a man.

'Everything is—the background is in perspective. It's just a beautiful scene, a scene of nature. It's very realistic but the figure is distorted. It's almost as though the figure is stretched out—on top of something: no, against something. Everything is going—everything is swirling around him, but nothing is really moving. I don't know if he's moving, swirling, spinning around. No. Everything around him is moving. He's standing still.'[10]

This is not a direct hit, a clear visualisation of the target picture, but it corresponds with both the theme of the picture and its predominant emotion: a man standing against a background of 'a scene of nature' in which he 'doesn't belong' and suffering agonies. As Beth was in a 'free choice' situation and could have imagined an infinite number of things, such a correspondence could hardly have occurred by chance and indicates a paranormal mode of perception.

Another researcher who has worked independently with subjects who have not previously exhibited psi ability is the hypnotist Lee Edward Levinson. Like Ryzl, he has discovered that about ten per cent of normal people possess latent psi faculties that can be brought out under hypnosis. He describes an experiment with one of his more successful subjects, a young artist and housewife who for the purpose of his report and to maintain her anonymity he named Kate. In the presence of two witnesses, a man and a woman, Levinson put Kate into a deep trance and told her that when she awakened she would leave the room for a while, then return and find an object which would have been hidden in her absence. Two assistants escorted her from the room when she was awakened, and Levinson asked the witnesses to supply or suggest an object which could be hidden. The man's door key was chosen, and Levinson put it high above a window-sill, but the man, perhaps thinking the hiding place too obvious or suspecting collusion between Levinson and his subject, suggested that it should be hidden in the woman's bra. Kate was then brought back into the room. She didn't consciously know what she was supposed to do, but obeying the post-hypnotic suggestion she crossed the room and said that she felt that there was something she had to find there. At the window-sill she stopped and concentrated for a moment. 'I feel it was placed here first,' she said, 'but I don't feel that it is on this side of the room any longer.' When Levinson asked her what she thought the object was, she said at first, 'It is small,' then, 'I feel that it is metallic', and after concentrating further, 'It's a key.' She walked over to the woman, pointed at her bosom and said, 'They've placed it inside there. But I'm not going to retrieve it.'[11]

Accounts of anecdotal and experimental evidence for clairvoyance could be piled up ad infinitum. There is not space in the present context to elaborate upon the evidence afforded by the phenomena of map dowsing, radiesthesia, lucid dreams and the voluminous technical literature produced by parapsychologists who have patiently worked through thousands of card-guessing experiments with gifted subjects like Ryzl's star discovery, Pavel Stepanek. By now, the fact that clairvoyance really occurs and that the evidence for it cannot be put down to chance, fraud or statistical anomaly hardly needs further proof, and in this chapter I have been chiefly concerned with surveying the work and theories of investigators who have asked how and under what conditions it occurs. The conclusion that such investigations point to is that man and nature, mind and matter, are more intimately and subtly interlinked than common sense and prevailing scientific concepts acknowledge, and that the mind has access to channels of information exchange that are not subject to the laws of cause and effect and the limitations that space imposes on physical interactions. In the next chapter we shall survey the evidence for the fact that mind can also transcend the limitations inherent in common-sense concepts of the nature of time.

5

Mind Out of Time:
The Evidence for Precognition

Sixteen people filed into the room and occupied individual chairs, each of which was numbered. On entering the room each person had drawn a number from a black bag, which indicated the seat that he or she should occupy. When they were all seated and attentive a tape-recorder was set going. The voice on the tape said, 'Seat number 14: a lady, height one metre seventy to one metre seventy-five, age group forty to fifty. Within the last year, accident in own house injuring the knee by slipping on the steps. Profession: helping other people to spend their leisure time.'[1]

The occupant of seat number 14 was a lady aged forty-two, an actress by profession, whose height was one metre seventy-two, and who confirmed that she had had an accident in her home some months before in which she had injured not her knee but her ankle. She had picked out the number of her seat at random when she entered the room, and the description given by the voice on the tape fitted her and nobody else present. The voice was that of a German psychic named A. Orlop. He had recorded his prediction two weeks before in Mannheim, Germany, and mailed it to Dr H. C. Berendt, President of the Israeli Parapsychology Society, who had assembled the participants for this meeting, which took place in Jerusalem.

The 'empty chair' test was devised by the French psychical researcher of the middle period, Eugene Osty, a man renowned for his critical acumen and scrupulousness in creating carefully controlled conditions for investigations, and whose book, *Supernormal Faculties in Man* (1925), remains a classic of its *genre*. In the 1920s Osty conducted a number of successful chair test experiments with a German clairvoyant named Ludwig Kahn, but this type of experiment was dropped during the period when evidence for psi was chiefly sought through card-calling procedures, and its recent revival is due to the work of Dr W. H. C. Tenhaeff of the University of Utrecht in

Holland, who discovered in Gerard Croiset a psychic with rare and consistent ability.

Croiset is mainly known as a clairvoyant who has often helped police solve murders and locate missing persons. In addition to these dramatic feats of clairvoyance, he has repeatedly demonstrated his precognitive ability in chair tests, which have the evidential advantages of being objective, easily assessable and foolproof. A film made in Holland in 1969 shows Croiset describing a man and a woman who were to attend a meeting in Denver, Colorado, some weeks later. The man, he said, would be wearing 'a coat with green spots made by a chemical from his work in a scientific laboratory'.[2] He said that the woman would have had an emotional experience connected with page 64 of a book she was reading. When the second part of the film was shot in Denver and the assembled people were asked to fill in forms answering questions about themselves, one of the men was found to have a jacket with green spots caused by a chemical, and one of the women admitted that she had been upset by a passage in a book dealing with the problem of putting a cat to sleep, and when the book was examined the disturbing passage was found on page 64.

On another occasion, when thirty people had been invited to attend a meeting in Rotterdam, Croiset was asked four days before the meeting to describe the person who would occupy chair number 18. But he said, 'I see nothing,' and though urged to try again he insisted that he could get no impression of the occupant of the target chair. The night of the meeting arrived and despite a heavy snowstorm 29 of the people invited turned up and occupied seats at random. The empty seat was number 18.[3]

Having written the above paragraphs, I have to confess to a minor crisis of conscience. It is doubtful whether the cause of parapsychology is served by the repetition of such evidence, the antecedent improbability of which is formidable. And when experiments with famous psychics become reminiscent of performances given by stage magicians or mentalists, it is difficult to know whether the phenomenon has elicited genuine supernormality in the performer or residual superstition in the observer. But this is the kind of evidence that the reader of parapsychological literature continually comes up against, and as crises of conscience and credulity are hazards inherent in the subject, it is perhaps as well to confront and examine them when they arise instead of bypassing them, even if doing so results only in a confession of perplexity. An all-knowing attitude, whether credulous or incredulous, is a singularly inappropriate one to adopt with regard to evidence for the paranormal. So, with the reservation that the Croiset material brings me close up against my own credulity threshold, I will allow the above paragraphs to stand, if only as illustrative of the kind of dilemma that must beset anyone who delves into parapsychological literature.

A chair test must be a very convincing proof of paranormal faculty for the person who conducts and controls it, but the person who observes or reads about such an experiment will hardly be able to suppress the suspicion that the result is accountable to collusion or some kind of subterfuge. Human fallibility, mendacity, vainglory and gullibility are realities more familiar to us than aberrations from the laws that causes must precede effects and that events take place in an orderly sequential manner in the context of linear time, and if the intelligent, open-minded man is to be convinced that such aberrations occur he will require more substantial proof than accounts of feats of prediction that resemble the performances of stage virtuosi.

Precognition is a bigger hurdle for the normal sceptic to take than either telepathy or clairvoyance. It is easier to believe that information can be received paranormally from other minds or even from material objects than that it can come from the future. This is perhaps because we are more ready to believe that our ideas of physical reality are at fault than that our ideas of temporal reality are. But this readiness is a cultural bias. In the West in the present century we have seen concepts of physical reality change dramatically; and as for time, this is of all the mysteries of the universe the one we have most thoroughly demystified and domesticated, with our clocks, calendars and schedules. Individuals, corporations and nations devote a lot of time to planning the future, making decisions and taking actions that will shape it, and making predictions that are extrapolations from current trends, but all these activities are based on the assumption that effects ineluctably proceed from causes, and our commerce with the future is programmed along such familiar lines that it is inconceivable that a future event that has no causal connection with the present can be known. An extra rung is added to the hurdle by the fact that the majority of people in our culture find utterly repugnant the idea that the future is in any way predetermined, for a philosophy that appears to lead to fatalism ill accords with a social ethic that preaches that self and circumstances can be improved by diligent effort, intelligent free choice and careful planning.

And yet statistical surveys have clearly established that precognition is the *commonest* type of spontaneous psi experience, particularly in dreams. This surprising fact suggests an interesting conjecture. According to Jungian theory, dreams are compensatory, i.e. the unconscious produces dream material that the conscious mind suppresses as irrelevant to its purpose, and by producing such material the unconscious seeks to maintain in the personality a 'total psychic equilibrium'.[4] As the very idea of precognition subverts the hegemony of the conscious mind, which is based on reason, logic, linear time and cause-and-effect, it would follow from Jungian theory that consciousness would suppress it and that it would emerge in dreams. And this appears to be what happens. An analysis of thousands of reported ESP experiences in the United States showed that about 40% of them were precognitive and 68% of these occurred in dreams. A similar survey in Germany established that 52% of 1000 reported cases were precognitive, and in an English survey precognition accounted for 34% of 300 cases.[5] However repugnant it may be to reason and logic, it seems that the paranormal acquisition of knowledge of future events is a rather widespread and common occurrence.

The evidence afforded by dreams is, however, for obvious reasons difficult to assess. Dreams are subjective events and are often elaborately symbolical, and to qualify as evidence for precognition a dream must be told to another person or preferably written down immediately after its occurrence and before the event that verifies it, and it must also contain enough specific detail to rule out the possibility of coincidence. Other possibilities that must be ruled out are that the dream is predictive rather than precognitive, i.e. that it is the product of an unconscious reasoning process, and that its fulfilment is a result of the dream itself, in other words that it is a self-fulfilling prophecy. When these stringent conditions are applied, however, there remain among the records of research numerous dreams that qualify as genuine precognitions.

Take an example. Dr Walter Franklin Prince, a clergyman and historian who became a professional psychical researcher, wrote that he had experienced in his life four dreams compared with which all his other dreams were 'as the glow-worm to the lightning-flash'. He knew that these dreams were special immediately upon awakening from them, for the imagery in them was extraordinarily vivid and the emotion they aroused particularly intense. Here is Dr Prince's account of one of his dreams:

'During the night following the day Jan. 7th, 1902, probably to-wards morning, I dreamed that I was looking at a train, the rear end of which was protruding from a railway tunnel. Then, suddenly, to my horror, another train dashed into it. I saw cars crumple and pile up, and out of the mass of wreckage arose the cries, sharp and agonized, of wounded persons. I could distinctly see some pinned under the wreckage. Then other persons hurried up, and seemed to be occupied in trying to get the imprisoned persons clear. And then what appeared to be clouds of steam or smoke burst forth, and still more agonizing cries followed. At about this point I was awakened by my wife, since I was making noises indicative of distress . . . my brain seemed to echo with the after-effects of the crash, the hissing steam and the frenzied screams. It was many minutes before they quite subsided. The dream was related to my wife before I went to sleep again.'[6]

Prince left home the following morning and was away all that day and the following night. In the afternoon, Mrs Prince was talking to a neighbour, who told her about a railway disaster that had occurred in New York that morning. Mrs Prince immediately recognised the parallels between the details of the neighbour's account and those of her husband's dream. Prince himself did not learn about the accident until he read the newspapers the following day. He, too, was struck by the parallels, and later he made a list of the 'coinciding particulars':

'(1) A collision of railway trains; (2) In a tunnel; (3) At the tunnel entrance; (4) A rear end collision; (5) The killing and injuring of people by the first impact; (6) The added horror of 'steam or fire'—what I saw in the dream being dense clouds of what might have been steam or smoke, and what occurred being that the steam-pipes burst and also the wreckage took fire; (7) The further infliction of death and injury by the steam; (8) The fact that men rushed in and began cutting away the debris and saving the unfortunate *before* the steam and flames broke forth; (9) Temporal proximity—the disaster proving to have been not more than six and probably not more than four hours after the dream; (10) Comparative proximity of place—the collision occurring not in some other country or some distant part of our vast land, but within seventy-five miles, in a locality familiar to me.'[7]

The dream, moreover, had no connection with any of Prince's conscious thoughts, fears or experiences; it was objective, extraordinarily vivid, and immediately recognised as belonging to a unique category. He did not keep a copy of the newspaper account, but the dream experience remained etched in his memory and when he wrote it down for the psychical researcher Dr Hyslop seven years later his account was found to tally in precise details with newspaper reports of the event. Prince himself never asserted that his dream was precognitive, but the detailed correspondences between it and the later rail disaster in New York certainly render the only alternative explanation of coincidence highly improbable.

Precognitions of disaster or death outnumber precognitions of happy events by four to one, and in about eight out of ten cases they involve a close personal relationship and occur within a few hours or days of the event precognised. These statistics are the findings of Dr Ian Stevenson, who has made a systematic study of precognitions of disasters.[8] Two of the most harrowing and unexpected disasters of the century, the sinking of the *Titanic* in 1912 and the burying of the schoolhouse in the Welsh village of Aberfan under an avalanche of coal waste in 1966, were apparently the subjects of a considerable number of precognitive experiences. In the case of the *Titanic* these have been collated and studied for their evidential value by Dr Stevenson. A London psychiatrist, Dr J. C. Barker, has made a similar study of the Aberfan tragedy.

In 1898 an American writer and ex-sailor named Morgan Robertson wrote a story, *The Wreck of the Titan*. Robertson was an unusual writer in that he conceived his stories in a state of trance and attributed them to his 'astral writing-partner'. In his trance vision he saw an immense ship ploughing through the icy waters of the mid-Atlantic in April. It was a luxury liner, much bigger and more powerful than any that existed in the world in 1898. The writer could see it clearly and he estimated its length as 800 feet, its speed as 23 knots, its displacement tonnage as 70,000 and its capacity as well over 2000 passengers. It had three propellers and twenty-four lifeboats—too few, Robertson judged, for a ship of its size. He could see the name, the *Titan*, on its side, and the word 'unsinkable' kept coming to him. In Robertson's vision the mighty ship rushed through the fog and hurled itself against an iceberg, and he heard 'nearly 3000 human voices, raised in agonized screams'.[9]

Fourteen years after Robertson wrote his story the *Titanic* set sail from Southampton on its fateful maiden voyage. It was a liner extraordinarily like the one Robertson had described: 882 feet in length, with a maximum speed of 25 knots and a displacement tonnage of 66,000, a capacity of nearly 3000 passengers, and equipped with three-propellers and only twenty lifeboats. It sailed in the month of April, vaunted as 'unsinkable', and in mid-Atlantic collided at full speed with an iceberg. There were well over 2000 people aboard, and of these 1502 lost their lives. The detailed correspondences with Robertson's story are staggering and, like the details in Prince's dream, make the chance coincidence explanation look very inadequate.

One of the people who perished in the *Titanic* disaster was another writer, W. T. Stead. Curiously enough, he too, twenty years before, had written a story about a steamship colliding with an iceberg in mid-Atlantic and many lives being lost because of the shortage of lifeboats, but it didn't have the detail corresponding with the actual tragedy that Robertson's story had. Death by drowning was a subject that kept coming up in Stead's life. He spoke about it in a public lecture he gave in 1910, envisaging himself struggling in the water and crying for help after a shipwreck. He visited two psychics, one of whom told him that he would be in danger from water and, specifically, that 'travel would be dangerous in the month of April, 1912'; the other said that Stead would go to America and that he could see a huge black ship, but, he added, he could only see half the ship. A friend, Archdeacon Colley, wrote a letter to Stead in which he predicted that the *Titanic* would sink. Despite these converging premonitions Stead booked his passage on the first and only voyage of the great liner. He had been invited by President Taft of the United States to speak at a peace conference, and no doubt felt that to turn down such an invitation because of a few insubstantial premonitions would be pusillanimous and unworthy of a rational man.

A London businessman, J. Connon Middleton, was not inhibited by such scruples. He had booked a passage on the *Titanic*, and as a result of two dreams he had about a fortnight before departure, he cancelled it. In the first dream he saw the ship 'floating on the sea, keel upwards and her passengers and crew swimming around her'; the second dream was identical, except that in it he saw himself 'floating in the air just above the wreck', an image that may plausibly be construed as a prevision of his not being one of the victims of the disaster.

When the *Titanic* was steaming out of Southampton, thousands of people stood on the shore, waving and cheering it on its way. One woman among them, a Mrs Marshall, suddenly had a vivid mental image of the imminent tragedy. She saw hundreds of people struggling in icy waters and she cried out, 'It's going to sink! That ship is going to sink before she reaches America!' On the same day a psychic, V. N. Turvey, wrote a letter to a friend in which he said that the ship would sink in two days. The *Titanic* was actually four days at sea before she sank, at 2.20 a.m. on April 14th, leaving hundreds of people floundering and screaming in the turbulent North Atlantic and hundreds of others precariously crowded into the few lifeboats. At the same hour, in New York, a woman awoke from a nightmare in which she had seen her mother in a crowded boat in mid-ocean. It had been a vivid dream, and she had actually felt the cruelly cold and salty wind on her face, heard the cries of the drowning and seen the great liner take its final plunge into the depths. She woke her husband and told him her dream, saying that she feared for her mother's safety, but he reassured her that as her mother was in London there was nothing to fear. But it later transpired that the mother, planning to pay them a surprise visit, had booked a passage on the *Titanic* and was one of the fortunate minority who were rescued from the life-boats.[10]

Well, the sceptic will argue, millions of people are having dreams and visions every minute of the day, and it is hardly surprising if a few of them coincide with actual events. And who can tell how many apparent previsions of disaster are *not* fulfilled? Every time a ship sails or an aeroplane takes off there is an obvious hazard which will prey upon the imaginations and exacerbate the unconscious fears of people connected with the event.

The argument is unanswerable because there is no possible evidence that would prove it wrong. But there is evidence that makes it highly unlikely. When the precognitions contain precise and verifiable detail, when they are experienced by people who have no emotional link with the event, and when subsequent analysis of their occurrence reveals a tendency for them to cluster towards the time of the event, only the most inveterate sceptic would continue to hold that they could be explained away as hysteria or chance coincidence.

All these evidential characteristics are to be found in the records of alleged premonitions of the Aberfan tragedy, in which 116 children and 28 adults died beneath a deluge of coal waste that engulfed the village school only a few minutes after they had assembled for morning classes. Some 200 people responded to newspaper appeals for accounts of such premonitions, and in assessing the material Dr Barker applied the strictest standards to establish authenticity. Premonitions had to be specific and to have been written down or reported to others before the event in order to qualify. Let us consider a few of the premonitions that satisfied these criteria.[11]

The disaster occurred at 9.17 a.m. on Friday, October 21st. Twelve hours before, at a spiritualist meeting in Plymouth, a Mrs Milden had a prevision of the event in astonishing detail. She saw an old schoolhouse in a valley and an avalanche of coal tumbling down a mountainside towards it. Then she saw a boy standing at the bottom of the mountain looking terrified as he watched rescue workers digging for bodies in the coal waste. The boy had a long fringe of hair, Mrs Milden noticed, and one of the rescue workers was wearing a strange-looking peaked cap. Watching television the following

Sunday, Mrs Milden saw exactly the same scene, including the terrified boy with the fringe and the worker in the peaked cap.

In the early morning hours of the fateful ·day an elderly man who lived in the north-west of England saw in a dream, spelled out in bright light, the word A-B-E-R-F-A-N, which he thought very curious because he had never seen or heard the word before. At about the same time, in Brighton, a telephone operator named Sybil Brown had a nightmare in which she saw a screaming child in a telephone booth, and another child coming towards her, followed by a 'black, billowing mass'. Another dreamer the same night had a vision of a school and a crowd of children ascending to heaven dressed in the national costume of Wales.

The precognition which came closest in time to the actual event was that of Mrs Monica McBean, a secretary in an aircraft plant. At 9.14 she had a vivid vision of 'a black mountain moving and children buried under it'. She was so shaken that she had to leave her desk and go to a rest room.

None of these people had the remotest connection with the mining village or anyone in it. The only recorded premonition of an inhabitant of Aberfan was that of a nine-year-old girl, Eryl Mai Jones, one of the victims. On the Thursday morning she told her mother that she had dreamed that she went to school 'and there was no school there. Something black had come down all over it.' Two weeks before, her mother later recalled, Eryl Mai had said a strange thing for a nine-year-old: 'I'm not afraid to die. I shall be with Peter and June.' On October 25, when the bodies of the children were buried in a common grave, Eryl Mai was placed between her classmates, Peter and June.

Out of the 34 precognitions of Aberfan that were the most specific and best authenticated, 18 occurred within 4 days of the event, 8 up to 14 days before and another 8 over a period of several weeks before. This temporal clustering and decline effect conforms with a statistical pattern observed in other cases of multiple precognition.

Some of the earlier precognitive dreams and visions were quite specific. A woman woke up screaming in the middle of the night a week before the event and said she had been dreaming about 'screaming children buried by an avalanche of coal in a mining village'. Also

93

a week before, a man told his wife 'something terrible is going to happen', and for days he couldn't shake off a pervasive feeling of depression. He was an amateur artist and he did a sketch of a human head against a black background. He kept thinking, he said, of coal dust. In a dream two weeks before, a woman had what could have been a symbolic prevision of the disaster. She saw 'hundreds of black horses thundering down a hillside dragging hearses'. And in many of the alleged premonitions that did not quite satisfy Barker's strict evidential criteria there were recurrent themes and images relevant to the tragedy: blackness, avalanches, mountains, children, school, buried buildings, screams, digging.

It was as a result of his study of the Aberfan material that in 1967 Barker set up in London the British Premonitions Bureau. The following year his initiative led to the establishment of the Central Premonitions Registry in New York. Writing in a medical journal, Barker said that while analysing the Aberfan material he 'realized that the time had surely come to call a halt to attempts to prove or disprove precognition. We should instead set about trying to harness and utilize it with a view to preventing further disasters.'[12] He foresaw the day when the fact that certain people are able to receive information from the future would be generally recognised, and when the data derived from possibly precognitive dreams, visions, intuitions or trance states would be processed by a computer, which would detect 'peaks or patterns', thus enabling an 'early warning' system to be put into action. That day is not yet with us, but the London and New York Registries have in their files enough well-substantiated cases of correct premonitions to make Barker's own vision of the future a plausible proposition.

Before leaving the subject of precognitions of disaster, we must mention the patient and significant research of William Cox.[13] Investigating 28 serious railway accidents in the United States over a number of years, Cox found that the number of passengers on accident-bound trains was always considerably fewer than the number on corresponding trains seven, fourteen, twenty-one and twenty-eight days before the accident. The pattern was so consistent that it is difficult to see how it can be explained otherwise than as the operation of a precognitive faculty at an unconscious level. The finding suggests, as Broad's and Stanford's theories suggest for telepathy and clairvoyance, that precognition is not a rare and freakish faculty but one that a lot of people possess and make use of, even though they may not be conscious of doing so. The implications of Cox's research are reinforced by the fact that in the week before the *Titanic* sailed an unusually large number of people cancelled their passages, and several were able to give no better reason than that they thought it unlucky to travel on a ship's maiden voyage.

There is no lack of evidence for precognition to satisfy those who look to the laboratory and the controlled experiment for proof rather than to anecdotes or statistical studies derived from life situations. Some of the most convincing evidence for ESP obtained in the Rhine era of card-guessing experiments came through subsequent analysis of the records, when results were discovered that were not sought or expected at the time when the actual experiments were conducted. Of all such retrospective discoveries the most dramatic and unexpected were those made by the British mathematician and parapsychologist, Dr S. G. Soal. Soal was highly sceptical of the sensational results that Rhine had obtained at Duke University and announced to the world in his 1934 monograph, *Extra-Sensory Perception*, so he decided to replicate the experiments and see if he could obtain similar results. Over a period of five years he patiently tested 160 people and recorded 128,350 card guesses, taking the most elaborate precautions against any kind of error. He finally came to the conclusion that 'there seemed indeed little evidence . . . that the persons tested . . . possessed any faculty for either telepathy or clairvoyance'.[14] And there the matter might have rested had not another British researcher, Whately Carrington, working in Cambridge, come up with some quite odd findings from his own experiments. Testing for long-distance clairvoyance, Carrington drew a picture on ten successive evenings and hung it in a locked room in his house. His percipients were scattered throughout England and the United States, and on each of the evenings allocated to the experiment they too drew a picture and mailed it to Carrington, who compared all these drawings with his own target pictures for evidence of ESP. When all the results were in, Carrington noticed a persistent odd phenomenon. Many of the percipients' drawings matched well with drawings in his target series, but the match was not always with the target drawing for the particular evening. A highly significant number of them matched with a picture one ahead in the series, which meant that they had been drawn before Carrington had made his target drawing and even before he had decided what it should be. The percipients had apparently quite unwittingly exercised precognitive clairvoyance. The phenomenon was so clear, so improbable, so staggeringly unaccountable to chance, that Carrington urged his colleague Soal to work through his records again to see if they contained corroborative evidence of what he termed the 'displacement effect'.

Soal was understandably reluctant. He felt he had put in enough time on ESP testing to convince him that so far as he was concerned as an experimenter he could only ever expect negative results. But Carrington persisted and prevailed, and Soal discovered, buried in his records, clear evidence that two of his 160 subjects had consistently made guesses at the target cards which showed a time-displacement effect. He sought out these subjects, Basil Shackleton and Gloria Stewart, and carried out a further series of thorough experiments with each of them. The displacement effect remained consistent and unmistakable. For some unaccountable reason, Shackleton and Stewart were able to guess, with odds of millions to one against chance, the card that was going to come up next in the series. Soal noticed that Shackleton scored consistently one ahead when his guesses were spaced at intervals of 2.8 seconds, and that when this interval was halved he guessed with equal consistency two cards ahead, which suggested that his precognitive faculty focused on the event 2.8 seconds in the future.

Critics of the ESP hypothesis maintain that extra-chance results obtained in guessing tasks can be explained by the fact that occasionally the target materials will fall into a pattern that happens to coincide with the subject's guessing pattern. In other words, the target sequences are not always truly random. To guard against this possibility, parapsychologists in recent years have been using some ingenious test machines that reflect one of the most random processes in nature—the radioactive decay of the nucleus in a Strontium-90 atom—to generate targets. This nucleus can decay at any time without apparent cause. In the machine developed by Dr Helmut Schmidt of the Institute for Parapsychology in Durham, North Carolina, radioactivity emissions from Strontium-90 are used to randomly light up one of four lamps. Beneath the lamps on the panel of the machine are four corresponding push-buttons which the subject uses to predict which lamp will go on next. In his first experiments with this machine, Schmidt tested 100 people and discovered among them three subjects who consistently scored significantly above chance expectation. Moreover, with repeated testing these subjects were all able to improve their scores, and when one of them was asked to try to miss the lamp that would light next, she was successful in doing so, which proved that the targets were genuinely random and that the subjects were using ESP to identify them.[15] Similar positive results have been obtained by other experimenters using Schmidt's machine. A further development in machine-testing for precognition was the addition, in a device invented by the physicist Russell Targ, of a 'pass' button to enable the subject not to have to make a guess if he doesn't feel like doing so. The idea of this is that a person can learn to exercise ESP if he pays attention to his subjective feelings when he makes a correct guess and subsequently only attempts a guess when it 'feels' right.

Any gambler knows that there is a correlation between subjective states and success or failure, that there are times when he intuitively knows that he will win and other times when he knows with equal certainty that he will lose. The majority of gamblers are compulsive and do not heed these feelings, but what would happen if a gaming system could be devised that used such subjective signals to determine when to wager and when not to do so? The parapsychologists Robert Brier and Walter Tyminski have worked out such a system and tried it out in casinos, using the predictions of subjects who showed precognitive ability in ESP tests. The experiments were conducted in the interests of psi research rather than pecuniary profit, but they did produce consistently positive and profitable results.[16]

In an earlier chapter I referred to the research done at the Maimonides Medical Center with the English sensitive Malcolm Bessent. In addition to the dream telepathy experiments, Bessent co-operated with the Maimonides team in a series of experiments designed to test whether he could dream precognitively. The targets in these experiments were randomly selected after Bessent had recorded his dreams, and then the dream reports and the targets were assessed for correspondences by three outside judges working independently. Before he went to sleep in the dream laboratory, Bessent was told by an experimenter, 'Tomorrow evening you will be shown a series of slides accompanied by sound effects. You are to try to dream about that slide-and-sound sequence tonight.' At the time nobody knew what the target material would be, so Bessent had no possible way of receiving cues as to what to dream about by normal means or by alternative paranormal means such as telepathy or clairvoyance. This was a pure test of precognition, and its success was indisputable. On five nights out of eight Bessent incorporated in his commentaries on his dreams imagery corresponding to the target material that he would experience the following evening.

Here is an example. Awakened from his third dream one evening, Bessent reported, 'It involved Bob Morris [the parapsychologist Robert L. Morris]. His experiments with birds. . . . The target is of emotional interest to Bob Morris. The colour of deep blue is important. The sea or the sky.'[17] Bessent had four dream periods in the course of the night, and on being awakened from three of them he spoke about the sky and the colour blue. Then in a post-sleep interview the following morning, conducted by inter-com with an experimenter immediately on awakening, he elaborated: 'Bob Morris does research on animal behaviour and more specifically birds. . . . He's been doing various research and studies with birds and he's taken me out to see his sanctuary where all the birds are kept. . . . I remember seeing various different kinds of doves. Ring-tailed doves, ordinary doves, Canadian geese. . . . The only thing I think about is just water. Just a lake of water. . . . Kind of greeny-blue. A few ducks and things. It's fairly misty, but there are quite a lot of mandrake geese and various birds of some kind swimming around in rushes or reeds. . . . Birds . . . I just have a feeling that the next target material will be about birds.'[18]

It was. The following evening the elaborate procedure that led to the selection of the target material randomly turned up the theme, 'Birds'. Bessent was shown slides of birds in the water, on land, and in the sky, and the accompanying tapes that he listened to contained recordings of a variety of bird-calls. This method of presenting the target material as a multisensory experience was designed in order to make the controlled laboratory situation approximate as closely as possible to the conditions under which precognition functions in spontaneous cases, by involving the emotions and the senses of the subject. The target was an experience rather than an object or an abstract theme, and when Bessent incorporated the relevant imagery in his reports on his dreams it was as if he was 'remembering' something that had not yet happened to him.

In ancient and modern cultures throughout the world the fact that certain individuals are capable of prophecy and foreknowledge has been widely accepted. Within our own culture we have a vast anecdotal literature of well-attested spontaneous experiences of precognition, to which in recent decades there has been added a substantial literature describing sophisticated and carefully controlled laboratory experiments. Precognition is a phenomenon that doesn't worry physicists unduly. Russell Targ has written, 'Of these three phenomena [telepathy, clairvoyance and precognition], we believe that contemporary physics will find the least trouble in assimilating precognition.'[19] Contemporary psychology, too, has experimental data and theoretical developments that have bearing upon precognition and make the phenomenon less outlandish than it appears to the common sense point of view.

Rudyard Kipling, who professed disbelief in psychical experiences, had a dream in which he saw himself standing in a line of formally-dressed men in a large stone-floored hall. Some kind of ceremony was in progress, which he couldn't see for the crowd, and when it was over a stranger came up to him, took his arm and said, 'I want a word with you.' Six weeks later Kipling remembered the dream when he was attending a war memorial service in Westminster Abbey. The place and his situation were exactly as he had seen them in the dream, and at the end of the service a stranger took his arm and said, 'I want a word with you, please.' Writing about the incident in his autobiography, Kipling asked, 'How, or why, had I been shown an unreleased roll of my life film?'[20]

Kipling's question expresses the common sense view of time and common sense bafflement faced with the phenomenon of precognition. Time, as we know it in our everyday experience, unrolls like a film, sequentially and at a consistent pace, and even if we can make the vertiginous speculative leap of assuming that the future in a sense already exists rather as the unprojected frames of a film already exist, we will find it very difficult indeed to take the further step of allowing that we may acquire knowledge of future events before they are presented to consciousness through the mediation of sense impressions. The problem of precognition thus has two aspects which need to be distinguished before we can begin to explain it or speculate about it: it is a problem that conflicts with common sense views both of consciousness and of time. If we approach it as a problem of consciousness we will look to psychology for enlightenment, and if we seek an explanation in terms of the concept of time we will look to modern physics. In fact, neither psychology nor physics can satisfactorily answer Kipling's question, but the evidence and theories that they contribute towards the understanding of precognition are nevertheless important, for they considerably diminish its antecedent improbability.

Consider first the psychological evidence. Everyone knows from experience that our consciousness of time is relative, that an hour spent with a lover passes quicker than one spent listening to a boring sermon. This common experience has far-reaching implications. When we say that 'time flies' or 'time drags' the assumption normally is that we are confessing to an illusory experience, and that what we are really saying is that time *seems* to fly or drag. We assume that there is such a thing as real time, objective time, and we further assume that this is the time that we measure with clocks and calendars, and if our subjective sense of time races or slows in relation to 'real time' we automatically conclude that it is our subjective time that is 'wrong'. In other words, we postulate the existence of a 'biological clock' and make it a criterion of the reality of experience that this 'biological clock' must keep pace with our objective and consistently paced chronometers. It takes but little reflection to realise that these assumptions and criteria are arbitrary, customary and convenient but by no means absolutely necessary or true. The temporal consciousness we use to actively participate in the world, to plan our days and make appointments, is not our only mode of temporal consciousness. It is as subjective as the different temporal consciousness of the lover, the poet, the mystic or the pregnant woman, and the fact that it is inter-subjective does not make it more true, nor does it justify the assumption that time itself is linear, sequential and an even-paced flow. What is it that we speak of as flowing, flying or dragging? The words are metaphors, for time is not an objective entity but a function of consciousness, and when we describe our experience with such metaphors we are really talking about a process of interaction between our consciousness and our environment.

'Flow', 'fly' and 'drag' are verbs of motion, and there is a close correlation between our perception of motion and our experience of time. The relation has observable physiological correlates in our brainwave rhythms. The brain cells 'fire' bursts of neural energy at varying frequencies per second depending on the person's state of consciousness, and this process can be measured, observed and recorded on an EEG machine. To illustrate the correlations between the perception of motion, brainwave rhythms and the experience of time, the psychologist Keith Floyd has developed an illuminating analogy. When we watch a film the illusion of motion is created when the frames are projected at a rate of twenty-four per second. Our normal, waking state of consciousness, which is characterised by the production of beta brainwaves, processes incoming information at this rate, and thus constructs its version of what constitutes reality. If the projection of the film is progressively slowed down we will see it first in slow motion, then with a flickering effect, then—at about eight frames per second—as a series of jerky movements. Eight frames per second would correspond to the brain's alpha rhythm, five frames to its theta rhythm, and two frames per second to the delta rhythm that the brain only produces during deep sleep. As the projection of the film slowed down, the events portrayed in it would seem to take up more time and could be observed in greater detail, and at three or four frames per second the observer would begin to discriminate the separate stills out of which the illusion of motion was created.[21]

In the states of mind conducive to creativity, meditation and visionary experience the brain's activity progressively slows down.

Poets and mystics have often written about experience of 'timeless moments', of time standing still, of seeing eternity in an hour, and these expressions are in fact quite literal descriptions of how the world looks when the brain is producing low frequency waves. Furthermore, people who have had this type of experience generally report an enhanced sense of reality, a feeling of liberation from ultimately arbitrary conceptual constraints, and a conviction that the experience has given them a truer picture of reality than they have in normal states of consciousness. As T. S. Eliot expressed it in his poem, *Burnt Norton*,

> the end and the beginning were always there
> Before the beginning and after the end.
> And all is always now.

This feeling that 'all is always now', that past, present and future are not arranged in a sequential, linear way, but merge and simultaneously co-exist in consciousness, has also been expressed by psychics. Thus Mrs Eileen Garrett: 'At clairvoyant levels time is undivided and whole, one often perceives the object or event in its past, present and/or future phases in abruptly swift succession.'[22] And Alan Vaughan, a psychic who has sent some correct premonitions to the New York Central Premonitions Registry, writes: 'Another by-product of going into a psychic state is disorientation to the conventional time and space around me. As I become highly activated, sufficiently enough to lose my sense of ego-identity, then conventional time loses its meaning as I get caught up with extradimensional adventures in the future.'[23] The concurring testimony of poets, mystics and psychics, supported by the findings of modern brain research, leaves no doubt that there are other modes of temporal experience than the linear, sequential mode. And as the psychologist Robert Ornstein has said, 'For us, an event is considered "paranormal" if it does not fit within the coordinates of ordinary linear time. But if linear time is but one possibility, these unusual events, unusual communications, may in fact occur, even though they cannot be charted in the coordinates of linearity.'[24] In other words, from the viewpoint of modern experimental and theoretical psychology, precognition is quite a plausible phenomenon.

It is from the viewpoint of modern physics too. Targ and Puthoff write, 'The reason we believe physics will find precognition the easiest of psi to describe lies in this fact: in physics, everything that is *not* forbidden occurs. And . . . physics does not forbid the transmission of information from the future to the present. The difficulty that one has in dealing with this problem is more linguistic than physical.'[25]

The temporal anomalies implicit in relativity theory are by now common knowledge, having been used by dozens of science fiction writers. If a man could travel into outer space faster than the speed of light and still observe events on earth he would be able to witness historical events as they occurred, and moreover if he spent several years space-travelling he would be younger when he returned than his erstwhile contemporaries. If he could visit a planet with a gravitational field stronger than the earth's, such as Jupiter, time would pass more slowly for him than on earth, and if he could exist within a black hole—an immense star that has collapsed into a super-dense mass under its own gravitational force—time would stand still and he would stop ageing. Modern physics has not only established the relativity of time, but also the theoretical possibility of time-reversal, of time's flowing backwards instead of forwards. This concept, which violates common sense and everyday experience, has had such far-reaching repercussions on modern physics that the man who elaborated it, Richard Feynman, received the Nobel Prize for it in 1965.

Targ and Puthoff have developed a tentative model for precognition which seeks to demonstrate that it may be a natural phenomenon, though admittedly a rare one. Their hypothesis is 'that significant events create a perturbation in the space-time in which they occur, and this disturbance propagates forward and, to some small degree, backward in time.'[26] As a rock thrown into a pond creates ripples that move out in all directions from the point of entry, so an event in space-time may propagate waves that flow along the time axis both in the $+t$ and in the $-t$ direction, i.e. towards the future and the past. Thus a person at a $-t$ point on the time axis might intercept a precursor wave before the actual event occurs. The greater the magnitude of the event, i.e. its significance for the experient, the stronger the precursor waves will be and the further they will travel along the − t axis. So a shock or an intense emotional experience will be more likely to be precognised than a trivial one. This in fact happens. As we have seen, deaths and disasters are more often precognised than happy events, and the tendency for events to be precognised close to the moment of their occurrence is also an observed fact. The Targ–Puthoff model enables us to think about precognition and may alleviate some of the intellectual discomfort that the very idea naturally causes, but of course it is only a model, a conceptual aid, and it does not explain how precognition works, particularly what kind of energies are involved in the perturbations in space-time and in the propagation of waves along the time axis. But physicists are not deterred by the lack of empirical evidence for their models. Enough of them have won Nobel Prizes for ideas that in any other discipline would be considered baseless and metaphysical. In 1929 Paul Dirac proposed the existence of a sub-atomic particle with negative energy, the antiparticle of the electron, although at the time the ideas of negative energy and antiparticles were innovations without any known meaning. Then in 1933 C. D. Anderson discovered the particle proposed in Dirac's theory, the positron, in cloud-chamber experiments. Physicists interested in paranormal phenomena are fond of quoting this example of bold but informed speculation preceding and guiding empirical discovery. Who is to say that the Targ–Puthoff model for precognition may not in due time find empirical support? Or of course it may be some other model, yet to be elaborated, that ultimately proves relevant. At this stage nobody can say. But at this stage, too, nobody can deny that the phenomenon exists, and nobody can dismiss it as impossible or irrelevant by invoking common sense concepts of time and causality that in the light of modern psychology and physics are demonstrably true only over a limited range of the events that occur in nature, even though those events agree with the evidence we derive from our sensory and physiological mechanisms and are the building blocks we use to construct our consensus view of what constitutes reality.

6

Mind Over Matter:
The Evidence for Psychokinesis

Coin-collecting would appear to be a safe and reliable hobby, combining the advantages of occasional satisfaction and long-term investment. But apparently it is not without its hazards. A collector in East Germany recently claimed compensation of DM50,000 because his entire collection had bent while he was watching Uri Geller on television. The collection was worthless to him, he said, but it must surely be invaluable to parapsychologists.[1] He was wrong. Parapsychologists are not short of evidence of the power of 'mind over metal'.

Here is a very odd situation. Before 1973 nobody had considered metal-bending as a possible psychokinetic phenomenon, and now seven- to twelve-year-old children are doing it. It all began in November 1973, when the Israeli psychic, Uri Geller, appeared on British television and, before an audience of millions, gently stroked a fork and caused it to bend. The following day the newspapers were full of stories from all over the country of domestic cutlery simultaneously bending in viewers' homes. The same thing happened when Geller appeared on television in other countries. In Sweden a woman even announced that the Geller effect had caused a metal birth-control device in her uterus to straighten and she had consequently become pregnant!

One is naturally sceptical, and inclined to wonder whether the phenomena might not be explained as trickery on Geller's part and hysteria on the part of some members of his audience. There have been other alleged paranormal phenomena which have been widely manifested for a time and then have been abruptly dropped from the psychic's repertoire. We hear little about levitations or materialisations of living forms today, though these were common occurrences in the age of the great 'physical' mediums. The sceptic's explanation of course, is that the incidence of the phenomena diminishes as the control conditions become stricter and the observers become wiser as to how the 'trick' is done. The stage illusionist Milbourne Christopher claims that professional magicians could reproduce all Geller's effects, and in a recently published book he reveals some of the tricks which he alleges Geller employs to deceive his audience.[2] Geller ought not to be investigated by scientists, he claims, but by members of the Magic Circle, for scientists are likely to be as ignorant as anyone of the psychology and techniques of deception. This, I think, is untrue. Scientists who are investigating paranormal phenomena today are generally very thorough in the precautions they take. I recently mentioned Milbourne Christopher's book in conversation with Professor John Hasted, who has investigated Geller, and when I did so Professor Hasted said, 'Let's see if we can add to these,' and read from one of his own notebooks a list of possible means of deception or causes of malobservation that included numerous possibilities that Christopher does not mention. And the fact that the 'Geller effect' has been produced by young children surely makes the explanation that it is all clever conjuring highly improbable. Odd though it is, it appears that in metal-bending we have a manifestation of PK (psychokinesis) which is without precedent.

Geller visited Birkbeck College, London, where Hasted is Professor of Physics, on three occasions in 1974. He had impressed Hasted some months before by bending two sturdy keys, which Hasted produced for the purpose, just by stroking them gently. Hasted was convinced that he had kept his eyes on the keys all the time and that there could be no question of fraud, and he was keen to investigate Geller in his laboratory. He prepared a number of experiments designed to test Geller's powers in relation to a variety of materials and also to explore whether the energies involved might be known physical energies. He gave him a Geiger counter, an instrument that registers cosmic radioactivity, and asked him to hold it and try to increase its count-rate. Operating normally, the Geiger counter clicks once or twice per second, but held by Geller it soon showed a burst of 25 counts per second and later reached a peak approaching 200 counts. It seemed as though Geller could produce pulses of nuclear radiation at will, though Hasted favoured the explanation that it was electrical rather than nuclear energy that caused the increase in the count-rate. He was satisfied, however, that the energy emanated from Geller, for when the Geiger counter was left to run for control periods without his holding it, it immediately began to register at the normal rate.[3]

A scientist monitoring a gaussmeter during this experiment had noticed significant fluctuations in the chart record which corresponded with the periods of most intense clicking activity. A gaussmeter registers variations in the magnetic field, and Geller was now asked to try to produce a deliberate variation of magnetic field. He could do nothing at first, probably, Hasted thought, because he didn't understand clearly what was required of him, so a compass was produced and he was asked to concentrate on it and see if he could deflect the needle. This he did, and the gaussmeter recorded a corresponding change in the magnetic field.

The most extraordinary occurrence at these experimental sessions was what Hasted calls a 'disappearance event'. He had assembled a variety of metal objects and single crystals on a metal surface plate. Among them were three tiny discs of vanadium carbide, a substance as hard and brittle as thin glass. Each of these discs was enclosed in a cellulose pill-case, of the type normally used to administer powdered drugs and which consists of two halves which slide together. In the experiment, Hasted held his hand outstretched over the metal plate and Geller slowly moved his hand a few inches above Hasted's. Suddenly Hasted experienced a warm sensation when Geller's hand was directly above his knuckles. Then to his astonishment and that of the onlookers the capsule just under his knuckles gave a little jump. Geller removed his hand and Hasted and a colleague examined the capsule. They simply could not believe what they saw. The disc within it had not only fractured, but half of it had completely disappeared. It could not have passed through the wall of the capsule, for this was undamaged, and it could not have been removed by anyone, for this would have required a very delicate operation and anyway nobody had touched it. There was simply no plausible scientific explanation of the observed fact that the disc had just broken up and half of it had utterly vanished.[4]

Another English scientist who has investigated Geller systematically, John Taylor, Professor of Mathematical Physics at King's

College, London, had even more alarming events occur in his laboratory. After Geller had broken a spoon and bent some strips of metal sealed in glass tubes, Taylor asked him to try to bend a brass strip which was taped to the platform of a balance so that it projected horizontally out from it. The idea was that Taylor would be able to observe the amount of pressure he applied when he stroked the metal by watching the scale of the balance. Geller not only caused the brass strip to bend upwards, i.e. against the light pressure he applied, but also bent the needle on the scale of the balance through 70°.[5]

Then the alarming events started. A strip of brass fell to the floor at the far end of the laboratory. Taylor had put it on a table about 20 feet from where it landed, only a few minutes before. A small piece of copper that had been near it also flew across the laboratory. A perspex tube with an iron rod sealed in it struck Taylor on the back of the legs, and when he picked it up he noticed that the rod inside it was bent. While they were walking along a corridor a piece of metal which Taylor knew he had left on the desk in his office suddenly fell at his feet. Another piece of metal seemed to disappear completely, though when he searched the room later Taylor found it under a radiator at the opposite side of the room from where it had been. 'These events seemed impossible to comprehend', Taylor wrote, 'and I should certainly have dismissed reports of them as nonsense had I not seen them for myself.'

After their initial experience with Geller, both Hasted and Taylor sought other subjects to continue their experiments with. Largely through reports carried by newspapers after the television broadcasts, 46 people with metal-bending abilities were found in Britain. One was a man, three were women, and the rest were children under seventeen with girls outnumbering boys in the ratio of 3 to 2. From bending of cutlery, some children have gone on to bigger things and produced effects that could not possibly be achieved by the application of manual or even mechanical force by a child. One twelve-year-old girl bent a chromium-plated steel towel-rail through an angle of 40°, an effect that would have required a force of at least a quarter of a ton. Another girl, eleven years old, bent strips of metal by holding them between the toes of one foot and rubbing them between the toes of the other. Many of the children can cause bending without direct contact. A ten-year-old boy produced a variation now known as the 'scrunch' effect. A number of straightened paperclips were sealed in a box and the child concentrated on the box and thought of the paperclips folding and twisting over and round themselves. When the box was opened they were found to have formed themselves into a tangled mass.[6]

Finding that children did not work well under impersonal laboratory conditions, Hasted devised a way of enabling them to produce effects that would be acceptable as evidence of paranormality while allowing them to work in their own time and in their own homes. He sealed strips of metal inside glass tubes and spheres in such a way as to ensure that they could not be bent physically without the glass being broken. A child would be allowed to take a tube or sphere home and handle it whenever he wished, and was asked to return it when he had managed to make the metal inside bend or when he was satisfied that he was unable to do so. Most of the children found this task too difficult, but one seventeen-year-old boy has produced several remarkably successful bendings, the first of a strip of brass sealed in a bent tube, and the second a really complex bending and twisting of a brass strip and a 'scrunching' of a mass of paperclips into a shape resembling a model of a seated man, both of which were contained in a glass sphere with only a small hole. They could not be removed afterwards without breaking the sphere.[7]

There has been a lot of controversy recently, both in public and in private, about the 'Geller effect', and a view that is often expressed is that even if the phenomenon is real, the ability to apply mental power to the bending of cutlery is a singularly useless possession. Of course, such an argument does not affect the parapsychologist, who is concerned with the investigation of paranormal abilities, not with their application. He might argue, in fact, that it is precisely because it is of little practical use that this particular PK effect has not been discovered earlier, and that PK, like the other psi faculties, has fallen into disuse because man can deal much more efficiently with his environment by using his sensory and motor mechanisms and the technologies that are extensions of them. The important point about the evidence for PK is that if it is true, our knowledge of the ways in which mind and matter interact is incomplete, and if our knowledge is incomplete, it is surely up to science to investigate the phenomenon and pursue its implications. Yet scientists like Taylor and Hasted, though they have applied unimpeachable scientific procedures in their investigations, have drawn the fire of their colleagues, been accused of dabbling in the occult, and are well aware that they have to proceed with circumspection lest they should jeopardise their professional credibility. They no doubt remember the case of Sir William Crookes, the distinguished nineteenth-century physicist, who was ridiculed by the scientific world when he published his researches into the PK effects produced by the medium D. D. Home, a man who produced phenomena quite as startling as Geller's and who also willingly submitted to laboratory investigation under strict scrutiny and control.

Contemporary orthodox science is rather less hostile to investigation of the paranormal than it was in Crookes' day because it has fewer dogmatic certainties. Even disregarding the evidence of parapsychology, scientists today cannot maintain the view that mind can only act upon matter through the mediation of motor mechanisms, i.e. through the muscles and nerves of the body. The idea that illnesses or cures can be *psychosomatic*, which was regarded as heretical and occult not long ago, is now widely accepted although it implies an interaction between mind (*psyche*) and body (*soma*) that cannot be observed or measured and that obeys no known laws. The fact that mind can act directly upon the material world was clearly demonstrated by the neurophysiologist Dr W. Grey Walter, who reported his researches to the scientific world in 1969. Walter situated his subjects in front of a TV screen on which they were told that when they pressed a certain button an 'interesting scene' would appear. Attached to the subject's frontal cortex were electrodes which transmitted electrical impulses from the brain through an amplifier to the TV set. Walter found that the brain produced a small 'expectancy wave' about one second before the subject pressed the button, and that, amplified by his circuitry, this wave would itself change the scene on the TV screen. Some subjects learnt to change the picture literally at will, without even bothering to reach for the button.[8] Grey Walter's data were not ridiculed, for they were not obtained in the pursuit of parapsychological research, but his experiments clearly demonstrated that thought is a kind of energy and that PK is not theoretically implausible. Though the electrical energy produced by the brain in his experiments was minute and had to be amplified to trip the TV switch, it does not necessarily follow that mental energy is always so minute or that electrical circuitry is the only way of amplifying it. Grey Walter wrote that the effort his successful subjects made required 'a peculiar state of concentration, a paradoxical compound of detachment and excitement'.[9] Readers acquainted with the literature of the techniques of mysticism and magic will recognise a familiar note in this. It is normally in an altered state of consciousness that the psi faculties are enhanced and the strongest paranormal effects obtained.

A group of British researchers have obtained results reminiscent of Grey Walter's under séance room conditions. Believing that a positive and expectant attitude is essential to the manifestation of PK, and that laboratory conditions with all their precautions and monitoring devices inhibit such an attitude, Ken Batcheldor and Colin Brookes-Smith have conducted numerous experiments in 'sitter-group PK' in which the registering and control apparatus is unobtrusive. Among many paranormal effects obtained with a small group of 'sitters' who shared a positive attitude towards the possibility of producing phenomena was the following. An electric bulb was placed in the middle of a table around three sides of which the 'sitters' were assembled. Mounted on an extension to the table on the fourth side and well away from any of the 'sitters' was a hinged flap which, when raised, completed an electric circuit and caused the bulb on the table to light up. The 'sitters' found that with practice they could put themselves into the right state of consciousness and generate a kind of group PK by means of which the light could be made to go on and off to order.[10] This effect was achieved when they collectively concentrated on the bulb and not on the flap, which lends support to a theory, proposed by Helmut Schmidt, that PK is a 'goal-oriented' function, that is to say, it is one 'that aims successfully at a final event, no matter how intricate the intermediate steps'. This suggests that PK effects are not accomplished by an act of will, in the sense of a consciously controlled and directed force, but are, like mental psi phenomena, functions of the unconscious. To speak, as Professor

Taylor does, of successful PK subjects as 'superminds' is probably misleading, for it suggests that they deliberately focus a beam of 'willpower' to accomplish an effect upon the material world, whereas in fact the mental concomitants of successful PK appear to be a combination of relaxation, expectancy, concentration and detachment. To conceive and hold in mind a goal, but not to strive after it and not to allow the conscious mind to inhibit the process by questioning how it might be achieved, seems to be the formula. And the work of Batcheldor and Brookes-Smith suggests that PK is often effectively manifested as a product of the *collective* unconscious, which would explain why its occurrence suddenly diminished when psychical research became parapsychology and moved out of the séance room into the laboratory, and might also explain the spate of spontaneous PK events that were reported while millions of people sat expectantly before their TV sets watching Uri Geller.

Possibly the most objective and best authenticated evidence for the occurrence of unconscious spontaneous PK is that afforded by the investigation of so-called 'poltergeist' phenomena. Parapsychologists prefer to speak of RSPK (recurrent spontaneous psychokinesis) rather than of poltergeists, for the latter term suggests the existence of supernatural spirit entities, but it is widely held today that the phenomena are produced by the (paranormal) action of a single person. They constitute good evidence for the reality of PK, for they have been reported down the ages and from all parts of the world and the correspondences within these anecdotal records clearly point to the fact that the phenomenon is genuine, recurrent, and tends to develop and abate according to a pattern. It was Frank Podmore, a co-worker with the pioneers of psychical research, Gurney and Myers, who first observed that when 'poltergeists' are active there is usually an adolescent in the vicinity. He did not draw the modern conclusion, that RSPK is an unconscious expression of repressed hostility and frustration, but suggested rather that the naughty children consciously faked the phenomena to deceive, mock and avenge themselves upon the adult world.

A brief digression is relevant here. Independent investigators have discovered that some of the metal-bending children that Professors Taylor and Hasted have worked with have sometimes cleverly cheated. Taylor and Hasted acknowledge this and yet maintain that most of the bendings are genuinely paranormal. There are similarities between reported 'poltergeist' activities and events that Taylor and Hasted have observed in the presence of Geller and of some of their child subjects, for example paranormal displacement of objects and apparent matter-through-matter penetration. Some 'poltergeist' cases have been proved to have been fundamentally contrived or to have been initially genuine and then fraudulently exploited, yet nobody familiar with the literature would maintain today that all 'poltergeist' cases can be dismissed as fraud or delusion. It would therefore seem prudent not to dismiss the metal-bending phenomena as totally fraudulent, as many scientists are inclined to do, and at least to give such investigators as Taylor and Hasted the benefit of the doubt and encouragement and facilities to pursue their researches.

In a public opinion poll conducted in Germany in 1959, eighteen per cent of the people stated that they believed that 'poltergeist' events really happened. Ten years later the believers were twenty-eight per cent of the poll. The reason for the increase was the publicity given to the 'Rosenheim poltergeist' case of 1967–8 and to the careful investigations of the parapsychologist Dr Hans Bender. The bizarre events that occurred in a lawyer's office in the Bavarian town of Rosenheim suggested to the victims the existence of a 'boisterous spirit' (the literal translation of 'poltergeist') possessed of technical expertise. Electric bulbs exploded, neon lights kept going out and were found to be unscrewed from their sockets, automatic fuses blew without cause, the four telephones rang simultaneously, conversations were abruptly cut off and the firm's telephone bills rose astronomically, for the counter at the post office registered innumerable calls, sometimes as many as six per minute. When Bender and his colleagues from the Freiburg Institute for Border Areas of Psychology were called in they were able to collect evidence from about forty first-hand witnesses, including employees and clients of the firm, puzzled municipal and post office technicians, journalists and police officers. It turned out that the phenomena were RSPK effects connected with a nineteen-year-old employee named Anne-marie. Apart from the originality of the phenomena, an outstanding feature of the Rosenheim case was that the investigation was sponsored by the German Association for the Advancement of Science and distinguished physicists participated in it. One of them, Dr Friedbert Karker of the Max Planck Institute in Munich, subsequently issued a very significant statement: 'We have investigated with particular intensity a case of RSPK. This was the Rosenheim case, 1967. In the course of this investigation we came to the conclusion that it cannot be explained by the means of today's theoretical physics. On the other hand we ascertained its existence by means of the same experimental physics. I cannot offer any model which seems to fit these phenomena. That they really do exist could be established with the utmost certainty'.[11]

In 1972–3 Hans Bender and members of the Freiburg Institute investigated another unusual 'poltergeist' case in the village of Scherfede in Westphalia. In September '72, in a small house on a modern estate, puddles of water suddenly started to appear, first on the floor of the bathroom, then in the kitchen and other rooms. Mechanics checked all the pipes and could find no leakage. In October and November pools of water also appeared outside the house, interior and exterior walls developed damp patches and carpets became wet. Then on December 10 a literal flood of events began. The family, which consisted of the father, mother and a thirteen-year-old girl, were sitting in one room in the house when they heard a loud splashing sound in another. They investigated and found a big puddle of water on the floor. Then friends who lived in the next house but one came in and asked for help because water was flooding down their staircase from the second floor. In the course of the evening two other houses in the row suffered inundations. The phenomena continued to occur for three days, although the water supply was cut off at the main. Building technicians, geologists and hydrologists were baffled. A specimen of the water was analysed and found to be identical with the water in Scherfede's water supply, though nobody could explain how it could get out of the pipes. Bender's investigations finally identified the girl from the house where the phenomena first occurred as the unconscious cause of them. He found that she was a frequent visitor at all the other houses in the row except the one immediately next door, which was the only one where no inundations occurred. Of the many interesting features of the Scherfede case, Bender wrote, 'the most striking one is for me the matter through matter penetration which seems to be involved'.[12] Matter through matter penetration, in the form of what Hasted calls 'disappearance/reappearance events', is another often-reported aspect of the Geller effect, which again suggests that 'poltergeist' and metal-bending phenomena may have something in common.

RSPK phenomena constitute good and well-authenticated evidence that mind can interact with matter in quite powerful and dramatic ways, but as they are always involuntary and unconscious effects and appear to be related to unstable and pathological mental states they arm the opponents of the evolutionary view of psi functions with a strong argument. If psi energy is so uncontrolled and destructive, the argument might go, then the purposes of evolution are not served by enhancing it but by suppressing it. The only counter-argument to this is that psi energy, like electrical or nuclear energy, is not in itself good or bad, but manifests itself in a variety of ways. Lightning is destructive, but man learnt a century ago to harness electrical energy and now could hardly survive without it.

One of the more positive manifestations of PK is in psychic or paranormal healing, a phenomenon as old as recorded history and attested in the scriptures of all the world's religions. A modern healer, Oscar Estebany of Montreal, a former Hungarian army colonel who is said to have discovered his healing abilities by chance through massaging cavalry horses, has cooperated in controlled experiments with two researchers, Dr Bernard Grad of McGill University and Sister Justa Smith of the Human Dimensions Institute at Buffalo, New York. In his experiment Grad used mice as Estebany's 'patients' in order to rule out the possibility of cures being effected by faith or suggestion. A small area of skin was removed from each of 300 mice under anaesthetic and the mice were then divided into three equal groups; one was treated by Estebany, the second by people who claimed no healing powers, and the third was left without any treatment. All the mice were put in cages, and the cages were enclosed in heavy paper bags. Some of the mice that Estebany treated were in cages in completely sealed bags so that he could only touch the outside, and others were in open-ended bags to enable him to put his hands inside and touch the sides of the cage. Estebany and the control group of non-healers handled the bags twice daily for fifteen minutes over a period of sixteen days. Then the wounds were measured by members of Grad's team who did not know which mice belonged to which group. There were marked differences in the rate of wound-healing. The mice that Estebany had treated in cages with open bags had healed the most rapidly, and those in the sealed bags that he had handled had also made significantly greater progress than those treated by the non-healers or not treated at all. The experiment seemed to demonstrate that some kind of energy had emanated from or been channelled through Estebany's hands to interact with the living tissue and accelerate the healing process.[13]

Sister Justa Smith, who is an experimental biochemist as well as a nun, heard about Grad's work and formulated the hypothesis that 'if an energy exchange takes place, it should be detectable at an enzyme level'.[14] Enzymes are catalysts, the 'brains' of individual body cells, and without them cells undergo no radical changes. To test her hypothesis, Smith prepared a quantity of the enzyme trypsin, which digests proteins, in solution and divided the solution into four equal parts, which were put into flasks. One flask was put aside and held at a constant temperature as a control. Two flasks were given to Estebany for treatment, one of which contained normal healthy enzymes and the other enzymes that had had their molecular structure slightly damaged by exposure to ultraviolet light. The fourth was exposed to a high magnetic field in order to compare the effects of such exposure with those of Estebany's treatment. Estebany was given the two flasks and asked to do to the solution in them whatever he did when he tried to heal. When the experiment was completed and the enzyme solutions were examined, it was found that the control enzymes were unchanged, the damaged ones had been 'healed' to a significant extent, and the level of activity of the normal enzymes, both those treated by Estebany and those exposed to the magnetic field, had been significantly raised. The results suggest, as did Grad's, that from the healer's hands emanated some kind of energy, and the similarity between the two positive results suggests that the energy involved may be electromagnetic. However, when a sensitive gaussmeter was placed between Estebany's hands, no magnetic field effect registered, so precisely what kind of energy input caused the increased activity in the enzymes remains an open question.

Smith followed up her experiment with Estebany by conducting further researches with other healers and different enzymes. To promote bodily health, the chemical actions of some enzymes need to be accelerated and those of others need to be slowed down. The healers who co-operated in these further experiments did not know which kind of enzyme was in the flask they were given to treat, nor did they know whether they were supposed to accelerate or slow down its reaction. However, Smith found that the changes they caused in the reactions were always positive, that is to say they were the kind of changes that would promote health or healing if the enzyme was functioning in the body. This evidence is consistent with Helmut Schmidt's theory that PK is a 'goal-oriented' function, and that although it operates at a totally unconscious level it incorporates in its actions purposive and discriminative factors that we would normally associate with consciousness.

Recent experiments with animals and plants appear to confirm this. However, the possibility of the effect emanating from the experimenter himself has not been satisfactorily eliminated in the control conditions of these experiments, so it would be premature to take them as evidence that all living organisms produce energy fields that can interact with and effect changes in their environment. This is probably the most contentious area in parapsychology today. The most widely publicised developments in the field in recent years have been the alleged discoveries of 'Kirlian' photography and of plant-polygraph studies. Many people with no particular interest in parapsychology will have seen in magazines the colourful pictures of energy discharges from human finger-pads and from leaves, and many have gathered from such popular books as *The Secret Life of Plants* that plants respond to human thoughts and produce electrical impulses that can be monitored by a polygraph and that signify processes analogous to human thought or feeling. Neither of these discoveries, however, may be quite what it seems; the reality of the effects may be indisputable, but what causes the effects is still a matter of conjecture. Considerably more research needs to be done before it can be established that all living organisms under certain conditions manifest psi functions, though the pointers to this conclusion are not to be lightly dismissed.

The investigations so far surveyed in this chapter illustrate how psi research today, particularly research into PK, converges with mainstream sciences such as biology and physics. These convergences will be discussed in detail in Part Two, and to conclude the present chapter we shall consider the evidence for PK afforded by less sensational manifestations than metal-bending, 'poltergeists' and psychic healing. The statistical evidence obtained through patient research in parapsychological laboratories over four decades constitutes for some people more acceptable evidence than any that carries a whiff of occultism, religion or the stage.

From 1934 to 1940, in the heyday of the Rhine era at Duke University in North Carolina, the parapsychology lab echoed continually with the sound of rolling dice. A professional gambler had told Rhine that when he was in a certain frame of mind he could influence dice to come up as he wanted them, and it was his claim that set the experimental dice rolling. No results were published, for Rhine and his colleagues were loath to over-tax the credulity of the scientific community at a time when they were having enough trouble convincing them of the reality of ESP. The procedure initially adopted was to have a subject throw a pair of dice twelve times and will either high or low combinations of numbers to come up. Twelve throws constituted a 'run' and with a chance expectation of five 'hits' per run it was a simple matter to calculate the statistical deviation from chance over a large number of runs. The first results were encouraging. In a series of 562 runs there were 3,110 hits, exactly 300 more than should have occurred by chance, which was a result that yielded odds of about a billion to one against chance. The experimental conditions were tightened up and varied, precautions were taken against the results being due to bias in the dice or the exercise of skill by the thrower, and highly significant extra-chance results continued to be obtained. Rhine was convinced that he had demonstrable evidence of the operation of PK, but it was not until 1943 that he ventured to publish his findings.[15]

While preparing his material for publication, Rhine discovered in his records of ten years of dedicated dice-rolling a consistent pattern which he considered really clinched the argument. The pattern was of 'position effects', i.e. a tendency for hits to cluster at the beginnings and the ends of runs. Records of ESP experiments had revealed a similar pattern in the positioning of high scores, so the discovery of the correspondence suggested that ESP and PK were related functions. But what particularly excited Rhine about this discovery was that it was objective evidence that a genuine psychological process was at work, and moreover evidence that no critic could say he had cooked up, for it had been in the records for years without anyone realising it or suspecting its significance.

Dice-rolling, like card-guessing, has tended to fall into disuse with the development of electronic means of generating targets. Schmidt's nuclear-powered random generator (see p. 97) has been adapted for PK testing. Radioactive decays are used in this device to stop a very rapidly oscillating switch in one of two possible positions, which for convenience Schmidt calls 'heads' or 'tails'. The subject concentrates on a display panel of nine lamps arranged in a circle which light up one at a time either in a clockwise or anticlockwise direction depending on whether the generator produces a head or a tail. The PK task is to make the lights go on in a clockwise direction, and success in enforcing such a movement means in effect that the subject has influenced the subatomic particles to arrive at the Geiger counter when the switch is in a 'heads' position with significantly greater frequency than when it is in a 'tails' position. The subject is not instructed to attempt to exercise a PK influence on the subatomic particles, for such a task would be incomprehensible to the layman and too daunting for anyone with a knowledge of physics, but just to concentrate on making the lights go on in the desired direction. It was the success of some subjects in achieving this that led Schmidt to his conclusion that PK is 'a goal-oriented principle . . . that aims successfully at a final event, no matter how intricate the intermediate steps'.[16]

Schmidt's own report on the first subject who exhibited PK ability using this device will serve as an example of the kind of apparently marginal statistical evidence that for parapsychologists constitutes firm proof of the operation of psi faculties:

'The first outstandingly positive subject was an outgoing girl who had come to me because she had felt herself to be very 'psychic' in everyday situations, mainly in the way of receiving psychic impressions about other people. This girl obtained in a first experiment, comprising 50 two-minute test runs of 128 trials each, a scoring rate of 52.2% on the desired heads, instead of the 50% expected by chance, and an even higher scoring rate (53.5% in 25 test runs) in a later, follow-up test. These results are far outside the range of possible chance fluctuations. The odds against chance are more than a billion to one. Even with this very gifted subject, however, PK results did not come easily or in a routine manner. Each session required a new, special effort, and on many days we did not hold tests because the subject did not feel up to the task.'[17]

Whether you are impressed by metal-bending, 'poltergeists', psychic healing or marginal statistical deviations that over long series yield astronomical odds against chance, the evidence for the reality of PK is substantial and unambiguous. Mind interacts with matter in mysterious ways that cannot be satisfactorily accounted for in terms of prevailing concepts in psychology, philosophy or physics. Paranormal effects in the physical world that in past ages could be put down to the intervention of demons or spirits can no longer be so naively accommodated to a consensus reality. They pose a challenge, particularly for physics, the science that has dominated this century both with its findings and its methodology. Which is why psychical research, which began as an offshoot of spiritualism and an eccentric interest of leisured, literate gentlemen with private means and 'immortal longings', has today become 'paraphysics' and the concern of an ever-increasing but still small number of distinguished mainstream scientists.

It is every man's privilege to adopt what attitude he chooses to the mysterious. He can ignore it, investigate it, dwell on it, morbidly or wonderingly, he can love it, hate it, even worship it. What he can't do is deny its existence or opt not to live with it. Queer and inexplicable things happen in everyone's experience, and if they are frequent or intense enough a man begins to wonder whether reality is deviant or he is. A socio-cultural orthodoxy confident in its priorities has enforced the latter conclusion upon the educated Westerner these last three centuries and more, but over recent decades the former conclusion has steadily become less heretical. The Western consensus view of reality has begun to look a bit thread-bare, and the priorities derived from it have turned out to be pre-scriptions for disaster rather than for the millenium. In these circum-stances more and more people have begun to wonder whether the mysteries that were peripheral in the prevailing culture might not have a central and saving relevance in the new.

The preceding chapters have surveyed a selected sample of these mysteries, and have put forward enough evidence, I trust, to establish to the satisfaction of the open-minded that psi is real, though probably not enough to convince the sceptic that it is important. So now let's look at the evidence in a broader context, and consider more fully why and how psi research is important and where it con-verges with other areas of perennial human interest and concern.

PART TWO

Convergences and Divergences

7

Psi and Science

The nuptials of 1969, when the Parapsychological Association was admitted to membership of the American Association for the Advancement of Science, were generally celebrated as a triumph. Parapsychology had at last made the advantageous marriage it had long sought, had gained the accolade of respectability and the prospect of future prosperity conferred upon it by membership of the scientific community. The betrothal had been long, the suitor had been rejected several times, and right up to the last moment there were members of the bride's family who strongly opposed the match. Just before the final vote was taken, one member of the AAAS said, 'The so-called phenomena of parapsychology do not exist and it is impossible to do scientific work in this area, so that we have a null science. I therefore will vote against this motion.'[1] His view was shared by others, and although they proved to be in the minority their very existence indicated that the marriage was going to be no idyll, and that the parvenu was going to be given a rough passage by the older members of the clan if he ever stepped out of line.

Henry Sidgwick, one of the founding fathers of psychical research, said in his presidential address to the S.P.R., 'If they [the scientific community] will not yield to half-a-dozen decisive experiments by investigators of trained intelligence and hitherto unquestioned probity, let us try to give them half-a-dozen more recorded by other witnesses; if a dozen will not do, let us try to give them a score; if a score will not do, let us make up the tale to fifty.'[2] The S.P.R. was founded in 1882, the AAAS recognition was grudgingly granted in 1969, and in the interim the number of decisive experiments done in the field of parapsychology had run into thousands. In the interim, too, science itself had changed radically both in its methods and its concepts, and had evolved theories quite as mind-boggling as any put forward by parapsychology. Yet in 1969 a scientist could state categorically and with confidence that psi phenomena 'do not exist'. Here, surely, is a phenomenon that itself demands investigation. Why have some scientists been for so long and so inveterately opposed to the evidence and the hypotheses of parapsychology?

We have one answer, that of the AAAS member: there is no evidence and 'it is impossible to do scientific work in this area'. Well, those are discussable points and we shall come to them. But first, consider the import of another quotation. It is not from a scientist, but it expresses, in revealingly immoderate language that most scientists would eschew, an attitude that many of them would endorse. It is from a German public prosecutor, writing in a professional journal about the 'Rosenheim poltergeist' investigations: 'There is a close connection between the disgusting and bloody superstitious belief in witches and parapsychology. We are sick of the cadaverous smell that professors of old blew into our nostrils with their atrocity stories . . . Did the sun of the Enlightenment shine in vain?' I have borrowed this quotation from Hans Bender, who says, 'We often cite this remarkable statement as an example of negative superstition.'[3] It is an example, too, of the difficulties parapsychology has undergone through its association with the occult. The association is unavoidable, for parapsychology is concerned with the investigation of occult phenomena, although its theories and explanations are usually very different from the occult ones. Indeed, the substitution of the concept of RSPK for that of 'poltergeists' could be regarded as quite consistent with the aims of the Enlightenment.

Objections to parapsychology, then, can be ostensibly rational, like the AAAS member's, or unequivocally emotional, like the public prosecutor's. For the sake of clarity and the purposes of discussion, let's reduce the main objections to simple statements:

a) psi phenomena do not exist;
b) they may exist, but they are unimportant, irrelevant to science;
c) their nature is such that they are not amenable to investigation by scientific method;
d) to attempt to investigate them is to engage in a trivial and possibly dangerous pursuit;
e) psi hypotheses fail to qualify as scientific hypotheses not because they cannot be proved but because they cannot be disproved;

f) parapsychological literature, voluminous though it is, does not constitute a body of scientific knowledge, with a coherent rationale and conceptual framework, but merely a congeries of anecdotal and experimental demonstrations of miracles.

There are, no doubt, other objections, but I think the above are the most fundamental and common ones, and they certainly raise enough issues. In fact, in the space available my discussion can only be sketchy and in the nature of an overview rather than a depth analysis. For the latter purpose, a lengthy examination of concepts would be necessary, particularly of the terms 'science' and 'scientific method'.

Points and arguments relevant to the objections listed above will arise later, but it is not possible to deal with the objections in sequence, for they raise complex and cross-referring issues, so at this stage I will simply list summary answers to the objections which will be supported and elaborated upon in the ensuing discussion:

a) Psi phenomena do exist.
b) To maintain that they are irrelevant to science constitutes an arbitrary and drastic demarcation of the scope of science. On the contrary, the investigation of psi phenomena may spearhead a revolution in science in the future.
c) Granted, psi has not been convincingly elicited by methods that meet the stringent requirements of control, verification and particularly repetition applied in the physical sciences. But there is evidence that these requirements inhibit psi functions, and surely it should be a part of the business of science to design methods of investigation that are flexible, unbiased by pre-conceptions as to what is possible, and even hospitable to the phenomena under investigation, without compromising scientific standards.
d) Psi investigation is not a trivial pursuit, but it may indeed be a dangerous one. The danger, however, does not consist in meddling with occult forces, but in the consequences of witnessing the overthrow of ideas and priorities in which, both as individuals and as a society, we have a substantial vested interest.

e) The argument that psi hypotheses are unscientific because they are not disprovable applies to some but not all of them.

f) Granted, parapsychology lacks a coherent rationale and conceptual framework that all its practitioners would assent to at present, but many people are working towards such a formulation and the problem at the theoretical level is one of proliferation rather than of paucity. The possibility that a parapsychological Einstein might emerge with a unifying theory cannot be ruled out.

The day is long past when science lent support to the common sense view of reality, or when common sense could be appealed to as arbiter of the probability of scientific statements. Einstein defined common sense as 'merely the residue of prejudices deposited in our early experience by inadequate teaching',[4] and since his day and with the development of quantum mechanics science has departed not only from common sense but from the very idea that reality can be even approximately represented by a visual model. It was possible to visualise the corpuscular theory of matter and the mechanical theory of its interactions that derived from Descartes and dominated scientific thought up to the end of the nineteenth century. So long as the layman could visualise the atom as a tiny solar system, in which the nucleus corresponded to the sun and the orbiting electrons to the planets, he could rest assured that he understood the fundamentals of physical reality, and marvel at the principles of law and order that prevailed in the microcosm and the macrocosm alike. But as science probed deeper into matter it discovered that the solar system analogue became less and less apt. And to the further dismay of the layman, with his common sense and his need to form a 'mind's eye' visualisation of realities, at the subatomic level the sense-mediated properties of matter—mass, weight, shape, size, colour, velocity, position in space—disappeared and were replaced by properties quite as arcane as (but not corresponding to) those in the occult lore of alchemy. The laws that obtain in the world of sensory reality, of cause and effect, of the spatial location of matter, of the irreversibility of time, no longer obtain in the queer world of quantum mechanics, which is so remote from the world where common sense holds sway that it not only cannot be visualised but cannot even be explained in language but only in mathematical formulae.

Arthur Koestler, in his book *The Roots of Coincidence*, has expatiated on the wonders of the quantum world and argued that 'the seemingly fantastic propositions of parapsychology appear less preposterous in the light of the truly fantastic concepts of modern physics'.[5] And the psychologist Sir Cyril Burt, in his essay *Psychology and Parapsychology*, has made the same point: 'The recent advances in physical science . . . have now so drastically diminished the antecedent probability *against* so-called paranormal occurrences that it is more than counterbalanced by the high empirical probabilities in their favour which emerge from the accumulated results of numerous experimental studies.'[6] It is not for me to labour a point which has already been so ably and authoritatively made. It is surely unarguable by now that psi phenomena do not conflict with science but only with the scientific philosophy and world-view of the nineteenth century. Why, then, is parapsychology almost as suspect and unacceptable to the scientific community as a whole as psychical research was nearly a century ago?

I would suggest three reasons. There are undoubtedly others, but there is a point where prejudice becomes idiosyncrasy and unworthy of serious discussion. These three are, I think, common enough to be worthy:

Because it threatens to reinstate the supernatural, from which science only emancipated itself after a long struggle.

Because it is not its data that are unscientific, but its methods of investigation and verification.

Because the scientific community is not 'a whole', the quantum physicist belongs to an untypical minority within it, and the scientific world-view of the nineteenth century is by no means totally defunct today.

Its relations with the supernatural do pose a problem for parapsychology. They cannot be totally repudiated, although they were in the Rhine era when the infant science was trying to prove itself a man among men and to toe the behaviourist line. When clairvoyance, prophecy, out-of-the-body experiences and reincarnation form part of your area of investigation, it is difficult to avoid the charge that you are dabbling in the supernatural, that you have forfeited reason or that your motives are impure. Parapsychologists are sensitive, some perhaps over-sensitive, to this problem, although few of them today would subscribe to a spiritualistic or supernaturalistic explanation of the paranormal. The supernatural is only inimical to science when it is invoked as an explanation of phenomena and thereby curtails investigation. However, as much of the research reported in Part One illustrates, modern parapsychology aided by electronic technology has come up with substantial evidence that psi functions are *natural* in human beings and that 'paranormal' cognition occurs much more commonly than we realise. This surely does not constitute a reinstatement of the supernatural, but rather a contribution to the emancipation of the human mind from superstition, which is quite consistent with the aims of science.

There is another way of looking at this question of the relations between parapsychology and the supernatural, a way that few parapsychologists would confess to entertaining for a moment, but which I know some would assent to in private. It is the view that by totally repudiating the supernatural and setting out to demystify and desacralise nature, science at the beginning of the modern era embarked on a road to disaster. 'May God us keep / From Single Vision and Newton's sleep!' prayed William Blake, and in our day of ecological crisis and threatening social anarchy the poet's passionate opposition to scientific rationalism looks less quixotic than it did to his contemporaries. In the Baconian and Cartesian prospectus for the scientific revolution there were no built-in safeguards against science becoming the dupe and handmaiden of the technocracy it created, a tamed, domesticated functionary enmeshed in the comsumption-oriented, environment-ravaging political-industrial complex of Western societies. This is perhaps immoderate language, betraying as partial a view of science as Hans Bender's prosecutor had of the supernatural, but sometimes the clash of expressed partialities yields more insight into a situation than a well-moderated debate. Few scientists would consider themselves responsible for the banes that science has brought upon the world, for it is a responsibility that devolves upon them by default rather than because of anything they have actively done. Repudiating the supernatural, science repudiated not only superstition and sorcery but also that vision of the *cosmos*, the universal order, the interrelation and interdependence of man and nature, that was fundamental to the religious world-view and was celebrated by the poets, the mystics and the magi of old. Through parapsychology, science may stand now to regain the dimension it vacated with such ill-considered haste and such dire consequences, and it does not behove the parapsychologist to kowtow to the demands of the science of 'single vision' or to join the chorus of sweeping and uncritical disparagement of the supernatural.

One parapsychologist who doesn't is Charles Tart, a professor at the University of California. Conventional science, Tart has argued, is a science of *one* state of consciousness, and as such it affords access to only one order of reality. This point has direct bearing upon the second main argument against parapsychology mentioned above: that its methods of investigation and verification are unscientific.

Conventional science is the science of *objective* consciousness. When parapsychologists first sought admission to the scientific community they endeavoured to qualify themselves and their science by adopting a conventional scientific approach. The term 'scientific approach' implies two things: an attitude towards the phenomena under investigation, and a method, a way of conducting the inquiry and validating its results. The conventional scientific attitude is objective, alert, inquiring and emotionally uncommitted; it situates the phenomena 'out there' in the world and involves no reciprocity between the investigator and what he investigates. The conventional scientific method proceeds by isolating and analysing discrete phenomena; its motto is 'divide and conquer'; it sets up a hypothesis, develops it into a theory, devises controlled experiments to test the theory, has other researchers repeat the experiments, and if all goes smoothly announces to the world a discovery that carries the imprimatur of science's approval. This attitude and this method have predominated in parapsychology since Rhine began his campaign to win respectability for his subject in the 1930s, but although they have produced positive results time and again, these have not been so impressive or so consistent as to convince science that psi is a phenomenon it should take seriously. Parapsychologists have not been able to produce the kind of proof that conventional science demands. They have not been able to say, 'If you do this in this way under these conditions, you will get this result.' In other words, they have not been able to produce the repeatable experiment. Soal's conscientious attempt to repeat Rhine's work in the 1930s (see p. 95) is typical. He obtained null results, and although the records of his experiments were later found to contain evidence for psi different from Rhine's, other researchers still could not repeat his procedures and obtain corresponding results. All kinds of methods have been tried to elicit a stable and consistent demonstration of psi functioning, but invariably quantifiable laboratory experiments have shown a 'decline effect' and with repetition scores or 'hits' have dwindled to chance expectation. So science is not impressed.

Soal did not suspect Rhine of cheating, as many of his critics have done, but assumed that Rhine possessed an ability to encourage psi performance in his subjects which he himself did not have. He was probably right. Modern experiments designed to study the best psi-conducive conditions, in which experimenters have deliberately adopted cool and clinical or warm and friendly attitudes to their subjects, have shown that the experimenter has a much more involved function in the psi experiment than that of an objective observer. There are 'sheep' and 'goats', psi-promotors and psi-suppressors, among experimenters as well as among subjects. Consequently the conditions of the conventional scientific experiment —objectivity, isolation of the phenomenon, control of all the variables, and above all repeatability—cannot be fulfilled in the psi experiment. It is simply not in the nature of the phenomenon to manifest itself to order under these conditions. To maintain on these grounds that it does not exist is surely like Nelson putting his blind eye to the telescope at the Battle of Copenhagen and declaring, 'I have a right to be blind sometimes . . . I really do not see the signal!'

Jule Eisenbud, a professor of psychiatry at the University of Colorado, has put forward a theory that the purpose of psi forces is to maintain order and balance in the universe and keep things running smoothly, and that since it is not in the interests of the maintenance of universal order for them to come under human surveillance and control, accordingly it is in the nature of things that they should remain elusive and unpredictable.[7] It is a theory that no doubt will delight the mystics among psi enthusiasts, but it is the kind of speculation that drives scientists up the wall, for it can neither be proved nor disproved.

A more promising approach to the problem of getting scientific principles of investigation and verification revised so that they are more flexible and hospitable to psi functions lies in invoking as a precedent the principles applied in modern physics. Although a series of subatomic events is predictable in terms of probabilities, an individual subatomic event, like a psi event, is quite unpredictable. Nobody can predict on the basis of antecedent conditions when an atom of strontium-90 will emit an alpha particle. The physicist simply has to watch and wait. If he makes an observation and takes careful note of all the ambient conditions, he still cannot say to a colleague, 'Do this in this way under these conditions, and you will get this result.' Verification by replication is only possible with effects that proceed from known causes, and to hold that in order to qualify for scientific recognition phenomena must be capable of such verification is to maintain that there are no uncaused events in nature, which implies a mechanistic model of the universe which is quite untenable in the light of quantum physics.

The parapsychologist William Roll recalls visiting the physics department at Duke University, where at the time they were 'very interested in some new atomic particles. I went to the laboratory to look at some of the equipment they use for this and I saw a row of about a hundred young ladies sitting in front of projection apparatuses examining cloud pictures. Each of these young ladies looked at hundreds of pictures from cloud chambers searching for a particular configuration that would indicate the existence of the particular particle they were interested in. There were hundreds of thousands of these pictures and I was reminded of our own situation, looking at tens, perhaps hundreds of ESP subjects until we had someone who can produce, and I asked myself the question, "What is the difference between . . . our situation and their situation?"'[8] The only difference he could see was not in the experimental design or method, but in the fact that physicists had 'a central framework on which to hang this particle when it appears', whereas, he felt, parapsychologists had no such framework to accommodate psi phenomena.

This problem of the central framework, the rationale, the conceptual scheme to embrace psi phenomena, is probably the greatest barrier to their acceptance. As William James put it, 'Every other sort of fact has some context and continuity with the rest of nature. These alone are contextless and discontinuous.' This is less true today than it was in the nineteenth century, when James wrote, but it is still a problem, as Roll testifies.

The corresponding methodological problems of the physicist and the parapsychologist are not only problems of the elusiveness of their data but also of the role of the observer in the experimental situation. In the investigation of the subatomic world the behaviour of particles is influenced by the act of observation. In the words of the physicist Werner Heisenberg, 'Observation plays a decisive role in the event and . . . the reality varies depending on whether we observe it or not.'[9] Correspondingly, in psi research the experimenter plays a decisive role in the event. A Rhine can get results where a Soal cannot. This is now generally recognised as a fact that has to be taken into account in the design of parapsychological experiments and in the quantifying of their results, at least, it is a fact generally recognised by parapsychologists, but there are other members of the scientific community who still hold that immediately the subjectivity of the observer becomes involved in the experiment the results are automatically invalidated.

'Contemporary science', wrote Burt in his magisterial essay, 'tends to think in terms of interactions rather than mere transmission, and I am inclined to suggest that parapsychologists would do well to adopt this change of tactics, and frame their hypotheses on the assumption that the processes involved are essentially reciprocal.'[10] The principles of reciprocity and interaction, as distinct from cause and effect, are not new to science. Newton pointed out that the movement of the tides shows that the moon attracts the earth as well as the earth the moon. The bias of nineteenth-century science was to explain everything in terms of causal actions, whereas modern science, as Burt says, thinks in terms of reciprocal interactions. The change should make the scientific climate more hospitable to the psi hypotheses, and should also make it possible to establish principles of method and verification that take account of the experimenter's active role.

Such principles have in fact been developed in parapsychology in recent years, and although they have not yet received general acceptance by academic science they constitute a methodological revolution that could eventually spread to other sciences. Tart, proceeding from his argument that orthodox science is a science of *one* state of consciousness, has proposed the development of 'state-specific sciences'. Opposing the behaviourist contention that mental states are irrelevant to the scientific study of man, Tart argues that subjective experiences, particularly in altered states of consciousness, are real and meaningful, and that to dismiss them as mere imagination or hallucination is to impose arbitrary and unnecessary limitations upon knowledge. 'Observations of internal processes', he writes, 'are probably much more difficult to make than those of external physical processes, because of their inherently greater complexity. The essence of science, however, is that we observe what there is to be observed whether it is difficult to not.'[11] Mental states, he suggests, can be studied and compared and common features can be charted by using experimenters trained in the phenomenological method. If such experimenters can experience an ASC and report on the specific states they go through, and such reports are subsequently analysed and compared, a number of maps of specific states of consciousness will be obtained, which because of the elements of consensus and repetition will stand as objective and scientifically acceptable descriptions of realities.

Religions, Tart observes, are 'state-specific technologies, operated in the service of *a priori* belief systems'. He realises that the ineffability of experiences undergone in altered states of consciousness, the gratification they afford and the natural tendency of experiments to construe them in the context of an existing belief system, are obstacles that stand in the way of the translation of subjective experiences into objective 'Gestalten' that is the object of a state-specific science. 'Investigators of ASCs', he writes, 'would certainly encounter an immense variety of phenomenon labeled religious experience or mystical revelation during the development of state-specific sciences, but they would have to remain committed to examining these phenomena more carefully, sharing their observations and techniques with colleagues, and subjecting the beliefs (hypotheses, theories) that result from such experiences to the requirement of leading to testable predictions. In practice, because we are aware of the immense emotional power of mystical experiences, this would be a difficult task, but it is one that will have to be undertaken by disciplined investigators if we are to understand various ASCs.'[12]

To assist the experimenter-subject to make specific state-of-consciousness reports, Tart has prepared scales of levels of consciousness and in the experimental situation has required subjects to name at intervals the level that they have reached. He has discovered by this method a pattern of correspondences between levels of consciousness and the occurrence of particular phenomena and experiences. Tart's work has attracted the attention of other parapsychologists, and it looks likely that the 'state-specific' approach will become increasingly common in psi research in the future, replacing the statistical method and the use of ordinary subjects in normal states of consciousness. This approach, combined with the use of electronic technology for monitoring and training psi performance, has made it possible for parapsychologists to plot with accuracy the experimental, cognitive, conative and physiological correlates of a range and variety of states of consciousness.

'We have to remember', wrote Heisenberg, 'that what we observe is not nature in itself but nature exposed to our method of questioning.'[13] The significance of Tart's approach is that it suggests a change in the method of scientific questioning, and also that it expands the concept of 'nature' to take in human nature and consciousness as part of the field of investigation. Traditional Western science has depended for its data on sense-mediated information obtained in normal states of consciousness, with a heavy bias towards information supplied by the sense of vision. But modern psychological theory and experiment have made it very clear that our senses were not evolved for the purpose of acquiring knowledge of the universe but for survival within our environment, and that the function of sensory systems is to *reduce* the amount of information that reaches consciousness. What Tart's proposals amount to is a prescription for establishing a broader empirical basis for science and for bringing into operation those parasenses which, it is plausible to assume, man is endowed with for the purpose of gaining knowledge of the universe. The fact that many of the major discoveries and insights that have advanced science in the past have come to men in altered states of consciousness, in dreams, visions, reveries, moments of inspiration, lends powerful support to the state-specific approach and the theories upon which it is based. And any scientist who remains sceptical of Tart's methodology or considers it merely a modish innovation would do well to recall the saying of the German chemist F. A. Kekulé, who discovered the ring structure of benzene in a hypnagogic vision and thus initiated a revolution in organic chemistry. Addressing a scientific convention in 1890, Kekulé said, 'Let us learn to dream, gentlemen, and then we may perhaps find the truth.'

'The conceptual activities of the human mind', wrote Burt, 'are as imperfect and as limited as its powers of sensory perception, and the conceptual procedures of the scientist are the most limited of all.'[14] The reasons why they are so limited were analysed by Thomas Kuhn in his book *The Structure of Scientific Revolutions*. Although I have very briefly summarised Kuhn's ideas earlier (see p. 18), a fuller exposition is pertinent in the present context, for they suggest reasons why parapsychology is anathema to many scientists and also suggest that its methods and data may be of central importance in a new scientific revolution that has already begun to take place.

Normal science, Kuhn says, is a puzzle-solving activity and does not 'aim to produce major novelties, conceptual or phenomenal'. He uses the word 'paradigm' to refer to a set of assumptions, derived from a particular achievement or discovery, about how scientific work should proceed, what kind of discoveries it might expect to make and what areas of investigation are relevant. 'A paradigm can', he writes, 'insulate the community from those socially important problems that are not reducible to the puzzle form.' Paradigms are necessary to facilitate scientific work of any kind, but no paradigm can ever 'explain all the facts with which it can be confronted'. So paradigm-based science becomes 'a strenuous and devoted attempt to force nature into the conceptual boxes supplied by professional education', and it 'suppresses fundamental novelties because they are necessarily subversive of its basic commitments'.[15]

Kuhn uses a well-known experiment of the psychologist Jerome

Bruner as an illustration. Subjects were required to name a sequence of cards as they were quickly exposed one at a time. Breaking the sequence were some anomalous cards; for example a red six of spades or a black four of hearts. At the first exposure, most subjects named all the cards and none showed any hesitation or puzzlement over the anomalous ones. A black four of hearts would be identified as a four of either spades or hearts, i.e. 'it was immediately fitted to one of the conceptual categories prepared by prior experience'. When the process was repeated with the exposure time lengthened, some subjects began to hesitate, to become confused, even annoyed. They became aware of the existence of anomaly, but couldn't say precisely what was wrong. After further exposures of longer duration most subjects would suddenly realise that the suit and the colour were not consistent on some of the cards, and thereafter they had no difficulty in correctly identifying the other anomalous ones. But a few subjects were never able to make the mental adjustment, and even at forty times the duration of exposure required to recognise normal cards they still got the anomalous ones wrong. 'In science,' Kuhn writes, 'as in the playing card experiment, novelty emerges only with difficulty, manifested by resistance, against a background provided by expectation. Initially, only the anticipated and usual are experienced even under circumstances where anomaly is later to be observed.'

Though paradigms exert a tenacious hold upon the scientific mind, they do eventually collapse under the weight of accumulated anomaly, to be replaced by a more inclusive formulation, which in turn becomes the prevailing paradigm. The process takes time, and Kuhn's description of it, though he never specifically mentions parapsychology, could be a description of the relation of psi research to orthodox science over recent decades: 'Discovery commences with the awareness of anomaly, i.e. with the recognition that nature has somehow violated the paradigm-induced expectations that govern normal science. It then continues with a more or less extended exploration of the area of anomaly [the situation today in parapsychology]. And it closes only when the paradigm theory has been adjusted so that the anomalous has become the expected. Assimilating a new sort of fact demands a more than additive adjustment of theory, and until that adjustment is completed—until the scientist has learned to see nature in a different way—the new fact is not quite a scientific fact at all.'[16]

While scientists go on debating among themselves whether parapsychology qualifies for membership of the club, research work in the area continues apace, with imaginative innovations in method and theory that show a decreasing conformity with the paradigm of orthodox science, and which arguably puts parapsychology alongside quantum mechanics in the vanguard of the new scientific revolution.

8

Cultural Constructs

Reality is structured differently in different cultures. Just as in science the prevailing paradigm establishes rigid lines of demarcation between the possible and the impossible, the real and the unreal, the important and the unimportant, so in a culture the underlying metaphysical assumptions determine what is real and what is possible. It is not just a matter of reality being *regarded* differently in different cultures, of there being an unchanging world 'out there' which *seems* different from different cultural viewpoints. Cultural constructs are literally different worlds, in which different things happen and can happen and different laws obtain.

In June 1966 an Afro-American woman was admitted to the Baltimore City Hospital. She had been suffering from chest pains for a month and had difficulty with her breathing. The doctors were puzzled because there was no apparent physical cause. After she had been in the hospital for two weeks without her condition improving, the woman told her doctor that he had a serious problem and only three days to solve it. She was fated to die before her twenty-third birthday as a result of a 'hex', or spell, that had been laid on her at birth.

She told the doctor the full story. She had been born on a Friday the 13th and delivered by a midwife who had delivered two other girls that day. The midwife had told the mothers that the girls were hexed and that the first would die before her sixteenth birthday, the second before her twenty-first birthday and the third before her twenty-third birthday. The girl in the Baltimore hospital was the third and she was going to be twenty-three in three days' time. The first girl, she said, had been killed in an automobile accident the day before her sixteenth birthday. The second had survived without mishap until the evening of her twenty-first birthday, when she had called up a friend and suggested going out to celebrate the end of the hex. They had gone into a saloon, where she had been hit by a stray bullet and killed instantly.

The doctor's reaction to this tale is not on record, but no doubt he assumed that the prior deaths were coincidental and the patient's symptoms were psychosomatic. But he could not allay the girl's fears. Her anxiety increased, and on the day before her twenty-third birthday she died. The cause of death was diagnosed as 'primary pulmonary hypertension'.[1]

Here is a graphic example of the incompatibility of the reality principles of two different cultures, and of the incompetence of one culture to cope with problems that arise in the context of another. The only explanation that Western psychology could put forward would be that hex deaths occur as a result of suggestion, but as external circumstances brought about the deaths of the first two girls suggestion is as unlikely an explanation as pure coincidence. Commenting on the case, the assistant professor of medicine at Johns Hopkins Hospital said, 'I have no doubt that the pathologist will be able to demonstrate anatomic changes which can be held accountable for her death. However, I am equally certain that he will not be able to rule out the hex as the real cause of her death. . . . It is not a part of our society and hence we know little about it; I suspect many of us would prefer to think it did not exist. Special circumstances and beliefs in a community must exist before an individual can die by hex, but once the proper background and individual conditioning exist, there is no reason why the physiological processes cannot occur and lead to death, at the proper time.'[2]

In other words, reality is structured differently in different cultures.

In 1973 the Parapsychology Foundation of New York organised a conference in London on the subject, 'Parapsychology and Anthropology'. It was one of the contributors, Mrs Joan Halifax-Grof, who told the above story. But the most valuable and riveting contribution, it was generally agreed, was made by an Englishman named Adrian Boshier, who gave a talk entitled 'African Apprenticeship'. Boshier is one of a new breed of anthropologist, who, probably without being aware of Charles Tart's recommendations, have adopted a 'state specific' approach, involving themselves intimately and unconditionally in the culture they have studied instead of just observing it from without. So intimately involved is Boshier, in fact, that he has himself been initiated as a witchdoctor. Equally at home in two very different cultures, Adrian Boshier is a rare individual whose life story and field-work comprise documentary evidence of a kind that is extremely valuable to modern parapsychology.

He went to Africa at the age of eighteen and spent several years wandering alone on foot in the bush. From tribesmen he learnt how to survive on the land. He earned a little money by catching deadly snakes, milking them of their venom and selling it on occasional visits to a town. He used to bed down in caves or rough rock shelters, and in these places he often came across prehistoric paintings connected with ancient magical rites. A South African professor who had written a book on cave paintings happened to hear of Boshier and contacted him through a bush farmer whom he stayed with from time to time. The result of this was that Boshier was invited to study anthropology and archaeology under Professor Raymond Dart in Johannesburg. After three years' study he went back into the bush as an anthropological field worker. He lived with tribesmen, accepted by them as a brother, and eventually was invited to undergo the twelve degrees of initiation that would qualify him as a witchdoctor. He learnt the secrets of the symbolism of the prehistoric cave paintings, which the tribesmen had previously professed not to know the meaning of, and discovered that the ancient magical rites connected with them are still practised today. From his privileged position as an initiate, Boshier has been able to collect ample evidence that living African *sangomas*, or witchdoctors, possess highly developed psychic abilities and exercise clairvoyance, telepathy, precognition and paranormal healing all in the course of a day's work.

Many of the *sangomas* are women. Boshier has described his first encounter with one. From an African store-keeper in the bush he heard that there was a strange demented woman living in a village some miles away, and from the description he realised that she must be a witchdoctor. He engaged guides to take him to the village and they found the woman sitting on the floor in a mud hut, surrounded by bones and shells, her instruments of divination. She didn't look up when they entered, but kept on picking up and throwing down her bones and studying how they fell. Then she suddenly said, 'One of you is here to ask me questions, he has his head full of questions, he is not a man of this land, but comes from over the big water.' And she proceeded to tell Boshier many details about his own life that were completely accurate. Among the bones that she threw and studied from time to time was a small knuckle-bone of an impala. This, she said, represented Boshier, who was like the impala because he would leave the herd periodically and go off into the wilds alone. 'You walk by day and by night,' she said, 'you sleep under trees, like the impala ram. You go wherever you feel, wherever your spirits lead you. When you return to your people, they ask why you go off alone into the wilds. They think you are mad. But I know why you do this—I do it too. You go out to learn, living in the wild places, the mountains, the desert. You go on doing this throughout your life, living with your people, then leaving them to walk alone in the bush with your spirits. This is your life's work.' This, Boshier says, was a perfect description in African idiom of his life since he had arrived in the country seven years before.[3]

Some time after this first meeting he spent a week with some tribesmen in a remote mountain region where he wanted to explore ancient copper mines and learn about the traditional rituals that the Bantu miners practised in order to appease the underworld spirits. One morning he had a narrow escape when a leopard bolted out of one of the old mine workings just as he was about to enter. His route back to Johannesburg took him near the *sangoma*'s village, so he called on her and found her, as before, sitting in her 'hut of the spirits' and throwing the bones. She became quite concerned and agitated, for she said she could make no sense of what the bones were telling her. 'All I can see is the underworld, the underground', she said. Boshier told her about his exploration of the ancient mines, which put her mind at rest. But she warned him, 'You must be very careful when you go down there as the gods of the underworld can be very dangerous. Also I see you here in my bones next to a leopard. The leopard too was in that place, and he does not like people in his home. You must be very careful of this animal—I see you were right next to him.'

Most of the African *sangomas* practise divination by bones, but some have other methods. Boshier quotes a very interesting statement made to him by a young female Swazi *sangoma* who often diagnoses and treats illnesses. When an African is suffering from any misfortune or ailment he simply goes to a *sangoma*'s house and says, '*Sia cou lega*', which means 'I want to know.' He gives her no further information, and the *sangoma* is then expected to tell him why he has come and what to do about his troubles. When she is approached by a patient in this way, the Swazi woman told Boshier, 'I leave him and go into my room, put on my clothes, pick up my switch and begin to sing. I ask my ancestors to tell me what is wrong with this person. I sing and sing, walking around until I feel the spirit coming. When it comes it feels like a heavy weight on the back of my head and shoulders. Very heavy on me. Then I must go to that patient and start to talk. I must talk until the spirit goes. I cannot stop until it is finished. Sometimes I don't even know what I was saying and the patient must tell me. Sometimes I can hear my words, but don't understand them. When I come back afterwards I feel like I have been dreaming.'[4]

This account corresponds in several details with descriptions of trance states and their induction which we find in other cultures, and I shall refer back to it later in the present chapter. It also corroborates, of course, the point that parapsychologists have over recent years been demonstrating in their laboratories: that psi functions are enhanced in altered states of consciousness.

Boshier conducted an experiment himself with this particular *sangoma* when she visited his office at the Museum of Man and Science in Johannesburg in the company of another witchdoctor. Here is his account of it: 'Leaving her in my office with the other witchdoctor and Miss Costello, I went to a neighbouring building and took out the skin of a gemsbok. This I hid beneath a canvas sail on the back of my Landrover. I then called her outside and told her I had hidden something which she must find. With the aid of the other witchdoctor, she knelt down and began to sing softly. Then, in a trance state, she informed me that I had hidden something across on the other side of that building, over there. She told me that it had more than one colour, that it came from an animal, that it was raised up off the ground. Suddenly she got up, ran around the building, out into the front where the Landrover stood and knelt down beside it. Again she began singing softly and within five minutes of this she tore off one of her necklaces and, holding it in front of her like a divining rod, she walked around the Landrover, climbed onto the back and took out the skin.'[5]

Whether it was accomplished through clairvoyance, telepathy or spirit guidance, this was a pretty convincing demonstration of paranormal ability. The African woman herself would have had no doubt as to how she came by the required information, for she belongs to a culture in which it is generally believed that the spirits of ancestors are always accessible, if invoked with the right rituals, to give help, advice or any information that may be requested. During one of Boshier's initiation ceremonies, the presiding witchdoctor told him that he had been accepted for initiation because his ancestors and those of the witchdoctor had agreed that it should be so. And when he asked her whether she had any regrets or doubts about initiating him, an Englishman, into a tribally oriented ceremony, she replied, 'Today you and I are different, we live differently, our culture is different, but long ago we all came from a common source and when we die we go back to the old people—back to the old days, to our ancestors, and on that side there is no difference, we are all the same.'

Only believe and you will see, say the leaders of religious movements down the centuries, offering a prescription for that expansion of consciousness and transcendence of quotidian reality that the human being needs for survival as much as he needs food, rest or water. Seeing is believing, retorts the Western scientific rationalist, dictating a criterion for reality that precludes experiences of expansion or transcendence and makes sovereign arbiter of the real a demonstrably fallible physiological process. And from these points of departure in fundamental belief spring world-views and worlds to view and to experience as different and as irreconcilable as sorcery and science.

One of the most remarkable examples of a society in which paranormal occurrences are commonplace and are easily explained in terms of the prevailing world view is in contemporary Brazil. Here the Spiritist religion, based on the writings of the nineteenth-century Frenchman Allan Kardec, flourishes, and some Spiritist mediums have produced paranormal effects quite as puzzling and challenging as any of Uri Geller's. An English psychic researcher, Guy Playfair, who has lived in Brazil since 1961, has recently written an account of his investigations. He explains the eccentric title of his book, *The Flying Cow*, by saying that Brazil is 'the most psychically-oriented country on earth, where nothing can surprise anybody', and if a Brazilian were to go home one evening and tell his wife he had just seen a cow flying over the road she would be likely to react not with incredulity but with a matter-of-fact question like, 'Oh really, what colour was it?'[6]

Of course, an ambience of unquestioning belief is just what the fraudulent psychic needs, and Playfair has no doubt that fraud does occur on the Brazilian Spiritist psychic scene; in fact he devotes a chapter of his book to relating the exposure of one such case. But he maintains that a large number of Spiritist mediums are genuine and do not work for personal profit or fame, and he appears to be a careful and knowledgeable investigator who is nobody's fool, so his testimony is valuable, particularly when he writes about his personal experience of psychic surgery.

Psychic surgery has had a lot of publicity recently, both in the press and on television, mostly unfavourable and designed to discredit its practitioners. Hundreds of Europeans and Americans, many of them suffering from terminal illnesses, have gone to Manila in the Philippines (where Spiritism also flourishes) to be operated on by Tony Agpaoa or one of the other Filipino psychic surgeons. Millions of others have watched on television Agpaoa at work, operating on a patient with his bare hands, kneading the patient's stomach until a profuse flow of blood appears, apparently plunging his hand into the body and removing some tissue or a tumour, then swabbing away the blood to reveal an expanse of skin that bears no mark of an incision. Of course, it must be achieved by sleight-of-hand, says the sceptic; the 'surgeon' must conceal a sachet of blood which he bursts open while he is kneading the flesh. Yet the British scientist and author, Dr Lyall Watson, who has investigated Agpaoa under conditions which he himself controlled, even to the extent of requiring him to be stripped and searched before beginning an operation, states, 'I have watched hundreds of these operations . . . and I can personally swear that there is no sleight of hand.'[7] Such authentication weighs heavily against the sceptic's view of the phenomenon, but that of Guy Playfair, who is not only an experienced and critical observer but has also had an operation by psychic surgery himself, is even more weighty.

The 'surgeon' in this case was Edivaldo Oliviera Silva (known as Edivaldo), a secondary school teacher from a town 500 miles from Rio de Janeiro who over a period of ten years had treated some 65,000 patients. Playfair had suffered for three years from stomach pains and digestive troubles, and he decided to consult Edivaldo both in the hope of alleviating his pains and in the interests of psychical research. It took considerable courage to go through with his project, however, particularly when he accepted an invitation to witness the operation before his own. It took place in a ramshackle hut in a run-down area of Rio, where the only furniture was a narrow bed, a chair and table. A lady assistant unpacked some bandages and cotton wool, but there were no surgical instruments. Edivaldo himself was a slight man, aged about forty, who had the air of a friendly bank manager. His first patient of the day was a lean, elderly man. He lay on the bed, his shirt was unbuttoned so that his stomach was exposed, and the operation began. Here is Playfair's account of what happened and of his own reaction: 'Edivaldo and two or three people were leaning over the bed, one holding the microphone and another with a large bandage ready. I rested my hands on the foot rail and stared in complete bewilderment at about two square feet of exposed innards. It was only a fleeting glance, as several hands intermittently blocked my view. But it was the kind of sight one does not forget in a hurry; the old man's body had been ripped wide open. There were a few spots of what looked like blood on the skin to either side of the opening, and the rest was a sickening bloody mess. . . . My first sight of a paranormally opened body was an overwhelming shock. Instinctively, I looked away, and when I looked again the man's stomach was all neat and tidy and being covered by the bandage the helper had slapped on. Then the man's wife came forward, helped him to his feet and led him out.'[8]

When it came to his turn, Playfair began to entertain thoughts of bolting from the scene, forgetting all about psychic healing and depending on conventional treatment to solve his digestion problem. 'If I was going to be carved open,' he says, 'I wanted a pretty nurse to hold my hand and assure me there was nothing to worry about.'

But it was too late to escape. An assistant asked him to lie on the bed. He lay and waited while Edivaldo saw about a dozen patients in rapid succession and scribbled prescriptions for them. Then, 'Edivaldo suddenly swung round in his chair, got up and hurried over to the bed as if he had just made up his mind to strangle me. . . . The hands just came at me and began to feel around the belly area. . . . Then came the unmistakable moment of truth. Edivaldo's hands seem to find what they were looking for, the thumbs pressed down hard, and I felt a very distinct plop as they penetrated the skin and went inside. My stomach immediately felt wet all over, as if I were bleeding to death. I could feel a sort of tickling inside, but no pain at all. . . . Then it was all over, as suddenly as it had begun. Edivaldo muttered something I could not understand, a bandage was slapped casually and quite hard on my belly, and a lady said I could get up and go home.'[9] Another assistant interpreted Edivaldo's muttered instructions about diet and rest and away Playfair went, feeling distinctly groggy and as if he still had a hole in his stomach. When he examined his stomach later he found a jagged red line about three inches long, which faded the following day, and two bright red dots where Edivaldo had pressed his thumbs, which did not subsequently fade.

He had to go for a second operation some months later, and this time he took a friend who was able to corroborate his account of what happened and compare the marks on his stomach before and after the operation. This time he was not so nervous at first, but he became alarmed when Edivaldo said, 'This is going to hurt.' It did hurt, he says, but only slightly and briefly. 'I felt a firm wrench in my innards—deep down, not just on the surface—and there was a slight pain, but not enough to make me yell. I had the curious sensation that there were two sets of hands at work on me; Edivaldo seemed to be doing no more than just keep his hands there while another invisible pair did the actual work.' Edivaldo prescribed some pills for him to take after this second operation, and after two further check-ups told him that he was fully cured. And he was.

When Playfair later interviewed Edivaldo, the healer had no recollection of having operated on him. He explained that he did all his healing work in trance, and had no conscious memory of any of the 65,000 patients he had treated, which was why he had tape-recordings of his sessions made at the time. He was only a medium and the actual work, as Playfair had felt during his own operation, was not done by him but by one of several spirit doctors who worked through him. Among these there was a Frenchman, a German, an Italian, an Englishman and a Japanese, all of whom spoke their own languages through Edivaldo. His chief control was a Dr Calazans, who spoke Spanish. Playfair had another opportunity to see Edivaldo–Calazans at work and the experience, he said, dispelled any lingering doubts he might have had about the reality of psychic surgery. Operations, he learnt, can be plasmic or ectoplasmic, i.e. they can be performed on the 'perispirit' body or the physical one, and on this occasion he witnessed both kinds. During the first, the healer simply moved his hands about above the bared stomach of a young man, giving a commentary as he did so, in the voice and language of Calazans, as if to a class of student doctors. When the operation was over the young man, who hadn't been touched by the healer, staggered over to a second bed where he lay for a time moaning and muttering; he was suffering, Edivaldo–Calazans said, from post-operative shock.

The second operation was on a young woman. The healer invited Playfair to put his hand beside his own on her stomach as he prodded her. Suddenly he found his fingers immersed in 'a pool of dark liquid that had simply appeared from nowhere'. It was of the temperature of blood, but lighter and thinner, and Playfair recalled that he had been told that in plasmic operations the red corpuscles were separated from the plasma. When the operation was over, 'the liquid pool on the woman's stomach simply vanished, like spilt water in an animated cartoon'. Playfair's fingers remained wet and sticky for some minutes. The experience, he says, 'was yet another moment of truth, not that I should have needed further proof'.[10]

I have devoted considerable space to Playfair's account of his experiences of psychic surgery because the subject is highly controversial and first-hand accounts by experienced psychic researchers are rare. I do not know Mr Playfair personally, but his book was brought to my attention by Dr Eric Dingwall, who has spent some sixty years in psychical research and whose guarantee of a parapsychologist's competence and integrity, as anyone professionally involved in the field knows, is very rarely conceded. If 'Ding' recommends a para-psychologist's work, it has to be work of quite extraordinary integrity. For this reason, and also because Playfair's accounts have many points of correspondence with Lyall Watson's of his experiences in the Philippines, I am disposed to believe that Playfair has reported his experiences conscientiously and truthfully and to maintain that such evidence constitutes a *prima facie* case for the reality of psychic surgery.

Paranormal healing is only one of many kinds of psychic pheno-menon that take place in the context of Brazilian Spiritism. Brazil's most prolific author, with (up to 1974) 126 books to his credit, is Chico Xavier, a Spiritist with little formal education (he left school at thirteen) who has written poetry, novels, children's books, history, and works of popular science and Spiritist doctrine. Chico, however, is not recognised by the Brazilian literary establishment, for he is a trance author who attributes all his works to spirit guides, issues them through Spiritist publishing houses, and donates his income from them to the Spiritist cause. Also, he maintains that he doesn't understand a word of some of the scientific works that flow from his pen. Several of Brazil's leading modern authors have created and published posthumous works through Chico's mediumship, and literary experts have attested that the style and subject matter of these works is unmistakably characteristic of the alleged authors. One writer's widow even took Chico to court to claim a share of the royalties, but although Chico offered to prove that her husband was the author by producing more specimens of his work in the court-room the judge ruled that the author was officially dead and had no rights in works not produced by his own hand in his own lifetime.

Even more impressive as evidence of paranormal if not discarnate authorship was a book entitled *Evolution in Two Worlds*, alternate chapters of which were written by Chico and another Spiritist, a doctor named Waldo Vieira. The two trance authors lived 250 miles apart and were not in communication during the book's composition, but when the chapters they had written down independently were put together they were found to follow logically one upon the other and the whole work had complete unity of style.

Mediums capable of producing extraordinary physical effects are to be found in the Brazilian Spiritist movement. Playfair summarises the feats attributed to the most versatile of them, Carmine Mirabelli, who surely puts Uri Geller in the shade: 'automatic writing in over thirty languages living or dead, speaking in numerous foreign tongues, materialising objects and people, transporting anything from a bunch of flowers to large pieces of furniture (including levitation of himself even when strapped in a chair), producing impressions of spirit hands in trays of flour or wax inside locked drawers, dematerialising any-thing in sight, himself included. . . . He could, they say, contact dead relatives or friends and paint portraits of them. He could sing or play the piano or violin with considerable skill while in a trance, although he had no musical talent or training. He could write a message of several pages in a few minutes while chatting away at the same time—in another language. He did, in fact, just about anything that any other medium has ever done, doing so for something like forty years . . . in broad daylight or in a well-lit room in front of anything up to five hundred witnesses.'[11]

Such a catalogue of miracles is enough to bring the most uncritical psi enthusiast up against his credulity threshold, and indeed tales of such virtuosity as Mirabelli's are more likely to be read as evidence of the gullibility engendered in a society by the prevailing belief structure than as proof that reality itself is structured differently. However, since it would not be relevant in the present context to attempt to disentangle the genuine from the fraudulent in accounts of Mirabelli's mediumship, let us just say that if he actually did any of the things that thousands of witnesses swore they had seen him do he confounded laws that science and common sense consider to be axiomatic and universal, and if he did them because he was a Spiritist he furnished substantial proof that belief can accomplish miracles.

My use of Brazilian Spiritism as an example of a cultural construct perhaps requires some justification. It might be objected that Spiritism, or Spiritualism as we know it in Britain and America, is not a culture in the sense of a total *modus vivendi* of an ethnic group, but a system of beliefs held by a minority of people living within Western society. The example of the African *sangomas* suggests the development of an argument that in non-Western societies, which are not inhibited by a scientific-rational outlook and a distrust of altered states of consciousness, events that we would call paranormal are regarded as quite normal. It would be interesting to have more evidence of this, and to consider the question whether there is more evidence for psi functioning in societies we would consider primitive, and if so what part it plays in the lives of these societies. However extraordinary the phenomena of Spiritism may be, they do not prove that reality and the limits of the possible are different in different cultures, but only that 'faith can move mountains'. So let's be clear about this: are we talking about the convergence of parapsychology with religion or with anthropology? And are 'cultural constructs' anything more than systems of belief?

By way of answering such questions an initial point to make is that ethnic purity and integrity are rare in the world today, and even in 'backward' countries it is generally only a minority that keep alive the old cultural traditions and ways of life. The African store-keeper from whom Boshier learnt about the existence of the clairvoyant *sangoma* regarded her as a mad old woman, and when Boshier told him he had just described to him a witchdoctor he refused to accept the fact. Boshier's evidence is in fact very similar to Playfair's, in that it describes people who accomplish paranormal feats and attribute them to the work of spirits, and the main difference between the two accounts is that one relates to a group that we tend to think of as alien and primitive and the other to a group we regard as familiar and perhaps a bit cranky. But Spiritism is not just a century-old phenomenon in the West; it is an ancient tradition that under different names was an integral part of the Roman and Greek cultures and survived in esoteric forms throughout the Christian era, although the Church, claiming a monopoly on the miraculous, attempted to put it down whenever it surfaced. If it survives only in pockets today and its devotees do not constitute an integral and localised culture, this surely does not disqualify it as a subject of interest to the anthropologist, particularly when, as in Brazil and the Philippines, it develops as a movement strong enough to create an ambience for the performance of miracles. The stories of the miracles performed by Christ, his disciples and rivals (such as Simon Magus), as recorded in the New Testament and Apocrypha, may all be fictions, delusions or cynical lies, but who would not give a great deal to have been there to see for himself? Unfortunately we cannot travel to ancient Galilee or Rome, but contemporary Brazil and the Philippines are not out of reach and the evidence seems to be substantial that there the age of miracles is not a dubious historical tag but a living reality.

To the question, Are 'cultural constructs' anything more than systems of belief? the answer is that they are nothing more unless they are entered into and lived through. The question of the relation of belief to experience is a thorny one. On the one hand, as Bruner's anomalous card experiment demonstrated, the reality we perceive is conditioned by our antecedent belief and expectation. We don't see what we don't expect to see or believe to exist. Belief limits accessible reality. On the other hand, antecedent belief can also produce delusions and hallucinations, totally subjective convictions of reality. That there are planes of non-ordinary reality which are accessible in altered states of consciousness is attested by the world's religions, by psychical research, by esoteric traditions and by a great deal of literature, and that these are not merely delusory but are planes upon which things happen that have observable effects in the physical world is also well attested. But when a man is in an ASC and believes that something is going to happen, how is he to know when it does happen whether he has entered upon another plane of reality or is merely hallucinating? This was the question that continually worried Carlos Castaneda throughout his long apprenticeship to the Yaqui Indian sorcerer, don Juan, and his evidence is among the most convincing we have for the existence of other realities and the inadequacy of the mere hallucination hypothesis.

In Castaneda's don Juan quartet, published between 1968 and 1974, we have the most detailed account of a contemporary Western-educated man's experience of an utterly alien culture. Some critics have maintained that the books are pure works of fiction, pointing out that nobody else has been able to locate the now legendary don Juan. I suppose it is just possible that Castaneda would have been capable of synthesising his immense work, with its coherent philosophy, its knowledge of esoteric tradition, its system of consciousness training, its wealth of anecdote and epigram, its superbly complex, strange and profound character portrayal, out of the raw material and the suggestions he could have picked up from Professor Mircea Eliade's classic study, *Shamanism*, which was first published in English in 1964. But he was a young man, a graduate student of anthropology at the University of California at Los Angeles, when he began his apprenticeship, and would have had to have been the prodigy of prodigies to have invented the seventy-year-old don Juan and all his wisdom, knowledge and poetry. It is more likely that the books are what they purport to be: an anthropological study written from a 'state specific' point of view.

In the summer of 1960, Castaneda went to Arizona to collect information about the medicinal and psychotropic plants used by the Indians. Here he met an elderly Mexican Indian who was reputed to be a *brujo*, i.e. medicine man or sorcerer, and to be very knowledgeable about plants. Castaneda offered to pay him for information and help with his field-work, an offer which don Juan scornfully declined. He would talk to him about numerous other subjects, however, about animals and hunting, about life and death, about some of Castaneda's personal problems and experiences, even experiences of his childhood, about which he seemed to have an extraordinary knowledge. Castaneda was intrigued and bewildered and went back to don Juan's house time and again, and about a year after their first meeting don Juan told him that he had chosen to make him his apprentice, to initiate him into the Indian traditions of sorcery and make him a 'Man of Knowledge'. He warned him that by accepting he was committing himself to a long and arduous training. Castaneda accepted, and let himself in for the bizarre series of adventures that he recounts in his four books.

When the first appeared in 1968 it immediately became a kind of Bible of the counter culture, for its theme was the exploration of non-ordinary reality through the use of hallucinogens. *The Teachings of Don Juan* covered the first period of Castaneda's apprenticeship, from 1961 to 1965, and from it don Juan emerges as a kind of master of hallucinations, sometimes sinister and sometimes benign but always inscrutable as he instructs his apprentice in the use of various psychotropic plants, orchestrates his visions and experiences under their influence, and expounds the fundamentals of his philosophy. In

Journey to Ixtlan (1972), Castaneda returned to this first period, saying that in the earlier book he had given the erroneous impression that the only way to learn don Juan's lessons was through the ingestion of psychotropics, and proceeded to make the portrait of his mentor much more substantial by relating him to his environment, showing him as a natural philosopher, a hunter, a man on intimate terms with nature. Castaneda abandoned his attempt to become a Man of Knowledge after a harrowing experience of 'psychic attack', which nearly cost him his sanity if not his life, but he resumed his apprenticeship in 1968, and *A Separate Reality* (1971) and *Tales of Power* (1974) recount further adventures in the company of don Juan and his prodigious and clownish fellow-sorcerer don Genaro. Between them the two old men utterly confound Castaneda's sense of reality by involving him in their world of mystery, magic and power, and through a weird and arduous course of instruction they cultivate in him a certain modest facility in the practice of their occult arts.

Towards the end of the first period of his apprenticeship, Castaneda had an experience of flying, or what parapsychologists would call an OOBE. Don Juan had told him that a sorcerer can soar through the air for hundreds of miles to see what is happening or to strike a fatal blow to an enemy. After drinking a potion concocted by don Juan from the root of datura, or devil's weed, Castaneda took off: 'I soared. I remember coming down once; then I pushed up with both feet, sprang backwards, and glided on my back. I saw the dark sky above me, and the clouds going by me. I jerked my body so I could look down. I saw the dark mass of the mountains. My speed was extraordinary. My arms were fixed folded against my sides. My head was the directional unit. If I kept it bent backwards, I made vertical circles. I changed directions by turning my head to the side. I enjoyed such freedom and swiftness as I had never known before. . . .'[12] Eventually he descended and landed amid landscape he recognised as being about half a mile from don Juan's house. He was completely naked and it was nearly dawn. He tried to run and hurt his feet on the stones of the road. He hid behind the bushes when he saw someone approaching up the road, but when the figure drew closer he saw that it was don Juan and that he was bringing his clothes.

The experience was real and vivid, but was it an hallucination? 'Did I really fly, don Juan? . . . I mean, did my body fly? Did I take off like a bird?' he asked. He wasn't satisfied with the answer that the purpose of the devil's weed was for flying, and that he would learn to fly perfectly as he took more of it. 'Where was my body?' he asked. 'In the bushes,' don Juan said. If a friend had been there, would he have seen him flying? he insisted. That depended on the friend, don Juan said. Exasperated, Castaneda asked what would have happened if he had been tied to a rock with a heavy chain. Puzzled by his insistent questions, don Juan said he would have to fly holding the rock with its heavy chain.

In this exchange, two radically different conceptions of reality clashed. 'The trouble with you', don Juan said, 'is that you understand things in only one way.'[13] A point he continually repeats throughout his teachings is that the world as we know it is not the real world, it is only a description. 'We are perceivers. The world that we perceive, though, is an illusion. It was created by a description that was told to us since the moment we were born.'[14] Thus, in a sentence, don Juan brings together the fundamental insights behind the work of the anthropologist Claude Lévy-Strauss and the psychologist Jean Piaget: Lévy-Strauss's idea that a culture constitutes a 'semantic universe', i.e. a description of reality, and Piaget's that the process of creating this consensus reality begins in earliest childhood. Elsewhere, don Juan says, 'The world is such-and-such or so-and-so only because we tell ourselves that that is the way it is. If we stop telling ourselves that the world is so-and-so, the world will stop being so-and-so.'[15] This process of telling ourselves, of continually reconfirming that reality is as we have learnt to regard it, goes on both between people and within the individual. 'The internal dialogue is what grounds us,'[16] he says. Reality is much more awesome, mysterious and charged with possibilities than our linguistic or conceptual functions can grasp, and by relying on these to tell us what the world is really like, we shut ourselves off from knowledge of realities that lie outside our conceptual and semantic universes. 'You insist on explaining everything as if the whole world were composed of things that can be explained,'[17] don Juan tells Castaneda. He can't answer his question, 'Did I really fly?' for it is a question that presupposes a description of reality quite different from the sorcerer's description and experience. He can only toss it back, emphasising the incompatibility of their conflicting reality principles: 'You don't think a man flies; and yet a *brujo* can move a thousand miles in one second to see what is going on. He can deliver a blow to his enemies long distances away. So, does he or doesn't he fly?'

Don Juan's world is full of strange powers, both benevolent and malevolent, that dwell in every object and living thing. It is not a comfortable world, it is full of hazards, but it is, he insists, the world in which everyone lives, though most people go about unaware of the forces that are acting upon them. In this world—which, incidentally, anthropologists would tag 'animist' and regard as a primitive conception—spirits dwell in rivers, mountains, trees, waterholes, and a moth might be an 'ally' and a bird a witch. 'The world is indeed full of frightening things,' don Juan says, 'and we are helpless creatures surrounded by forces that are inexplicable and unbending. The average man, in ignorance, believes that those forces can be explained or changed; he doesn't really know how to do that, but he expects that the actions of mankind will explain them or change them sooner or later. The sorcerer, on the other hand, does not think of explaining or changing them; instead, he learns to use such forces by redirecting himself and adapting to their direction.'[18] His rewards are knowledge, power and control far surpassing the capacities of other men, and for these he pays with tireless vigilance, discipline and strenuous labour. For don Juan, there is simply 'no other way to live',[19] for none of life's satisfactions can equal 'the happiness that comes from doing things deliberately'.[20]

In the course of his apprenticeship, Castaneda had many demonstrations of the sorcerer's paranormal powers, both from don Juan and from his friend don Genaro. 'Sorcery', he learnt, 'is interference. A sorcerer searches and finds the key joint of anything he wants to affect and then he applies his will to it.'[21] This could be a definition of PK, and don Juan proceeded to illustrate his point in a manner that would delight any parapsychologist. 'Your car is the spark plugs', he said. 'That's its key joint for me. I can apply my will to it and your car won't work.'[22] They got into the car together, and after a few minutes of ritual preparation for his task don Juan told Castaneda to turn the starter. He did so, and kept turning it repeatedly for ten minutes, but the engine wouldn't fire. Don Juan laughed and then eventually told him that he had released the car and he should try again. This time it started at the first turn!

As well as having clairvoyant knowledge of circumstances and events in Castaneda's life, don Juan also knew or could foretell what he experienced during his 'trips' under the influence of drugs. Bizarre and sometimes terrifying though these visions and experiences were, they were coherent and logical within don Juan's conceptual scheme, and they differed from dreams or hallucinations in that they were not arbitrary and evanescent but extraordinarily concrete and stable. In don Juan's philosophy, to enter upon a plane of non-ordinary reality and to meet the beings and creatures that existed there, was not an exercise designed merely to 'blow the mind', but to acquire by paranormal means knowledge that could be applied in the world of ordinary reality. 'Every man is in touch with everything else,'[23] he claimed, but to be aware of being in touch, to 'see' (a key word in his philosophy), required either a process of prolonged and strenuous training or disciplined use of psychotropics. On one occasion he taught Castaneda to use lizards as a channel for clairvoyant perception. 'Ask them about anything you cannot find out for yourself',[24] he told him, and said that with their help he could find out about persons he did not see ordinarily, about lost objects, or about places he had not seen. Castaneda pondered for a while, then asked the lizards, in the manner that don Juan prescribed, to identify a person who had been stealing books from a certain library. Later, under the influence of the datura potion, he had a clairvoyant vision of the thief in action and recognised him as a young man he had seen occasionally.

Don Juan says he has given up exercising his sorcerer's powers just for the sake of it. There was time when he would toss boulders that twenty men couldn't move, or jump so high that he chopped the top leaves off the highest tree, but 'it was all for nothing. All I did was frighten the Indians—only the Indians. The rest who knew nothing about it did not believe it. . . . It was different when there were people in the world . . . who knew a man could become a mountain lion, or a bird, or that a man could simply fly. So I don't use the devil's weed any more. For what? To frighten the Indians?'[25] A

man can be a sorcerer, he says, without really being a Man of Knowledge and without being able to 'see', which are the important aims
of life. However, he will exercise his powers for the purpose of training his apprentice. On one occasion, for instance, he told Castaneda
to look at a certain tree and watch a leaf that would fall from the very
top. They watched together for several minutes and then, sure enough,
a leaf cracked loose from the top and fell to the ground. 'You would
say that the same leaf will never again fall from that same tree, true?'
said don Juan. Castaneda agreed, but when he looked at the tree he
saw the leaf fall again, hitting the same leaves and branches on its
way to the ground as the other had done. 'Look!' said don Juan a few
moments later, and a leaf fell for a third time, describing exactly the
same pattern. 'It's impossible', Castaneda said. 'You're chained . . .
chained to your reason', don Juan said, and explained that the leaf
had fallen again and again so that he would stop trying to understand. 'Understanding is only a very small affair,' he said, 'so very
small.'[26]

If don Juan was sparing in his acts of sorcery, his friend don
Genaro was by contrast lavish and flamboyant, and his numerous
feats are the most incredible and entertaining part of Castaneda's
narrative. He could, apparently, materialise or dematerialise objects,
disappear and reappear at will, levitate, cause tremendous and
terrifying noises like that of an avalanche. Once he made Castaneda's
car disappear, and after a crazy pantomime search for it under rocks
and amid bushes, which the two sorcerers enjoyed like children, he led
Castaneda some distance out into the chaparral, where they found it.
Castaneda suspected many times that don Genaro was a consummate
illusionist, which no doubt he was in a sense, but in the sorcerer's
philosophy the word has a rather different connotation than we
would normally give it. 'Yesterday the world became as sorcerers tell
you it is,' don Juan said; and, explaining the car incident: 'Genaro
never moved your car from the world of ordinary men the other day.
He simply forced you to look at the world like sorcerers do, and your
car was not in that world.'[27] In other words, he was not creating an
illusion in the sense of a deceptive perception, but was transporting
Castaneda on to a plane of non-ordinary reality that was as concrete
and substantial as the world he ordinarily inhabited.

Perhaps the key passage in don Juan's teachings is the following, from the end of Castaneda's first book: 'The particular thing to learn is how to get to the crack between the worlds and how to enter the other world. There is a crack between the two worlds, the world of the *diableros* [sorcerers] and the world of living men. There is a place where the two worlds overlap. The crack is there. It opens and closes like a door in the wind. To get there a man must exercise his will. He must, I should say, develop an indomitable desire for it, a single-minded dedication.'[28] He must also, before he can take the first step, arrest the persistent chatter of his internal dialogue, stop telling himself and being convinced by others that the world is so-and-so when it is demonstrably much more and when with a simple shift of consciousness he can 'see' that it is much more.

Even if Castaneda's incredible books were proved to be pure allegory and their hero to be fictitious, the words of this 'primitive' Indian shaman would still stand as an eloquent critique of the prevailing Western world-view and the reductionist paradigm. 'To turn that magnificence out there into reasonableness doesn't do anything for you', he tells Castaneda. 'Here, surrounding us, is eternity itself. To engage in reducing it to manageable nonsense is petty and out-right disastrous.'[29] The disasters created by reductionism and 'single vision' are all around us, and don Juan's teachings could not be more timely. From him, or from Castaneda, hundreds of thousands, maybe millions of Westerners have learnt to regard their world as but one of several possible cultural constructs, and have learnt too that there is more to 'primitive' philosophies and cultures than superstition, barbarism and black magic. And some have even come to the conclusion that to seek the 'crack between the two worlds' might be to take the first step towards restructuring our own reality principles and thereby changing the world.

9

The New Sciences

If anything suggests that Castaneda is an allegorist rather than an anthropologist, it is not the incredibility of his material but its consistency with some of the most advanced ideas of paraphysics, one of the new sciences that has emerged in recent years. The view of reality expressed by the sorcerer don Juan and that held by some avantgarde physicists have much in common. It could be argued, of course, that one is derivative from the other; but on the other hand it could be that they support and corroborate each other, and that the plausibility of the views they have in common is enhanced by their having been arrived at from such disparate points of departure.

Don Juan told Castaneda that don Genaro had not removed his car from the world of ordinary reality, but had 'simply forced you to look at the world like sorcerers do, and your car was not in that world'. This explanation implies that reality is a construct of consciousness, dependent upon observation, and that there exist multiple worlds, all equally real and mutually exclusive. Compare the following statement by the theoretical physicist Evan Harris Walker: 'Quantum mechanics states explicitly that between observations of a system the system is not in a single state but is in a combination of states, even though observationally these states are mutually exclusive.'[1] The physicist is stating a principle that the sorcerer applies in the practice of his craft.

Modern theoretical physicists are telling us that there may exist— and they mean really, not figuratively—many worlds. Considered in the light of the theories of Toben, Sarfatti and Wolf (*Space-Time and Beyond*, 1975) and de Witt and Graham (*The Many-Worlds Interpretation of Quantum Mechanics*, 1973), don Juan's statement that 'your car was not in that world' is simply a statement of fact.

The many-worlds view of reality is one of several theories developed from quantum mechanics which are relevant to paraphysics, i.e. the physics of paranormal processes, and to parapsychology. The theories had their origin in what is known as the quantum theory of

161

measurement. In classical, Newtonian mechanics, a system or object was taken to be in a single, constant state, and to be observable at any time in that state. When physicists got down to the investigation of the subatomic world, this single-state principle was found to be quite inadequate. Subatomic systems are in a state of continual fluctuation, and as these fluctuations are not determined by laws of motion or of force-fields it is not possible to predict what state the system will be in at any particular time; it is only possible to describe the system in terms of calculable probabilities. So between observations, as Walker says, a physical system is in a combination of mutually exclusive states. This combination is known as the 'state vector' and a complete description of the system is the description of its state vector.

A famous illustration of this principle was dreamed up by the Viennese physicist Erwin Schrödinger. Imagine a cat, sealed up in a chamber for life but provided with adequate supplies of food, drink and air. And imagine that there is in the chamber a flask of cyanide poison which will kill the cat if it is broken. It could be broken by a hammer, but the mechanism to release the hammer is activated by an emission from a radioactive source, and it is impossible to predict by quantum theory whether the radioactive decay will occur during the natural lifetime of the cat. If we take this situation as an analogue of a physical system, the state vector of the system, i.e. its complete description, must include both situations: the cat living and the cat dead.

Now, what happens when an observation of the system is made? In quantum mechanical terms, the state vector is said to 'collapse', i.e. to become fixed in one of its probabilities or component states. But now another problem arises. Remember Heisenberg's statement that 'observation plays a decisive role in the event . . . and the reality varies depending on whether we observe it or not'.[2] This means that the observer is an integral part of the system, and although his act of observation collapses the state vector into a single state *for him*, the system within which he is one of the variables is still in a state of continual fluctuation so far as a second observer is concerned. The first observer is split up into numerous copies of himself in many probabilistic configurations until the second observer makes his observation, which act fixes him in a single state, but again only from the point of view of the second observer. For a third observer the state vector is still uncollapsed, multiple states of the system are simultaneously probable and a complete description of the system must include all the probabilities. And so on, down through an infinite regression.

Theoretical physicists are on the whole uncomfortable with the idea of an infinite regression, and various ingenious ways of arresting the process have been devised. But some have accepted that the process can never be arrested, that the state vector can never be finally collapsed into a single state, that there exist systems within systems in infinite number, and that it is the act of observation that fixes the components of reality into a configuration which is, for the observer, while he is observing, the most probable of the infinite probabilities. This is the position taken by the 'many worlds' or 'multiple universes' theorists. To them, don Juan's statement to Castaneda that don Genaro had forced him to look at the world as sorcerers do, and his car was not in that world, would make perfectly good sense.

A further problem that arises out of this interpretation of quantum mechanics is that it implies an intervention in the processes of a physical system by an extraphysical element: the mind or consciousness of the observer. As the mathematical equation that represents the state vector deals with the physical properties of the system, the role played by the observer's consciousness within the system is a variable that cannot be included in the equation. The theoretical physicist David Bohm has boldly overcome this implicit dualism by proposing that matter is a form of thought. This may seem a rather far-fetched idea at first sight, but it is really no more so than the by now well proven principles that matter is energy and an electron is both a wave and a particle, and it not only has some experimental support but also itself supports the reality of many observed paranormal phenomena such as materialisation and the projection of 'thought forms' that can interact with the physical world. Bohm's idea is not to be construed as a return to philosophical idealism of the Bishop Berkeley type, which regarded the world as a thought in the mind of God and ultimately non-physical and insubstantial; it does not render matter non-physical but on the contrary suggests that thought can generate energy which in turn can become matter with concrete and measurable physical properties. Furthermore, the idea of thought-matter identity is not just a neat way of getting out of the impasse of theoretical dualism but gives rise to a new and, to the dualistic-minded, improbable-sounding physics, the 'physics of consciousness', which is a subject I shall have more to say about later.

To return to the many worlds theory, to the obvious layman's question, Where do they exist? one of the pioneers of the new physics, Professor John A. Wheeler of Princeton University, gives the answer: in Superspace. Superspace is a dimension beyond the space-time of relativity theory, which Wheeler describes as comparable to a carpet of foam spread over a slowly undulating landscape. 'The continual microscopic changes in the carpet of foam as new bubbles appear and old ones disappear symbolize the quantum fluctuations in the geometry',[3] he writes. The bubbles, which he terms 'worm-holes', are points of exit and entry connecting the multiple universes. Toben, in his graphic cartoon-style exposition of the new physics, *Space-Time and Beyond*, writes, 'All things are interconnected in the microcosmos. Every part is directly connected to every other part through the wormholes of space. At this level of quantum gravity, there is no time or distance separating parts. The description of any part is inseparable from the description of the whole.'[4] This idea of interconnectedness is another fundamental concept of the new physics, one which aligns it with ancient occult philosophies and also explains paranormal events which were inexplicable in terms of classical physics.

If everything and everyone exists in multiple universes simultaneously, and if these universes are configurations that differ from each other in slight details, and if consciousness can effect a transition from one universe to another, the mysteries that psychic researchers and parapsychologists have puzzled over for a century are less mysterious. Time, as Feynmann demonstrated, can flow backwards or forwards at the quantum level, so in Superspace past, present and future are all accessible to consciousness through the connecting wormholes. Messages too, from other minds or from objects, can pass through the wormholes, which would explain telepathy and clairvoyance and also the fact that these processes of paranormal cognition are not affected by distance, for there is no distance in Superspace. Materialisation and dematerialisation or disappearance and reappearance are simply explained as transitions into universes where the objects concerned are displaced in relation to the universe that consciousness focused before the transition took place. Metal-bending can be similarly understood, as a displacement of atoms within an object, or, as Hasted has suggested, 'as poltergeist phenomena on an atomic scale'.[5] Poltergeist events themselves would be explainable as a series of consciousness shifts from one universe to another. Paranormal healing would be effected by the consciousness of the healer causing transitions at the biomolecular level in the patient and thus restoring the organism to a state of health. And so on. All psychic and paranormal phenomena are easily explainable in terms of the new physics if—and this is the crux of the matter—quantum processes can be assumed to take place on the macroscopic as well as on the microscopic level. Physicists generally hold that quantum events in large numbers produce results that correspond with the laws of classical mechanics, and therefore that the laws and processes of the subatomic world and those of the macroscopic world are different. But this dualism is by no means proven, and in fact physicists working in the field of superconductors and superfluids (the physics of very low temperatures) have observed that quantum effects occur on a macroscopic scale, and moreover maintain that it is theoretically possible for such effects to occur at room temperature, though these occurrences would be extremely rare. Well, psychic events are rare, and it remains an open possibility that they may be brought about by a consciousness change that temporarily suspends the physical laws that normally govern the macroscopic world and enables quantum effects to occur. Psychic events, in fact, are so similar to quantum events that one scientist has gone so far as to declare that 'psychic research, if it did not already exist, would have to be invented to fully explore the new experimental paradigm of "undivided wholeness"'.[6]

The fundamental problem that normal science runs up against when it tries to make sense of the paranormal is the energy problem. Where does the energy come from to convey information over a distance, as in telepathy or clairvoyance, and why doesn't the effect decline with distance as the energy is dissipated? And how is mental energy, which is a measurable and weak effect of neuronal discharges in the brain, amplified and converted into kinetic energy in the performance of PK tasks? No plausible answers to these questions have been put forward, and from the point of view of the new physics it begins to look as if they were the wrong questions. Energy is not required for information transfer between parts of a universe of 'undivided wholeness', for in such a universe there is no 'here' and 'there', no distance or travel, and all information is available at every point. And if energy is involved in transition events between the universes it is not kinetic energy, for such transitions are effected by shifts of consciousness and would require only a minute discharge of neuronal energy. So if the 'undivided wholeness' paradigm of the new physics—which, incidentally, endorses the ancient occult principle 'as above, so below; as within, so without'—holds good, the energy problem posed by psychic events is no more.

With so much vertiginous conjecture in the air—and the preceding pages have condensed only a fraction of contemporary theoretical paraphysics—it is natural that theorists should get excited about an observable and repeatable phenomenon that seems to illustrate their ideas. Much excitement has been generated in recent years by the discovery of a process of three-dimensional photography by laser which is known as holography. A holographic plate has storage capacity for an immense number of pictures. A large amount of visual information can be imprinted on and retrieved from it. This is a remarkable and suggestive enough characteristic in itself, but even more extraordinary is the fact that every point on the surface of a hologram contains an image of the whole. If it is cut up into small pieces, an image of the original whole structure can be retrieved from every single fragment. So holography stands as demonstrable proof of the principle of 'undivided wholeness', of the fact that the part contains the whole just as the whole contains the part. Bohm, one of the physicists excited by the development of holography, wrote, 'There is the germ of a new notion of order here. This order is not to be understood in terms of a regular arrangement of *objects* (e.g. in rows) or as a regular arrangement of events (e.g. in a series).

Rather a *total order* is contained, in some *implicit* sense, in each region of space and time.'[7]

On another level, the phenomenon of· psychic healing would appear to validate the 'undivided wholeness' or 'total order' concept. Healers generally maintain that their 'power' does not come from them but through them, that they accomplish their healings by making themselves a channel or by establishing in themselves a harmony with external forces which they may call God, Nature or the Cosmos. Lawrence LeShan, who developed paranormal healing abilities in himself and others through meditation, describes what happens in the healing process: 'Knowing for the moment that you are a part of the total One of the cosmos, and that there are vast energies which maintain the universe on its course . . . you attempt by total concentration and "will" to bend these energies to increase the harmony of the healee, another part of the cosmos. Knowing yourself a part of an all-encompassing energy system, you will the total system to divert additional energies to the repair and harmonization of a part that needs it.'[8]

Don Juan tried to teach Castaneda the art of 'not doing'. Mystics and psychics concur that no stress or effort is involved in their experiences or effects, and speak of stillness, openness, waiting, and 'the path of least action'. Remarkable physical effects may occur—levitations, teleportations, materialisations, healings—but they are not accomplished by physical effort. The key lies in consciousness; in LeShan's words, in 'knowing . . . that you are a part of the total One of the cosmos'. It would seem to be one of the neglected laws of life and nature that for actions to take place within a system less energy is required than for interactions between systems. The energy output from the brain involved in instructing the limbs and muscles to lift a heavy object is infinitesimal compared with the energy required actually to lift the object; because we think of the object as being 'out there', as having a certain mass which requires a certain output of energy to displace it. But what if consciousness can be expanded to contain the object within the system to which consciousness belongs, as the healer attempts to create the unity of healer-healee-cosmos? Movements and levitations of heavy objects are paranormal effects that have often been observed and have baffled seekers for an energy source proportionate to the effect. The bafflement is of the same kind as that caused by healing phenomena; it comes down to the question, Where did the energy come from? The answer that paraphysics gives is that the energy is a function of the structure, the system, or the totality. The term 'synergy' has been used by some scientists for this energy produced by bringing together components of a system rather than by causing physical interactions between them.

The trend of modern technologies is towards obtaining maximum effects from minimum energy investments. There is a possibility today of very efficient energy conversion by the development of MHD (magnetohydrodynamic) generators, which could contribute to the alleviation of the world's current energy problems. Laser technology is another example, and one which suggests an interesting analogy with psychophysical processes. The term 'laser' stands for 'light amplification by stimulated emission of radiation'. Lasers produce what are known as 'coherent' light rays. Normally, light energy is dissipated in all directions, but in the laser apparatus a tube with reflecting mirrors immensely amplifies light energy by causing the excited atoms to emit their waves 'in phase'. In other words, the energy output is a product of the ordering or patterning of the components of the system. The process is analogous to the healer's trying to create a harmony of self, healee and cosmos, and healers might well describe what they do as bringing the 'vibrations' of these components into step or 'phase'.

The chief characteristic that the new sciences have in common is that they are 'holistic', i.e. they are concerned with interactions and effects within expanded whole systems rather than between parts of systems. The concepts of interconnectedness and 'undivided wholeness' have opened up new areas of scientific investigation. Psychobiology, psychophysiology, psychoenergetics, psychotronics, biofeedback, biogravitation, biophysics, cosmecology: all these terms of quite recent currency stand for cross-disciplinary studies, the bringing together of areas of research that formerly were investigated independently and without reference to each other. Researchers in the life sciences now work upon the assumption that living organisms are influenced by and responsive to environmental forces and factors that traditional science completely ignored, such as cosmic rays, radio waves, negative and positive ion atmospheres. And this shift of focus in science from the analysis of the functions of separate parts of living systems to the investigation of interactions between parts within a whole has already produced inventions of great practical use. Puharich has patented a device which employs programmed radio waves to alleviate deafness, accelerate the healing of fractured bones and diminish memory loss due to senility. Negative ion generators are used by some airlines to establish optimal conditions in cockpits and reduce the possibility of pilot error. Colour, light and sound are other environmental factors that have been found by various researchers to have therapeutic effects when their interactions with living organisms are understood and controlled. Time was— and not long ago—when the various sciences all had their 'nothing but' views of man: he was nothing but a series of reactions to stimuli, nothing but a collection of chemicals worth a couple of pounds, nothing but a 'naked ape'. That situation has now radically changed. The new sciences regard man as a being of immense and irreducible complexity participating in continual and intimate interaction with his environment. And by environment they mean everything between his skin and the stars.

What parapsychology has done for the new sciences is to provide the data, the evidence for paranormal organism–environment interactions, which has enabled them to formulate new questions to put to nature. The scope of our knowledge, as Heisenberg remarked, is always limited by our method of questioning. What the new sciences have done for parapsychology is to provide techniques and instruments for monitoring, measuring, controlling and enhancing psi functions. Many researchers have felt the need for a neologism that will encompass all the parasciences, and in Russia and Eastern Europe, where a great deal of modern psi research has been done, the term 'psychotronics' is commonly used. Dr Zdanek Rejdák of Charles University, Prague, explains: 'Parapsychology dealt mostly with rarely occurring phenomena, trying timidly to indicate that these incidents probably will affect everyone to a small degree. Psychotronics, through its pluridisciplinary approach, seeks to establish that psychophysical phenomena affect 90 per cent of mankind.'[9]

The main emphasis in Eastern European and Russian psi research has been upon the investigation of biological fields and non-physical energies. It was the American biologist, Harold Burr, who first demonstrated, in the 1930s, that all organisms are surrounded by 'life fields' in which changes occur that correlate with both internal biological events and events in the environment. Burr devised instruments that could measure field effects at a short distance from the body, and showed that such measurements could be used as indicators of states of health within the organism and of the occurrence of major biological changes, such as ovulation in females. These findings appeared to confirm the ancient belief that there is an 'aura' surrounding the human body, and the claim of certain psychics that they could 'read' the aura and diagnose a person's physical and spiritual state from it. Burr's researches identified this aura as an electromagnetic envelope surrounding living bodies and serving as an extended 'life space'. The psychologist K. Lewin proposed that within this 'life space' informational interchanges between organisms might take place which, being non-psychological and non-physical, would be inexplicable in terms of known modes of communication. When Kirlian and Kirlian developed the method of electrophotography that is named after them, the pictures they obtained by this method certainly appeared to confirm that there were considerable energetic effects within the surrounding life space of, for example, human finger-tips, leaves, flowers and cockroaches (the process requires an object to be placed between two oscillator plates, so is only suitable for photographing small objects). The well-known pictures of healer's and healee's finger-tips before, during and after a session of the laying on of hands type, seem to show an energy-exchange process taking place, and the discovery of a correspondence between the points on the body where these apparent energy discharges are most intense and the points and meridians of Chinese acupuncture therapy suggest that the body may indeed have a 'bioenergetic' system for interacting with its environment which is supplementary to and much subtler than the sensory-motor system that Western science has always held to be its only mode of interaction.

It has long been known that individual body cells have electrical properties, but the complexity and potential power of their electrical systems is a recent discovery. It has led the Russian biophysicist, Alexander Dubrov, to postulate the existence of 'a new and previously unknown property of living systems and of man as the summit of creation',[10] which he calls 'biogravitation'. This property was first hypothesised to explain observed effects during the process of mitosis, or cell-division. When a cell divides, a number of paranormal effects are produced. Chromosomes move towards the poles in a manner that is incompatible with the effects of all known physical forces except gravitation. The liquid in the cell changes into a crystalline structure. High-frequency ultrasonic waves are emitted, and other forms of energy and fields are produced. Dubrov calls these fields 'biogravitational' and suggests that under certain circumstances a constant biogravitational field may be created in protein molecules in biological structures. Basing his conclusions on observed events at the cellular level of such structures, Dubrov lists the following properties of biogravitational forces: '(a) they may act at close or long range; (b) they can be directed and focused; (c) they can be positive or negative (and cause attraction or repulsion, respectively); (d) they can carry information; (e) they are able to convert the energy of a field into matter with weight; (f) a field of such forces can persist in the absence of the source which originally gave rise to them; (g) they can undergo transition into any form of field or energy; and (h) they are closely bound up with change of symmetry groups and with distortion of space at the sub-molecular level of biological structures.'[11] These are bold claims, and it will be noted that they allow for some of the most controversial psychical phenomena, such as materialisation (e), hauntings (f) and metal-bending (h).

Dubrov and his colleagues are convinced that they have discovered a hitherto unrecognised form of energy and cracked the mystery of psychic, or 'psychotronic', phenomena.

Dubrov's 'biogravitons'—wave particles in the biogravitational field—have not actually been identified and tracked under the electron microscope, but there are many examples in modern subatomic physics of particles being predicted by a theory and then empirically discovered some months or years later. In his 1953 publication, *The Neurophysiological Basis of Mind*, Sir John Eccles suggested that the brain might be a sensitive filter or receiver of as yet unknown physical processes, and it could be that in biogravitation Dubrov and his colleagues have identified the processes that Eccles' theory predicted. Eccles would, I imagine, find the biogravitation hypothesis convincing, for in his book he drew attention to a theory of Sir Arthur Eddington's which has a remarkable correspondence with Dubrov's ideas. Eddington postulated the existence of a 'correlated behaviour of the individual particles of matter, which he assumed to occur for matter in liaison with mind. The behaviour of such matter would stand in sharp contrast to the uncorrelated or random behaviour of particles that is postulated in physics.'[12] In the modern parasciences we keep meeting this idea that in the 'correlated behaviour' of individual parts of a system synergetic effects are produced that are not predictable from the characteristics of any part standing alone. Dubrov states that 'the biogravitational field could equally well (and correctly) be called a "conformation field", the waves could be called "conformation waves" and the wave particles "conformons"' because 'changes in conformation induce a strictly ordered, structured crystalline state in the hydrated protein molecules and their oscillations are synchronized, as a result of which a qualitatively new physical situation is established'.[13] Here is a fascinating example of the genesis and progress of a scientific principle: beginning as an abstract postulate (Eddington's, 1939), its relevance to his own investigations is appreciated by a scientist in another field (Eccles, 1953), and it eventually is subsumed in a hypothesis of broader application (Dubrov, 1974). The process has the characteristics of what Kuhn would call the pre-paradigm stage of a scientific revolution.

The great paradigm changes, or scientific revolutions, of the past have tended to reduce man's stature and impoverish his self-image. It has been said that with the Copernican revolution man lost his throne, with the Darwinian his soul and with the Freudian his mind. The encouraging thing about the revolution now taking place is that it reverses this reductionist tendency and promises to restore at least the latter two of these lost dimensions. The fact that one can speak today of 'the physics of consciousness' is symptomatic of the changed situation, for the phrase implies the reconciliation of the mind-matter dualism (Descartes' *res cogitans* and *res extensa*) which has underlain and limited Western thought for four centuries. It also implies that the phenomena of mind, or consciousness,· have become accessible to scientific investigation. Positivist science scoffed at the concept of mind as the 'ghost in the machine' and considered it an unwarranted and unprovable hypothesis, but with the development of modern investigative techniques and instrumentation this has become an obsolete view. Mind sciences—the field now sometimes known as 'noetics'—not only have their own scientific methods and unimpugnable data, but they shade into, overlap and cross-correspond with many aspects of the physical sciences.

Biogravitation is an example of this overlap. The process is observable on the physical level, in mitosis for instance, but it may account for paranormal mental effects, such as telepathy and clairvoyance. Memory, too, is now thought to be related to a physical process occurring at cell level, and not exclusively in the brain. Biologists today speak of 'memory molecules' and, adopting concepts from physics, conjecture that a single superconducting molecule might store an immense amount of information just as a hologram does. And when neurophysiologists investigate brain processes at the submolecular level they discover a world where the laws of classical physics no longer hold and the principles of quantum mechanics have to be applied. Physics, the life sciences and the mind sciences thus join forces in repudiating both a mechanistic model of mind and the behaviourist argument that alleged mind events can all be explained away in terms of verbal behaviour.

Biofeedback is a practical development of the mind sciences and itself constitutes clear proof that mind is not a mere 'ghost in the machine' but has powers of organisation and control that generally go untapped. It used to be thought that man had two separate and distinct nervous systems, the somatic and the autonomic, or the voluntary and involuntary. Such internal functions as heart beat, blood flow, temperature changes, muscle tension and brainwave frequencies were thought to be automatic and beyond man's conscious control. Tales filtered through from India of yogis, fakirs and swamis performing extraordinary feats of control of pain and bodily functions, but if Western scientists believed them they tended to regard them as behavioural anomalies. It was acceptable that with a prodigious investment of time and effort a few uncommon individuals could perform apparent miracles of control of supposedly autonomic functions, but Westerners didn't see any point in making such effort and anyway took the attitude that it was just as well these functions went on below the level of consciousness. The new science of biofeedback has both tremendously reduced the time and effort involved in conscious regulation of internal states and has demonstrated that such regulation can be of great practical use.

The most publicised use of biofeedback is for the production of alpha brain rhythms, which correlate with a pleasurable sense of relaxation, with certain meditative states and a capacity for what Dr Elmer Green calls 'passive volition'. The slower theta rhythm has been found to correlate with a semi-conscious state in which vivid imagery and intuitions occur and sometimes psychic events are experienced. Through feedback of information about brainwaves, therefore, it is possible to enter an altered state of consciousness. This aspect of biofeedback has received the most notice, but it is also the most dubious, for alpha and theta training have been found to produce undesirable effects for a number of subjects. There are dangers in seeking such a quick cut to mystical or psychic states of consciousness, and experts in biofeedback recommend its use for such purposes only under supervision, and also only for initial training purposes. On the whole they consider that its main value will be in the areas of health, both physical and mental, for the prevention or cure of psychological or psychosomatic disorders. Anxiety states, hypertension, migraine, heart disease and epilepsy have all been successfully treated by biofeedback, and at a time when allopathic medicine—treatment by drugs—is giving diminishing returns and health delivery systems in many western countries show signs of breaking down under the pressure of demands made upon them, the diagnostic and therapeutic potentials of biofeedback, which make the patient aware of and responsible for his own states of health, could revolutionise medicine.

The principle of biofeedback is simply that when a person is made aware of physiological functions of which he is normally unconscious he can quickly learn to regulate them. He is not aware how he does this, or of making a deliberate effort of will, and it seems that it is sufficient for the purpose of change from automatic to controlled functioning that the subject be kept informed about the processes going on inside his skin. All these processes produce minute electrical impulses which can be amplified and fed back to the subject through circuitry that translates them into visual or auditory signals, bars or flashes of light or notes sustained at a certain pitch. Control of the processes seems to be, like Helmut Schmidt's PK subjects' work, 'goal-oriented'. A person told to hold a bar of light at a certain level may do so without making a particular effort or knowing how he does it. Elmer Green says that 'there seems to be a correspondence between human physiological responses to volition and the way Nature responds in general to human initiative',[14] and he compares the process to farming. A farmer first desires and visualises a crop, then plants the seed, then allows Nature to take its course, and finally reaps his crop. Similarly, the biofeedback subject first visualises a certain kind of physiological behaviour, then plants the idea in his unconscious, allows it to develop there without the interference of anxiety or conscious effort, and finally attains the desired physiological result. The process is one of non-striving, of taking 'the path of least action', and Green's account of it has obvious correspondences with LeShan's account of how psychic healing is accomplished.

Green has been assisted in his researches by two adepts of mind–body control, an Indian yogi named Swami Rama and a 'Western Sufi' from Holland, Jack Schwarz. On visits to the Menninger Foundation laboratory at Topeka, Kansas, Swami Rama, wired to the electronic monitoring devices used in biofeedback, produced temperature differentials of 11 degrees between two spots on the palm of his hand, reduced his heart beat rate, and even, for a period of seventeen seconds, stopped his heart functioning completely. Schwarz drove knitting needles through his biceps and controlled not only the pain but the subsequent bleeding as well. When he told it to stop it did, to Green's astonishment. He made a point of rubbing the needle on the floor with his shoe before lacerating himself, and when asked why he did this he said, 'All the cellular material of the body can be controlled by the mind. Normally we cannot do it because we are unaware or unconscious. Yet such functions are under the mind's control, and if I give instructions for my body not to interact with any foreign materials, how can I get an infection?'[15] Swami Rama made a similar point about the mind's sovereignty, and he explained it in terms of traditional Indian 'occult anatomy': 'The physical body is an energy structure. What you see is only a small piece of the energy structure and the whole energy structure contains a lot of subtle parts which you can't see. The physical part is just the densest part of it. All of the body is in the mind, but not all of the mind is in the body. There is a large energy structure and the body is only the densest section of it, and every piece of the body, every cell, you can control, because it's all in the mind. There are ten energies connected with this, called "pranas", which a man can learn to control. And in addition to the ten pranas inside the skin there are numerous pranas outside the skin, some of which he can also learn to control.'[16] There are interesting correspondences here with contemporary Russian ideas of the body's subtle energies, and even more interesting from the point of view of psychic research is the statement that control can extend to outside-the-skin events. Green says that both Swami Rama and Jack Schwarz were able to report correctly on the past, present and future mental, emotional and physical conditions of persons whom they did not know and had never seen.

This chapter has surveyed the relevance of recent developments in the physical sciences to psi research and psi theory. Most of the developments are of the past ten years, and no unified theory has yet won general acceptance, but what has clearly emerged is evidence that psi is not an embarrassing anomaly in an otherwise orderly universe, as traditional science has regarded it, but an indication that beyond the laws that man's limited conceptual abilities have discovered in nature and the cosmos there are other and subtler laws yet to be fathomed. Psi phenomena have moved from the periphery to the centre of scientific interest in recent years because they afford man a glimpse of these laws and give him an incentive to extend his knowledge to contain them and his technologies to work in harmony with them.

Psi and Psychology

In a letter to Hereward Carrington, Freud said that if he had his life to live over again he would devote it to psychic research. Yet throughout his life he eschewed investigation of the paranormal, and in his published work he was studiedly cautious and noncommittal whenever he broached the subject of psi phenomena. His most explicit statement, a paper entitled *Psychoanalysis and Telepathy*, in which he discussed two evidential cases of telepathy, was written in 1921 but, significantly, was not published until after his death. The paper was written for a Conference of the International Psychoanalytical Association, and before offering the cases for his colleagues' consideration Freud remarked, 'Every contribution to their explanation, and every objection to their convincingness will be most welcome to me. My personal attitude toward such material remains one of reluctance and ambivalence.'[1]

Numerous psychoanalysts have experienced Freud's dilemma, have found themselves fervently wishing that psi did not occur while confronted with irrefutable evidence that it does. The intimate rapport that has to exist between a psychoanalyst and his subject appears to constitute a situation highly conducive to· telepathic interaction. In 1933 a Hungarian analyst, István Hollós, published the results of twenty years of observation, documenting some five hundred cases of telepathic events in the psychoanalytic situation, and noting that these tended to occur with greater frequency during difficult periods of the analysts' lives. The following year an Italian analyst, Emilio Servadio, published similar findings, and expressed his belief that ESP commonly occurs between analyst and patient.

Servadio gives an example from his own experience. A young woman doctor had been having thrice-weekly sessions of analysis with him for two and a half years, which had on the whole been satisfactory. One evening he was consulted by another young woman whose case interested him, for she 'presented a clear agoraphobic syndrome—such as nowadays one rarely sees'.[2] However, he was too busy to take the case and referred it to a colleague. The next evening when the woman doctor attended for one of her regular sessions, the first thing she told him was that the previous day she had suddenly experienced a strange feeling of giddiness on going out of a friend's house and had thought to herself, 'It would be very strange that after two and half years of analysis I should now begin to develop some agoraphobic symptoms.' When Servadio asked his patient when this experience had occurred, she answered, 'About six or six-thirty yesterday evening', which was precisely the time when he had been in consultation with the other young woman. 'I have little doubt', he wrote, 'that this episode had a telepathic nature.' His patient, he suggested, had telepathically picked up his interest in the other woman's syndrome, at a subconscious level had considered her a rival for his concern and accordingly manifested similar symptoms in order to assert her prior claim to his interest.

This is one case out of hundreds on record that afford evidence that in the psychoanalytic situation patients often use ESP to establish, cement or disrupt their relationship with the analyst. Of all the evidence for the occurrence of telepathy, that to be found in psychoanalytic literature is among the most convincing, for it is attested by men whose attitude to the psi hypothesis is, for the most part, like Freud's, one of 'reluctance and ambivalence'. The reason for this attitude is that psychic events do not fit into the paradigm of psychoanalytic theory, for although psychoanalytic theory is able to cope with most of the vagaries of the unconscious it is fundamentally a theory of psychic determinism, and psychic events are notably indeterminate and unpredictable. Confronted with an apparent psi phenomenon, therefore, the psychoanalyst will adopt a reductionist method to contain it within his own theoretical paradigm.

A good example of this process is given by the psychoanalyst George Devereux in an essay entitled *ESP and Psychoanalytic Epistemology*.[3] 'Let us suppose', Devereux writes, 'that at 8.00 p.m., EST, John Doe's Chevrolet collides with a Ford on the corner of Tenth Avenue and 34th Street in New York. Also at 8.00 p.m., Mrs John Doe, who remained in Boston, exclaims: "My husband's car has just collided with a Ford on the corner of Tenth Avenue and 34th

Street."' We would naturally assume that some kind of connection exists between these two events, but what kind of connection is it? Before jumping to the conclusion that Mrs Doe's exclamation was a psi phenomenon, Devereux argues, we should examine the facts from a psychoanalytic point of view; we might well then find that both Doe's accident and Mrs Doe's utterance were determined by antecedent causes traceable to their matrimonial difficulties. Mrs Doe's utterance might reflect a death-wish, spontaneously springing up with hallucinatory intensity from the unconscious. She might have fantasised that her husband had an accident because she knew he was in the habit of getting drunk and driving recklessly when away from home. The number 34 might be found to correspond with Mr and Mrs Doe's age, and the number 10 with the years they had been married. Further, 'a Ford may have been chosen as the means of "retribution" because on her honeymoon Mrs Doe read, and was much impressed by, Aldous Huxley's *Brave New World*, in which men piously exclaim: "Ford's in his Flivver, all's right with the world."' If psychoanalysis can discover such explanations, Devereux argues, 'not one individual component element of Mrs Doe's utterance can be held to possess *a priori* the characteristic of relevancy, i.e. to pertain to, and be a description of, Mr Doe's accident'. The hypothesis of an ESP connection between the two events is thus disposed of and their simultaneity loses its significance and becomes a mere coincidence.

This is a hypothetical case, an illustration of how the method of psychoanalysis can be employed to diminish the possibility that a connection between two events is paranormal. Devereux does not claim that all psi phenomena can be explained away in this manner, or that ESP is a null hypothesis, but simply argues that if an explanation of an apparent psi phenomenon in psychoanalytic terms can be found it must be given precedence, for it is a fundamental principle of philosophy that supernatural explanations of events should not be invoked until all natural explanations have been exhausted. This is a reasonable argument, and it is undeniable that psychoanalysis constitutes a useful tool for investigating the paranormal and for separating the genuine from the spurious, but Devereux' example also illustrates how the psychoanalytic method might be overzealously applied to propose connections between events quite as conjectural as the psi hypothesis.

Oddly enough, Freud's brief excursions into discussion of paranormal cognition produced evidence for its existence through application of psychoanalytic method. Freud's chief contribution to the understanding of the human psyche, the idea that repressed psychic material finds its way into consciousness in disguised forms, in symbolism or through transference, proved a useful conceptual tool for discovering telepathic events. Freud made the ingenious suggestion that the study of the unfulfilled prophecies of professional fortune-tellers might be fertile ground for the production of such material, and gave an example from his own experience. A forty-three-year-old woman told him, in the course of her analysis, that at the age of twenty-seven a palmist had predicted that by the time she was thirty-two she would be married and would have two children. The woman had remained childless, and her disappointment over the fact was the cause of her neurosis, but in her analysis the significant fact emerged that her own mother had had two children by the age of thirty-two. Freud surmised that the strongest wish of the woman's emotional life—the wish to put her husband in the place of her father, to whom she had had an unusually intense attachment, by giving him children as her mother had given children in her marriage—had been telepathically transmitted from her unconscious to the fortune-teller. This, Freud said, was one of several incidents from his experience that had convinced him 'that strongly emotionally coloured recollections can be successfully transferred without much difficulty' by telepathy. He further suggested that telepathic interaction might be a common occurrence, and that 'telepathic messages received in the course of the day may only be dealt with during a dream of the following night', and even went so far as to state that it was an 'incontestable fact that sleep creates favourable conditions for telepathy'.[4] In other words, his experience as a psychoanalyst had convinced him beyond doubt that telepathy occurs.

The irreducibility of psi phenomena to a philosophy of psychic determinism is not the only reason for the abhorrence with which the man trained in the concepts and methods of psychoanalysis regards them. We also have to take into account the facts that the philosophical foundations of psychoanalysis are positivist and anti-religious, that it insists on regarding all the higher human values and achievements as derived by sublimation or reaction from lower motives and drives, and that the voluminous data that support its philosophy constitute a biased sample of psychic facts derived from the investigation and treatment of states of psychiatric disorder and imbalance. Thus the psychoanalyst has two strong lines of defence against the challenge of psi phenomena. First, he can assert that belief in them is a mere indulgence of infantile omnipotence fantasies and a throwback to primitive superstition and the magical philosophy that science should have expunged from the human mind. Second, if he is confronted with clear evidence that psi occurs, he can argue that it is a vestigial function, a regression of the unconscious to an archaic mode of communication that man rejected in the course of his evolution in favour of more efficient modes.

The question whether human personality is a product of 'nature' or 'nurture' has exercised philosophers since Plato's day, and the question whether psi is a vestigial or an evolutionary function is a comparable one, tending sharply to polarise attitudes prior to a balanced judgement of the facts that can be marshalled to support either side of the argument. The negative hypothesis, that psi is an erratic and vestigial function, would seem to be supported by evidence afforded by studies of mental illness and abnormal psychology. People in hysterical or psychotic states, states of disintegration or dissociation of personality, more frequently manifest psi abilities than do well-integrated and balanced personalities. Also, psi occurs most frequently in the lives of normal people in experiences of crisis or emotional upheaval. Therefore, the advocates of the 'vestigial function' point of view maintain, psi must be a concomitant of regressive and pathological mental states and not a positive function of an integrated personality, and the fact that it sometimes manifests spontaneously in crisis situations with positive effect does not invalidate this point of view, for such occurrences may be regarded as cases of the unconscious temporarily resorting to an archaic mode of communication which can be triggered into action by an emergency but is normally dormant because man has outgrown it.

A lot of evidence can be put forward to support this view, but both the evidence and the view would more plausibly have argued in favour of the 'vestigial function' thesis some years ago than they do today, when traditional assumptions about abnormality and mental illness are being radically questioned and reviewed. A view that is gaining widespread acceptance today is that so-called mental illnesses are not failures or aberrations of mental functioning but altered states of consciousness, states that may depart from a norm and a reality principle that socio-cultural influences dictate but that should not in consequence be automatically designated pathological. In these circumstances, the demarcation of lines between what is regarded as normality and as abnormality, and between concepts of higher and lower mental functions, is now widely seen as having been arbitrarily made and to be a task more relevant to the social scientist than the psychologist. At the same time, and as a corollary, traditional concepts of mental health and balance have been called in question, particularly the psychoanalysts' vaunted principle of 'reality testing' as a criterion of sanity, for the cultural malaise and disaffection of the young have made it patently obvious that the consensus reality to which psychotherapists have sought to adjust their patients is nothing more than a form of consensus delusion.

These changes of attitude tend to undermine the 'vestigial function' thesis in so far as it leans upon the evidence of abnormal psychology and psychopathology, but they do not in themselves support the alternative thesis that psi is an evolutionary function. Nor does the fact that a majority of the people who manifest psi abilities are not conspicuously highly evolved types. At this point, the question hinges upon the definition of the terms 'evolutionary' and 'evolved'. Adopting the concepts of systems philosophy, we may take as a criterion of evolution the principle of *hierarchical structural organization*. All natural systems—and this applies to cognitive systems as well as to biological systems, to mental functions as well as physical ones—are, according to this philosophy, ordered wholes which display two tendencies in varying degrees. The first is a tendency to stabilise themselves in their environment around existing steady-states, and the second is a tendency to evolve themselves to more adapted, inclusive and informed states and 'in the direction of increasing hierarchical structuration'[5] (Laszlo's terminology: see note).

All systems are self-stabilising and self-organising ordered wholes, and the higher-level and more evolved systems are defined by their properties of inclusiveness and organisation. We can postulate, then, a quantitative criterion of evolution, based on the number of functions or the amount of information that a system contains and maintains in a state of structural organisation. Or as Laszlo puts it, 'The higher we raise our sights on the hierarchy, the more diversity of functions and properties we are likely to find.'[6] So let's see how this understanding of the terms 'evolutionary' and 'evolved' relates to what we know about psi functions.

Evidence afforded by studies of the phenomena of multiple personality and of psychic healing, and by observations of effects of consciousness-training disciplines such as yoga, indicates that psi is not necessarily a concomitant of states of mental disorder and imbalance, but on the contrary is a function that becomes more manifest with increasing structural integration of psychic factors, and which therefore satisfies the systems philosophy criterion of 'evolutionary'.

Multiple personality is a rare neurosis in which the sufferer manifests several completely distinct and dissociated personalities, each with independent temperamental characteristics which are often so incompatible and contradictory that the conflicts between them cause great distress. Cases of multiple personality would therefore appear to exemplify the characteristics of psychic disorder in their most extreme forms, and if the alleged correlation between heightened psi functioning and pathological mental states held good we would expect psi to occur in cases of multiple personality but to occur with diminishing frequency in proportion as the dissociated personalities were integrated in therapy. But in fact the opposite has frequently been observed to happen. Various forms of psi have occurred during therapy, and they have increased rather than diminished as the therapy progressed. The classic case of this type is that of Doris Fischer, reported by Dr Walter F. Prince, whose own precognitive dreams have been discussed in a previous chapter. Prince succeeded in integrating the several dissociated personalities that Doris Fischer manifested, and *after he had done so* she continued to exhibit and develop remarkable psychic abilities.

Consider next the evidence afforded by psychic healing, and particularly the relevance to the present discussion of LeShan's testimony that healing is effected through the establishment of an harmonious integration of healer, healee and cosmos: 'Knowing yourself a part of an all-encompassing energy system, you will the total system to divert additional energies to the repair and harmonization of the part that needs it.' The act of healing is the reinstatement of a condition of high structural organisation in an organism, and LeShan's demonstration that the ability to accomplish this can be developed through techniques of meditation suggests that there is a correlation between the effectiveness of the healer's abilities and the degree of his own psychic integration.

In the process of training others in meditative techniques with a view to developing healing abilities in them, LeShan has found that other forms of psi often spontaneously occur as by-products of the process. He regularly takes groups of selected individuals on a five-day course at a remote retreat in New York State, and has reported: 'Quite often by the third day certain people are receiving telepathic messages from others in the group. This is not our goal, but it just happens in the natural course of the week's training.'[7] The production of psi is not the goal of yogic training either, but the ancient *Yoga Sutras* of Patanjali testify that *siddhis*, or psychic powers, are developed automatically and spontaneously in the course of such training. The essence of yogic techniques is the practice of 'one-pointed' or 'centred' concentration, in other words the cultivation of mental states that are integrated and ordered to a high degree.

This kind of evidence lends support to the argument that psi is an evolutionary function, but the evidence on the other side of the case cannot be entirely dismissed and the overall picture would seem to justify the postulate that there are different levels of psi and that in relation to different circumstances and personalities higher or lower psi functions may be manifested. This is not a mere compromise solution to the debate between the 'vestigial function' and the 'evolutionary function' points of view, but in fact a conclusion that we might expect to reach if we assume that psi is a property of the unconscious, for, as numerous psychological observations and investigations over the past century have shown, the unconscious itself contains, sustains and motivates both the lower and the higher functions of human nature.

The psychology of the unconscious is the key to the understanding not only of some of the mental processes involved in psi but also of the polarisation of attitudes towards psi phenomena and functions. In his fascinating historical study, *The Unconscious Before Freud*, Lancelot Law Whyte has illustrated very clearly and eloquently how the concept of the unconscious evolved over a period of some two centuries from about 1750, and how in the course of its evolution it was subject to interpretations determined by temperamental, doctrinaire and ideological factors. This process and these interpretations clearly correspond to stages and variations in the development of the concept of psi. For instance, in a passage such as the following the word 'psi' could be substituted for 'unconscious' if the dates were changed: 'The discovery of the unconscious is the recognition of a Goethean order, as much as of a Freudian disorder, in the depths of the mind. But for two centuries, say from 1750 to 1950, many rationalists tended to regard the unconscious as the realm of irrational forces threatening the social and intellectual order which the rational consciousness, they imagined, had built up over generations. . . . For others who saw deeper the unconscious was not a realm merely of chaos, conflict and destructive passions, but the source also of all the forms of order created by the human imagination. . . .'[8] The dichotomies designated in this passage, between concepts of order and disorder and between corresponding attitudes of acceptance and rejection, have, as the foregoing pages on the debate between the evolutionary and the vestigial points of view illustrate, been exactly paralleled in the course of the development of the psi concept.

Whyte speaks of 'a Goethean order . . . in the depths of the mind'. And Goethe wrote, 'Man cannot persist long in a conscious state, he must throw himself back into the Unconscious, for his root lives there.'[9] Freud was by no means the discoverer of the unconscious, as is popularly supposed, but was simply the most thorough and intuitive diagnostician of its pathology. Before him many men, particularly the poets and philosophers of the Romantic movement, had celebrated the creative, ordering, healing, intelligent and life-enhancing functions of the unconscious, but Freud and the neo-Freudians stuck to and successfully promulgated their partial view and even managed to convince themselves and many others that Romanticism itself was a form of collective psychosis. They were, in their consulting rooms, so overwhelmed with evidence of disordered minds that they leapt to the conclusion that disorder is the natural condition of the human mind, and that therefore psychotherapy is a panacea of universal relevance. 'Freud was the genius of conflict in the psyche', states Whyte, and 'he should be followed by the genius of order in the organism illustrated in the human mind. Freud asked, "What is the origin and nature of psychic conflict?" The next question is: "What is *not*-conflict? What is the source and character of organic coordination?"'[10]

The last twenty years have seen the emergence of post- and anti-Freudian psychological concepts, the reinstatement of the idea of the existence of 'a Goethean order' and ordering principle in the unconscious, and the development of conceptual and technological tools able to investigate 'the source and character of organic coordination'. Freud and his school contributed too much to our knowledge of the mind ever to be discredited, but they had eventually to be superseded, for their tendency to base sweeping generalisations on the evidence of psychopathology resulted in an incomplete and fundamentally negative view of the psyche and its potentials.

'From the occult viewpoint my own life was a singularly barren one',[11] wrote Freud. The opposite was the case with Jung, the greatest of several distinguished defectors from the Freudian school. Jung's own life was crammed with paranormal experiences, and in his practice as a psychotherapist he encountered reports of many more; so many that he became convinced that no psychology or philosophy of man with pretensions to comprehensiveness could leave such experiences out of account. In his autobiography, *Memories, Dreams, Reflections*, he relates many experiences covering pretty well the full range of psi phenomena, of which the following is a typical example.

A patient whom Jung had been very close to throughout his therapy, and whom he had succeeded in pulling out of a severe depression, got married to a possessive and unsympathetic woman who cut him off from his former friends and associates. Foreseeing the possibility of a relapse, Jung told his patient to get in touch with him if he found himself falling into another depression, but about a year elapsed and he had no communication.

After delivering a lecture in a town away from home one evening, Jung returned to his hotel about midnight, sat up talking with some friends for a while, then went to bed, but he found it unusually difficult to get to sleep. To continue the narrative in his own words: 'At about two o'clock—I must have just fallen asleep—I awoke with a start, and had the feeling that someone had come into the room; I even had the impression that the door had been hastily opened. I instantly turned on the light, but there was nothing. Someone might have mistaken the door, I thought, and I looked into the corridor. But it was still as death. "Odd," I thought, "someone did come into the room!" Then I tried to recall exactly what had happened, and it occurred to me that I had been awakened by a feeling of dull pain, as though something had struck my forehead and then the back of my skull. The following day I received a telegram saying that my patient had committed suicide. He had shot himself. Later, I learned that the bullet had come to rest in the back wall of the skull.'[12]

This is a fairly common type of paranormal experience. There are scores of similar cases in the early classics of psychical research, *Phantasms of the Living* and the *Census of Hallucinations*. I have chosen it from among Jung's accounts of his numerous psi experiences not for its uniqueness but because in his ensuing discussion of it he introduces some of his fundamental concepts with regard to psi.

'This experience', he said, 'was a genuine synchronistic phenomenon such as is quite often observed in connection with an archetypal situation—in this case, death. By means of a relativisation of time and space in the unconscious it could well be that I had perceived something which in reality was taking place elsewhere. The collective unconscious is common to all; it is the foundation of what the ancients called the "sympathy of all things". In this case the unconscious had knowledge of my patient's condition. All that evening, in fact, I had felt curiously restive and nervous, very much in contrast with my usual mood.'[13]

Jung was not concerned to demonstrate that psi occurs or to prove the psi hypothesis to a sceptical scientific community; he had enough personal experience to satisfy himself beyond any doubt of its reality. The task he addressed himself to was the investigation of the processes involved in its occurrence and the elaboration of a conceptual framework to contain it. The terms 'synchronistic phenomenon', 'archetypal situation' and 'collective unconscious' in the above-quoted paragraph were fundamental in his conceptual scheme. They are abstractions, but what they were abstracted from was Jung's wealth of experience as a clinical psychotherapist, which constitutes substantial empirical validation.

'Synchronicity' was the most controversial of Jung's neologisms. His critics claimed that it was merely a label, and argued that human knowledge is not advanced by giving the incomprehensible fancy names. But this criticism misses, or deliberately ignores, the point that man inhabits what Lévy-Strauss calls a 'semantic universe' and a phenomenon that is not named cannot be discussed, investigated or accommodated to the consensus reality; so although naming a thing does not confer reality upon it, it is the necessary first step towards including it in the 'universe of discourse' and studying its manifestations and relations to other phenomena. It does scant justice to Jung to criticise his concept of synchronicity without taking it in the context of his total philosophy of the psyche, where it subtly interrelates with his concepts of the archetypes and the collective unconscious, which have won readier and more general credence.

Jung gave his essay, *Synchronicity*, the sub-title: *An Acausal Connecting Principle*. Many personal experiences had led him to the conclusion that there is a class of events, by no means uncommon, which are *meaningfully but not causally* connected. Such events we normally call coincidences and attribute to chance, but, Jung insisted, there is an important distinction to be made between 'meaningful coincidences' and 'meaningless chance groupings'. It is a distinction commonly made in esoteric and Eastern philosophies, but alien to modern scientific Western thought, in which the causality principle remains the only generally acknowledged mode of connection between events. Jung was well aware that the causality principle had broken down in modern physics, and he was intrigued by the speculation that a similar breakdown of the concept of psychic causality and determinism might lead to the discovery of the means of releasing psychic energy as the physicists had released the energy potential of the atom. This was not wishful or analogical thinking, nor was it an indulgence of what the Freudians would call an 'omnipotence fantasy', for in his studies of the literatures, religions and mythologies of distant ages and cultures Jung had come across a great deal of evidence that the affective and cognitive potentials of the psyche were far greater than modern Western philosophical and psychological thought conceived.

As we saw in the last chapter, recent developments in theoretical physics have led to the creation of a new experimental paradigm of 'undivided wholeness' in physical science. Jung would have been delighted by this development, for he would have regarded it both as supportive of his own conceptual innovations and as an encouraging sign that Western science had at last escaped from the prison of mechanism and causality and managed to recover at least a portion of the ancient wisdom of mankind. His own thinking had been greatly stimulated by the classic of ancient Chinese philosophy and divination, the *I Ching*, which he regarded as the supreme endorsement and illustration of the validity of the principle of synchronicity. The Chinese mind, he wrote, was unlike the Western mind, because it 'does not aim at grasping details for their own sake, but at a view which sees the detail as part of a whole', and the *I Ching* was 'one of the oldest known methods for grasping a situation as a whole and thus placing the details against a cosmic background'.[14] The object of science, too, was to grasp the whole, but its experimental method involved imposing conditions on Nature and 'forcing her to give an answer to a question devised by man', a procedure that completely excluded 'the workings of Nature in her unrestricted wholeness'. The divination method of the *I Ching*, on the other hand, did not involve imposing conditions on Nature, but allowed her 'to answer out of her fullness'.

A person who consults the *I Ching* is guided to the relevant text in it by performing the apparently arbitrary act of tossing three coins six times and noting the patterns of 'heads' and 'tails' in which they fall. He thus obtains a six-line 'hexagram' which corresponds with one of sixty-four hexagrams in the book, each of which has an accompanying text and commentary. While he is throwing the coins he has to hold firmly in mind the question that he is putting to the *I Ching*, and if he applies himself to the ritual with proper seriousness and concentration he will obtain from the text an answer to his question. This method, Jung wrote, 'like all divinatory or intuitive techniques, is based on an acausal or synchronistic connective principle'. There are two components in the situation, each with its own independent line of antecedent causality. There is the life situation at a specific moment in time of the person who throws the coins, and there is the act of throwing and relating the result obtained to the relevant text. These two components clearly have no causal connection, but, Jung maintains on the basis of both his understanding of Chinese philosophy and his personal experiences with the *I Ching*, they have a *meaningful relationship*, and by meditating on the text obtained the serious student of the *I Ching* will obtain an answer to his question.

The rationalist can plausibly object that the Chinese texts are so cryptic and symbolical that they are open to a wide variety of interpretations, and that the questioner is not participating in any cosmic process but conducting a dialogue with his own mind. Jung would deny that the questioner's intentionality enters into the process, but would agree that a kind of dialogue, or preferably an interaction, is involved between the mind at a deep unconscious level and external events. The unconscious, Jung suggested, has three distinct levels, the personal unconscious, the collective unconscious and the 'psychoid' level, and it is the two latter levels that are involved in synchronistic events. At these levels the psyche is unbounded, transpersonal; it is a microcosm that interacts with and reflects the macrocosm. From Leibniz's philosophy Jung adopted the model of the universe as a 'pre-established harmony, composed of a multiplicity of interrelated monads each of which contains an image of the whole. 'Every body', wrote Leibniz, 'responds to all that happens in the universe, so that he who saw all could read in each one what is happening everywhere, and even what has happened and what will happen.'[15] This corresponds remarkably with the philosophy underlying the *I Ching*, and Jung based his conception of the psyche and its relations with the external world on the Leibnizian model of interrelated wholeness, maintaining that at the collective unconscious and psychoid levels the psyche is thrown open to influences from all points on the continuum which is the universe at any given moment. The human being at a conscious level is enmeshed in a complex of social, economic and personal relations which he partially manipulates and is partially manipulated by; and at the deep unconscious level he is enmeshed in another complex of relations, transcending space, time and causality, which continually form meaningful patterns, or synchronicities, across the continuum of the universe.

Jung borrowed from the French psychologist, Pierre Janet, the term *'abaissement du niveau mental'* to elucidate the psychological process involved in synchronistic and parapsychic events. Through this 'lowering of the mental level', he wrote, 'the tone of the unconscious is heightened, thereby creating a gradient for the unconscious to flow towards the conscious. The conscious then comes under the influence of unconscious instinctual impulses and contents. These are as a rule complexes whose ultimate basis is the archetype, the "instinctual pattern".'[16] The archetype, Jung explains elsewhere, is 'an irrepresentable, unconscious, pre-existent form that seems to be part of the inherited structure of the psyche'[17] in the same way that instincts are part of its inherited structure. He originally used the term 'primordial image' for this component of the unconscious, but as the word 'image' implies something with a definite content he adopted the term 'archetype' to stand for an ordering or patterning principle in the psyche, a kind of field force determined only by its form. When specific contents were added by consciousness or by cultural influences, the archetype would become an archetypal image. The image might vary greatly from person to person or from culture to culture, but the archetype, the underlying form, was part of the collective unconscious of mankind, a transpersonal and transcultural phenomenon. And when an archetype was experienced, or activated, through a person's 'lowering his mental level', a situation conducive to parapsychic, synchronistic or even 'magical' events was created.

In the writings of the great mediaeval mage and theologian, Albertus Magnus, Jung came across a passage that bore out his theory: 'A certain power to alter things indwells in the human soul and subordinates the other things to her, particularly when she is swept into a great excess of love or hate or the like. When therefore the soul of a man falls into a great excess of any passion, it can be proved by experiment that it [the excess] binds things [magically] and alters them in the way it wants . . . Whoever would learn the secret of doing and undoing these things must know that everyone can influence everything magically if he falls into a great excess.'[18] The interest óf this passage for Jung lay in its assertion that a psychological state can affect events in the physical world without there being a mechanical cause-effect link between the two planes, for this was the fundamental assertion of the principle of synchronicity. Also, 'falling into a great excess' corresponded with 'lowering the mental level'. The only difference between his findings and those of Albertus Magnus was that the latter attributed a magical power to the soul (the unconscious) whereas Jung believed that synchronistic events, being by definition noncausal, could not have an energetic base but were produced by a patterning process in the psyche (the activation of an archetype) creating a field effect which drew into correspondence or meaningful relationship with it events in the external world; in other words, a process of reciprocal interaction between the psychic microcosm and the macrocosm.

Here again we have a convergence, which would have pleased Jung, of his ideas with those of contemporary theoretical physicists, who have observed energy-like effects produced without mechanical or cause-effect interactions, through the patterning or structuring of components within a total system. Towards the end of his life, Jung put a great deal of time and effort into canvassing his idea of synchronicity among physicists, and he gained at least one distinguished supporter in Wolfgang Pauli, who published a monograph titled *The Influence of Archetypal Ideas on the Scientific Theories of Kepler* in the same volume in which Jung's essay, *Synchronicity: An Acausal Connecting Principle*, first appeared. Pauli was the creator of a key concept of quantum mechanics, the 'Exclusion Principle', which states that in the atom only one electron can occupy any orbit at a particular time. Writing about it, the philosopher of science Henry Morgenau makes statements that could apply with equal validity to Jung's concept of the archetype: '. . . this principle has no dynamic aspect to it at all. It acts like a force although it is not a force. We cannot speak of it as doing anything by mechanical action. No, it is a very general and elusive thing; a mathematical symmetry imposed upon the basic equations of nature producing what appears like a dynamic effect.'[19] In the light of this explanation, it is easy to see what drew Jung and Pauli to each other. They have in common the idea that symmetry can produce an apparently dynamic effect, and they bring mutually corroborating evidence for it from areas of investigation that according to traditional scientific thinking are widely divergent. One of Jung's profoundest convictions was that the physical and psychological sciences had been arbitrarily differentiated and must eventually converge, for their fields of investigation, nature and man, matter and mind, were subtly interrelated and governed by the same fundamental ordering principle. The fact that developments in physics since Jung's death have tended to fall into 'meaningful coincidence' with his principle of synchronicity suggests that his conviction was not ill-founded.

The analytical and theoretical contributions of Freud and Jung constitute a tremendous intellectual achievement in exploring and charting the depths of the human psyche, and their 'depth psychology' immensely expanded the range of man's self-knowledge. However, their work initiated rather than accomplished a revolution in psychological thought, and since the 1950s developments from and variants of their theories have proliferated, leading to the creation of what are known as 'Third Force' and 'Fourth Force' psychology, or alternatively 'humanistic' and 'transpersonal' psychology. These developments, which have taken place chiefly in America, and were initiated and given momentum by the American psychologist Abraham Maslow, focus upon the study of the nature, functions and characteristics of the healthy human being, and are concerned less with exploring the ramifications of the unconscious than with investigating the potentialities latent in the 'superconscious' or 'ultraconscious' mind. They may be said to constitute a 'height psychology', though if such terms as 'depth' and 'height' are used it is essential to bear in mind that they do not imply 'inferior' and 'superior', and that Jung amply demonstrated that some of the acknowledged higher experiences and functions of human beings, such as creativity and religious ecstasy, are attributable to the opening of so-called lower levels of the psyche.

Fundamental to the new psychologies is the belief that their concern is with all of human life and experience, and not merely with their pathological aspects. They regard the frustration of man's 'meta-needs'—life-enhancement as distinct from life-sustaining needs—as potentially the cause of as much distress as the frustration of his biological and basic instinctual needs, and they investigate the conditions pertaining to the fulfilment of these needs. Psychotherapy, they maintain, was primarily an *adjustment* therapy, which was concerned with integrating the individual into society and did not question the values, purposes and normative principles of that society. The concern of humanistic psychology, on the other hand, is with growth and 'self-actualization', in other words with integrating the individual with a norm not determined by society but by his own personality needs and potentials. In this psychology, therefore, needs that have no direct social relevance, and that might even be socially disruptive, are recognised as real and important and are catered for. Maslow calls these 'B-needs' (being needs) as distinct from 'D-needs' (deficiency needs), and the prospectus of the Association for Transpersonal Psychology lists some of them in a passage defining the 'Fourth Force':

'Transpersonal psychology is the title given to an emerging force in psychology and other fields by a group of men and women who are interested in ultimate states. The emerging transpersonal orientation is concerned with the empirical scientific study and responsible implementation of the findings relevant to: spiritual paths, becoming, meta-needs (individual and species wide), ultimate values, unitive consciousness, peak experiences, B-values, compassion, ecstasy, mystical experience, awe, being, self-actualisation, essence, bliss, wonder, ultimate meaning, transcendence of the self, spirit, oneness, cosmic awareness, individual and species wide synergy, theories and practices of meditation, sacralisation of everyday life, transcendental phenomena, cosmic self-humour and playfulness, and related concepts, experience, and activities.'[20]

Here is a list to drive any behaviourist apoplectic. Behaviourism, the psychology of the 'empty organism', sought to expunge from psychological discussion all terms referring to subjective states, but now such terms are being reinstated, with a vengeance. Transpersonal psychology has no difficulty at all in accommodating psi experiences and phenomena and in refuting the behaviourists' dogmatic denial of the relevance of subjective states to a science of man. Whereas parapsychologists of the 1930s had to fight a defensive campaign and depend on statistical methods to get their data grudgingly acknowledged by a sceptical scientific orthodoxy, their successors of the 1970s find themselves allied with and supported by the *avant-garde* in physics, psychology and philosophy. They may still employ statistical methods to evaluate their data, but they no longer need them to validate them, for they have available the facilities for psychophysiological instrumentation and recording techniques, as well as the conceptual framework, by means of which transpersonal psychology has prosecuted its campaign to bring subjective states and what Maslow called 'the farther reaches of human nature' into the purview of science.

As a crystal is formed in an amorphous liquid matrix, cohering around an invisible and unpredictable axis, so at the point where psi research, modern physics and transpersonal psychology converge there begins to cohere a radically new image of man, an image that offers at once a challenge and an opportunity.

CONCLUSION

Consciousness Expansion
and the Strategy of
Repossession

Conclusion:
Consciousness Expansion and
the Strategy of Repossession

'Alienation' is a term that has long been bandied about in modish literary and social criticism, but not always with the realisation that it could precisely define man's terminal disease. To survive, man needs to repossess the earth and at the same time to repossess those dimensions of self that Economic Man, Rational Man, *l'Homme Moyen Sensuel*, discarded in order to pursue goals which not only produce diminishing returns but also some alarming and quite unforeseen consequences. As the 1972 Club of Rome's Project Report on 'The Predicament of Mankind' made us all aware, there are 'limits to growth', and if the world's major industrial powers continue to pursue economic growth and to foster an ethic based on ever-increasing production and consumption of goods the planet's resources will rapidly be depleted and the environment irremediably polluted. To create 'a steady state of economic and ecological equilibrium', the Report concluded, will require '*a Copernican revolution of the mind*' [my italics] and if the human species is to survive 'man must explore himself—his goals and values—as much as the world he seeks to change'.[1] That such exhortations should appear in a Report prepared by scientists, economists, industrialists and civil servants is surely a sign that we are living in what Hebrew-Kabbalistic mystical literature designates 'an end of days' period, witnessing and participating in the death of one world and the birth trauma of a new. In the most unexpected quarters there arises today the realisation that man's urge to growth must be redirected inwards, and that if he is to repossess the earth and reorientate his runaway brain-child, technology, towards goals that enhance human life instead of precipitating crises for it, he must first repossess and reorientate himself.

How apposite as an analysis of our times is this paragraph written by a Kabbalist: 'So long as the world moves along accustomed paths, so long as there are no wild catastrophes, man can find sufficient substance for his life by contemplating surface events, surface theories and movements of society. He can acquire his inner richness from this external kind of "property". But this is not the case when life encounters fiery forces of evil and chaos. Then the "revealed" world [i.e. the physical, surface world] begins to totter. Then the man who tries to sustain himself only from the surface aspects of existence will suffer terrible impoverishment, begin to stagger, then he will feel welling up within himself a burning thirst for that inner substance and vision which transcends the obvious surfaces of existence and remains unaffected by the world's catastrophes. From such inner sources will he seek the waters of joy which can quicken the dry outer skeleton of existence.'[2]

This passage is, as I say, apposite; but to take it as a justification of, or worse still an exhortation to, the adoption of an attitude of purely self-indulgent withdrawal into inner space, would be irresponsible and potentially disastrous. When 'the world's catastrophes' are not localised wars but the imminent planet-wide collapse of the symbiosis of social and organic systems, no one can long remain unaffected by them. To transcend 'the obvious surfaces of existence' and cultivate an 'inner substance and vision' should be one of the acknowledged Rights of Man, but like all rights it should exact responsibilities, particularly the responsibility to follow withdrawal with return, to spread the spiritual enrichment conferred by the visionary experience outwards from the self, to nourish the earth itself with what the Kabbalist calls 'the waters of joy'. For as Coleridge wrote:

> Joy, Lady! is the spirit and the power
> Which, wedding Nature to us, gives in dower
> A new earth and a new heaven
> Undreamt of by the sensual and the proud.

There are those who will remain unconvinced by the mystics and the poets that their transports are not mere self-satisfactions and escapism, and who will continue to look to science and technology for amelioration of the world's ills. And indeed it is not easy, if you have a cultural background of mechanistic cause-effect thinking, to see how consciousness expansion in the individual can contribute to the solution of problems that appear to be fundamentally social, economic and political. A solution in terms of behaviourist principles seems more plausible: the accomplishment of the 'psyche-civilization of society'[3] by means of techniques of behaviour modification such as 'operant conditioning' (the systematic control of behaviour through reward·and deprivation) or electrocranial stimulation. Such techniques have been tried and have proved effective in education, in psychotherapy and in altering the behaviour patterns of recidivist prisoners, and B. F. Skinner's advocacy of them as means of bringing about the establishment of a humane, rational and peaceful society is convincing if you accept the behaviourist premiss that man is a manipulable mechanism and that consciousness, will, freedom and dignity are meaningless concepts handed down from the pre-scientific age. This premiss purports to be scientifically and rationally based, but it is pertinent to ask what kind of science endorses it. Contemporary theoretical physics, with its paradigm of 'undivided wholeness', certainly doesn't. Behaviourism is a product of the nineteenth-century 'divide and conquer' approach to science, which was supported by the mechanistic, cause-effect paradigm. The fact that its techniques are demonstrably effective with the young, the 'maladjusted' and recidivists is no guarantee that they will be effective with people for whom freedom and dignity are not conceptual anachronisms but principles integral with their sense of personal identity. It is arguable, of course, that the sense of personal identity and its attendant values can be expunged by behaviourist technology, and a cautionary scenario of the future that includes the emergence of 'friendly fascism' is not only to be found in 'distopian' fiction like Huxley's *Brave New World* and Orwell's *Nineteen Eighty-Four* but also in the proven success of 'thought reform' techniques with conquered peoples and prisoners of war. Which only makes it all the more imperative that an alternative to behaviourist technology should be found, and that answers should be sought to the question of how individual consciousness expansion positively correlates with the collective good and contributes to the attainment of the goals and the amelioration of the problems of contemporary society. It's all very well for the poet to say that joy is a power that weds Nature to us and 'gives in dower / A new earth and a new heaven'; but what sort of statement is this? Is it poetic hyperbole or a testable hypothesis? The fact that this seems a funny question is an indication of the extent to which the objective consciousness of the scientist has usurped the visionary consciousness of the poet as the approved truth-seeking faculty of man in our culture. But such men as Coleridge, Wordsworth, Blake, Whitman, Rilke were not fooling about with words. As men they were seeking, and as poets they were trying to express, truth; and to add the rider 'as they saw it' is inapt, for truth is always as someone sees it, and even the principle of consensus, from which scientific truth derives its authority, is fallible and no guarantee of absoluteness. In modern philosophy phenomenological method has largely replaced the consensus principle of truth-validation, which is a development highly germane to the problem of studying subjective states and experiences and how they affect and correlate with objective realities.

Sam Keen, the theologian of the consciousness movement, has a passage in his book, *To a Dancing God*, which succinctly describes the phenomenological approach: 'If I am to appreciate the uniqueness of any datum, I must be sufficiently aware of my preconceived ideas and characteristic emotional distortions to bracket them long enough to welcome strangeness and novelty into my perceptual world. This discipline of bracketing, compensating, or silencing requires sophisticated self-knowledge and courageous honesty. Yet, without this discipline each present moment is only for the repetition of something already seen or experienced. In order for genuine novelty to emerge, for the unique presence of things, persons or events to take root in me, I must undergo a decentralisation of the ego.'[4]

The Club of Rome's Report drew attention to the need for 'a Copernican revolution of the mind', but it was no part of its brief to recommend how such a revolution might be brought about. Sam Keen's description suggests how the phenomenological method and discipline can contribute to the work. To 'put the world in brackets' (Husserl's phrase), to bring to the act of observation neither perceptual nor conceptual bias, to silence and decentralise ego-consciousness (paradigm commitment in the collective, societal context), are necessary preconditions for the emergence of 'strangeness and novelty' into the world, in other words for the bringing about of a revolution in thinking. 'True philosophy', wrote the phenomenologist Maurice Merleau-Ponty, 'consists in relearning to look at the world', and phenomenology 'is as painstaking as the works of Balzac, Proust, Valéry or Cézanne—by reason of the same kind of attentiveness and wonder, the same demand for awareness, the same will to seize the meaning of the world or of history as that meaning comes into being.'[5] There is a philosophically revolutionary concept here: that meaning is not something added to the world by consciousness, but something implicit which will become manifest to phenomenological observation and explicit in phenomenological description. This has strategic implications for the work of repossession and revolution that those involved in the consciousness movement are engaged upon: through observation and description they may expect those new facts *and meanings* to emerge that will trigger the paradigm and consciousness change that they want to effect.

For decades parapsychologists have been observing and describing a whole range of facts that from the point of view of the prevailing paradigm are anomalous, strange and novel. They may not always have succeeded in 'bracketing' their own perceptual and conceptual biases, but by now enough well-observed and well-described data have accumulated for their implicit meaning to become manifest. It is a meaning, moreover, that developments in theoretical physics and psychology, and in systems philosophy, corroborate. Bohm's concept of 'undivided wholeness', of 'a total order . . . implicit . . . in each region of space and time'; Jung's principle of synchronicity and of the meaningful interconnectedness of events in the collective unconscious and in the external world; the systems philosophy view of the hier- archical structural organisation of systems and sub-systems in living organisms: in these schematic formulations developed in different disciplines we begin to detect the lineaments of an emergent meaning that transcends and connects them. In phenomenological observation, wrote Merleau-Ponty, 'perspectives blend, perceptions confirm each other, a meaning emerges'.[6] Applied in the context of the present inquiry, this approach yields a meaning constituted by the principles of unity underlying diversity, wholeness, implicit order, inter- connectedness, reciprocity. The data and perspectives of psi research blend into this framework of meaning, support it and are supported by it, and thus cease to be, as they were for William James, 'con- textless and discontinuous'. The framework does not help explain how psi phenomena occur—the mechanics or dynamics of the processes involved are another problem—but it does make sense of the fact that they occur, which is a big step towards their contributing to the emergence of a new scientific paradigm and a new image of man.

In his book, *The New Religions*, which is a survey of the spread of Oriental religions and life-styles among the young in America in the 1960s, Jacob Needleman stresses the relevance of a cosmology to the quest for personal identity. 'If . . . the universe is unalive and indifferent, I will hope and work for something in myself quite different from what I will seek if the universe is laden with mind and life. I cannot with sanity search for radically new possibilities in my inner life unless there is a real place in the universe for them. . . . In sensing the vast order of the cosmos, I sense in myself and for myself possibilities beyond my imagining; for I am part of this order and I see that I do not understand it or myself. *At that moment I need knowledge that corresponds to this emotion*'[7] [my italics]. Here is a statement that makes explicit the connection between psi research and the counter culture. Psi research, together with the other areas of research and theory that it overlaps or merges with, provides the knowledge corresponding to the sense of a living and meaningful cosmos, a universal order, which in turn provides the motivation for the quest for new possibilities in the inner life.

To return now to the question of how individual consciousness expansion can contribute to the collective good: some relevant and suggestive evidence is afforded by Walter Pahnke's famous 'Good Friday Experiment', which is also an excellent example of how the phenomenological method can bring to light new facts and meanings. In 1966 Pahnke, a psychologist, used twenty Harvard theological students in 'an experimental examination of the claim that psychedelic drug experience may resemble mystical experience'.[8] All the subjects were given apparently identical capsules to swallow one and a half hours before attending a long religious service in a private chapel on Good Friday. Ten of the capsules contained the psychedelic drug psilocybin, and the other ten contained nicotinic acid, a vitamin that has no psychoactive effects but causes sensations of warmth and tingling of the skin. The object of the experiment was to see if the subjects who had taken the drug would respond differently to the religious service than the control group who were in an ordinary state of consciousness, and also to compare the subjective experiences of both groups with spontaneous mystical experience.

Comparison implies measurement, and the obvious problem with this type of experimental project is to find a yardstick for such a subjective thing as mystical experience. This is where the phenomenological method comes in. By studying a wide range of the literature of mysticism, Pahnke worked out 'a phenomenological typology of the mystical state of consciousness', which broke it down into nine categories as a basis for measurement. These were: a sense of unity, internal and external; transcendence of time and space; a deeply felt positive mood; a sense of sacredness; objectivity and reality (i.e. conviction that the experience is not a subjective delusion but the attainment of knowledge of an ultimate dimension of reality); paradoxicality (e.g. 'The "I" both exists and does not exist'); alleged ineffability; transiency; and finally 'persisting positive changes in attitude and behaviour (a) toward self, (b) toward others, (c) toward life and (d) toward the mystical experience itself'.[9]

Each subject participating in Pahnke's experiment recorded his individual reaction immediately after the service. During the following week he wrote an account of it and completed a 147-item questionnaire, which served as a basis for a recorded 90-minute interview. Six months later each subject completed another questionnaire and had another interview. At no stage in the experiment did any subject know whether he had been administered the psychedelic drug or the nicotinic acid, though when all the questionnaires, recordings and written accounts were analysed for their content and statistically evaluated it became clear that the two groups had undergone experiences that were qualitatively different both at the time and in their subsequent effects. The relative percentage scores of the two groups under the nine categories of the phenomenological typology of mystical experience were as follows (the percentage for the experimental group is given first): unity—62 and 7; transcendence of time and space—84 and 6; deeply felt positive mood—57 and 23; sacredness—53 and 28; objectivity and reality—63 and 18; paradoxicality—

61 and 13; ineffability—66 and 18; transiency—79 and 8; persisting positive changes in attitude and behaviour toward self—57 and 3, toward others—40 and 20, toward life—54 and 6. These figures not only support the experimental hypothesis that the psychedelic drug experience resembles spontaneous mystical experience, but also show that such experiences are not mere ego-satisfactions but positive life-enhancing experiences that can effect a permanent change in the orientation of attitudes.

Pahnke wrote about the ten subjects who had been given the drug: 'Although the psilocybin experience was unique and different from the "ordinary" reality of their everyday lives, these subjects felt that this experience had motivated them to appreciate more deeply the meaning of their lives, to gain more depth and authenticity in ordinary living, and to rethink their philosophies of life and values. The data did not suggest that any "ultimate" reality encountered had made "ordinary" reality no longer important or meaningful.' And on the subject of the socio-cultural implications of the experiment: 'Mysticism has been accused of fostering escapism from the problems of society, indifference to social conditions, and disinterest in social change. While the possibility of such excesses must always be remembered, our study has suggested the beneficial potential of mystical experience in stimulating the ability to feel and experience deeply and genuinely with the full harmony of both emotion and intellect. Such wholeness may have been neglected in modern Western society.'[10]

Maslow calls mystical experiences 'peak experiences', and his studies confirm Pahnke's finding that people who have such experiences are generally psychologically healthier and better integrated than 'non peakers', and that the peak experience often changes a person's view of himself, of other people and his relations to them, and of life and the world, in a positive way. The experience can also release in a person, says Maslow, greater creativity, spontaneity and expressiveness, enable him 'to dip into the unconscious and pre-conscious, to use and value their primary processes instead of fearing them'.[11] It also often produces in the experient a feeling of gratitude which 'leads to an all-embracing love for everybody and everything, to a perception of the world as beautiful, and good, often to an impulse to do something good for the world, an eagerness to repay, even a sense of obligation'.

These testimonies based on phenomenological studies show that the experience that a person undergoes in an altered state of consciousness can give him profounder self-knowledge and a broader philosophy of life than before and at the same time motivate him to engage in some positive mode of action in the world. Which suggests that cultivation of ASCs could be an important contribution to the strategy of repossession, both of the self and of the earth.

Charles Tart, the advocate of 'state-specific sciences', has drawn attention to and brought into the arena of public debate the question whether our normal, everyday rational state of consciousness is the best state for human beings to apply to tackling the problems of surviving on the planet and gaining knowledge of the universe. Participants in the consciousness movement would unanimously argue that it is not the best state, and some might support their contention with that apt quotation from *Proverbs*: 'Where there is no vision the people perish.' Rational consciousness, objective consciousness (which treats everything that is not self as an object) and 'single vision' can be held accountable for most of the political, economic, spiritual, psychological and social problems that threaten and perplex modern man. Instead of looking for solutions to these problems in terms of 'more of the same'—more and better technology, psychiatry, 'operant conditioning', 'man-management', rationality—would it not be preferable and more hopeful, since the problems arise from states of consciousness, to seek solutions by effecting changes at the level of consciousness?

It undoubtedly would, but it is one thing to propose such a project and quite another to carry it out. Any realistic strategy of repossession has to start with a clear understanding of the phenomenology of censorship in its biological, intellectual and social aspects. Maslow has stated the problem in a dramatic way in his chapter 'The Need to Know and the Fear of Knowing' in *Toward a Psychology of Being*: 'It is precisely the god-like in ourselves that we are ambivalent about, fascinated by and fearful of, motivated to and defensive against.'[12] The evidence surveyed in Part One of this book repeatedly suggested that though psi functions may be much more normal and continuous in human life than we realise, there is at work in us a kind of biological censor that suppresses and aborts them. It is generally assumed that the purpose of the censor is to preserve the integrity of the individual personality, and indeed it is easy to imagine that heightened psi functioning in the context of daily life would not be an unmitigated boon, and that to be clairvoyant, telepathic or precognitive all of the time would be to be subject to an inundation of impressions sufficient to disintegrate and incapacitate any personality. From this point of view it is easy to leap to the conclusion that the censor is a biologically wise function of the organism, that we shouldn't interfere with, and that the present-day interest in developing psi faculties constitutes an unwarranted and dangerous usurpation of the wisdom of the body and even of the will of God. Maslow's point that human beings tend to be ambivalent about and fearful of their higher functions and potentials needs to be borne in mind as a counter-balance to this kind of piety, and a plausible alternative conclusion would be that the present wave of interest in enhancing and con-trolling psi functions may be a case of the collective unconscious manifesting *its* wisdom and will towards species-survival.

It is by now a well-proven fact and even a cliché in psychological literature that perception is selective, or as the phenomenologists say 'intentional'. In 1959 a research team at the Massachusetts Institute of Technology conducted a famous experiment on the visual system of the frog, which is similar to that of human beings. Their report, published under the title 'What the Frog's Eye Tells the Frog's Brain', showed how out of hundreds of thousands of visual stimuli that could be presented to the frog's eye only four types registered and were transmitted as messages to the brain. The eye functioned only in order to select from the environment information relevant to the frog's survival, to escaping predators and obtaining food. Numerous other experiments since have demonstrated that sensory systems generally are information-reducing and -filtering mechanisms serving the survival needs of an organism within its environment. In other words, perceptual limitations are self-imposed and not in-herent in the sensory systems themselves, which are potentially capable of a far greater perceptual range. The same applies to human consciousness and its conceptual limitations. But man today does not exist in a state of homeostatic balance with his environment, and the real threats to his survival are not part of the informational feedback from his immediate environment. So to become aware of them and to combat them he needs to challenge and overcome the sovereignty of the biological censor, which served his survival needs well enough in less complex environmental conditions but in the ones currently prevailing only serves to subvert the purpose that it is designed to fulfil.

The supreme example of the censor at work on the collective, social level is to be found in official attitudes to and legislation against the use of psychoactive drugs. There seems little doubt that the use of both natural and synthetic types of such drugs is a phenomenon that has come to stay in our culture, and that in the future we shall see them increasingly used in private, in psychotherapy, in religious observances and for research purposes. Informed public discussion of the issues involved is essential in these circumstances, but up to now the debate has been vitiated by the fact that arguments both pro and contra have been ill-informed and have tended to revolve around questions of freedom and authority, conflicting life-styles ('pot is to the younger generation what alcohol is to the older'), addiction as a social problem, and various factitious 'moral' questions such as whether people have a right to cut-price mystical experience (the question whether they benefit from it is another matter, and can be investigated phenomenologically). The creation of the martyrs of the psychedelic movement, Timothy Leary and Richard Alpert, who on being sacked from their posts at Harvard embarked on more colourful careers as rebels and gurus (Alpert under the adopted name Baba Ram Dass), alerted the mass media to a source of sensational copy and further obscured the important questions posed by the increasing use of psychoactive drugs in our culture. It also led to panic legislation which managed at the same time to curtail the individual's right to explore his inner world and to put a stop to responsible scientific work in a developing area of research. It was not only Leary and Alpert's Harvard Psilocybin Project that was halted, but also further research by such pioneers as Walter Pahnke and the husband and wife team of Robert Masters and Jean Houston, whose highly informative and intelligent book, *The Varieties of Psychedelic*

Experience, reports and discusses valuable research that fortunately was able to be completed before the axe fell. For anyone who is aware of the extent to which research with psychoactive drugs has contributed to man's knowledge of his own psyche and to the methodology of psychotherapy, it is difficult to regard the blanket ban on their use otherwise than as a case of the biological censor's indiscriminate and short-sighted rejection mechanism at work at the societal level.

Of course the psychedelics are dangerous. The term means 'mind-manifesting', and for too much subconscious material to erupt too suddenly into consciousness, by whatever means, is always dangerous. Everyone has read in newspapers and magazines horror stories about 'bad trips'. And addiction, too, is a hazard, though discussion of the problem it poses is generally muddled by people attributing addictive properties to the drug when they should be considering the dependency syndrome of the addict. The dangers of the psychoactive drugs should neither be minimised nor sensationalised, but should be clearly understood and guarded against, as are other dangerous substances and forces that civilised man uses. The importance of 'set and setting' (preparation and environment), of prior psychological screening and of expert supervision throughout the drug session, has been stressed by several writers on the subject (see Masters and Houston, Robert S. De Ropp's *Drugs and the Mind* and *The Master Game*, W. V. Caldwell's *LSD Psychotherapy*) and need not be elaborated on here. The important point is that the drug experience, when it is undergone in a spirit of exploration and not just for 'kicks', and when its emotional impact is assimilated to a correspondingly broad interpretative philosophical framework, is a remarkably effective means of expanding consciousness, transcending egocentricity and positively reorientating thinking and living patterns. Comparing drug-induced mystical experiences with those obtained by the traditional arduous disciplinary methods, Masters and Houston have observed that whereas the latter involve a process of emptying the mind of all its empirical content and making consciousness virtually a vacuum, the opposite happens in the drug experience. 'Consciousness expands and reaches outward to encompass a wealth of phenomena unprecedented in the subject's experience.'[13] On the basis of their own research work with six subjects who had mystical experiences under drugs, they reached a significant conclusion: 'The beneficial effect of the psychedelic mystical experience . . . was to take the subject through a process of experiencing Essence in such a way that it illuminated all of existence, making him more interested in and responsive to the phenomena of existence than he had been before. Thus, instead of retreating from the phenomenal world, as often occurs with the traditional mystic, the psychedelic subject was inspired by the process of his experience to a kind of flight *towards* reality.'[14]

This confirms Walter Pahnke's finding that the ten subjects who were given psilocybin in his 'Good Friday Experiment' had a profound experience which lastingly invested their lives with a greater sense of meaning, authenticity and depth. Such data prompt the consideration that the expertly monitored and guided psychedelic trip may be the approach to mystical experience most appropriate to Western man, not only because it is relatively quick and easy but also because, with its wealth of experiential content and consequent tendency to return a person to the plane of ordinary reality with enhanced appreciation and motivation, it harmonises with the Westerner's preference for involvement with the phenomenal world, as opposed to the Easterner's tendency towards rejection and withdrawal.

The etymology of the word 'sanity' suggests the meaning 'healthy-mindedness', but the word is invariably used with the covert meaning of 'right-mindedness', and the concept of 'right' in its turn is pragmatically debased to stand for that which conforms, least disturbs the status quo, smooths over conflicts and anxieties and minimises problems. The prevailing criteria of health, both mental and physical in Western societies are hopelessly ad hoc and confused. Thomas Merton has some pertinent reflections on the subject in his essay 'A Devout Meditation in Memory of Adolf Eichmann': 'I am beginning to realize that "sanity" is no longer a value or an end in itself. The "sanity" of modern man is about as useful to him as the huge bulk and muscles of the dinosaur. If he were a little less sane, a little more doubtful, a little more aware of his absurdities and contradictions, perhaps there might be a possibility of his survival.'[15] In other words, to think of sanity in terms of adjustment is itself a form of insanity, for to be well adjusted to a world that is headed towards suicide is the ultimate infirmity of mind. And perhaps to seek temporary unbalance and disintegration with a view to re-integrating on the farther side of extended awareness is a counsel of ultimate sanity. Mircea Eliade repeatedly points out in his classic study *Shamanism: Archaic Techniques of Ecstasy*, that the shaman, the holy man of primitive societies who possessed paranormal powers of divination and healing, was generally *a sick man who had managed to cure himself*. And Andrew Weil, in *The Natural Mind*, has made a provocative contribution to the debate by pointing out that there are such things as 'positive paranoia', 'positive neurosis' and 'positive psychosis', and even goes so far as to claim that psychotics may be 'the evolutionary vanguard of our species' for 'they possess the secret of changing reality by changing the mind'.[16] It is a dubious proposition, perhaps, but it is a good line of propagandist argument which raises some of the profounder questions that the drug debate should revolve around.

Weil predicts that the 'revolution in consciousness that will transform human society . . . will be a change from straight to stoned thinking on a grand scale'.[17] As he is one of the more lucidly articulate spokesmen of the counter culture, it is worth examining what he means, and the first thing to note is that he is talking about *thinking*, i.e. a way of using the mind, and not proposing that the transformation of society will come about through people getting 'stoned' on drugs. 'Straight' thinking he defines as characterised by a tendency to know things through the intellect only, to depend on sense-mediated information and therefore to pay more attention to outward forms than to inner contents, which leads to materialism. 'Straight' thinking also tends to be discriminating and separatist, to focus on the differences between phenomena instead of on their similarities, particularly the differences between self and not-self, and such egocentricity inevitably leads to negative thinking, pessimism and despair. Above all, 'straight' thinking is 'unmodified by interaction with our unconscious life'.[18] 'Stoned' thinking, in Weil's definition, is not, as the term might suggest, wild and deranged, but is characterised by balance, the coordination of intellect with intuition and imagination, acceptance of ambivalence and anomaly as part of the nature of things, unitive consciousness, and the 'experience of infinity in its positive aspect', which fosters optimism, a sense of life's infinite possibilities and the realisation that 'the only limits we encounter in the world around us are those we first create in our imagination'.

It will be clear from these definitions that 'stoned' thinking is not a mental mode exclusive of the beneficiaries of chemical illumination, but is shared also by poets, artists in all fields, some philosophers and scientists and a multitude of 'ordinary' mature people. The momentum of the consciousness movement itself in our day is evidence that such thinking is not rare or the privilege of a handful of illuminati or evolutionary mutants, but the fact remains that what Weil calls 'straight' thinking is the predominant mentality in our society at the *institutional* level, in politics and international relations, in education, in industry and economics, in health care and delivery systems, in science, and in law enactment and enforcement agencies, to specify a few examples. In most of these areas in recent years innovations deriving from the 'stoned' thinking paradigm have surfaced and had an influence, but it is in the nature of institutions to be self-perpetuating and resistant to change, and for decisive breakthroughs and radical reorientations to be made will require a consciousness shift, as Weil says, 'on a grand scale'.

Humanistic psychology stresses the importance of the self-image to the process of growth. How we regard ourselves and our relationships is the key factor in determining what we can become. This is as relevant to the dynamics of social change as to the process of individual growth; it must start from a redefined image of man. Everything that contributes to this work of redefinition needs to be given maximum publicity, and that includes parapsychology and the convergent areas of anthropology, modern theoretical physics and Jungian and transpersonal psychology. The situation has greatly improved since 1964, when the psychologist S. Koch launched a bitter attack on his profession, stating that 'modern psychology has projected an image of man which is as demeaning as it is simplistic', and deploring the fact that psychologists had tended to abet rather than combat a cultural trend towards 'mass dehumanization . . . the simplification of sensibility, homogenization of experience, attenuation of the capacity for experience',[19] while scientists and scholars in other fields—physicists, biologists, philosophers, historians, humanists—were effectively working against this trend. The situation has considerably improved in psychology itself with the development of the 'Fourth Force' and of the holistic approaches of Gestalt therapy and psychosynthesis, and of powerful new technologies which have given man unprecedented knowledge of and control over his inner world—biofeedback, chemopsychiatry, electronic means of monitoring physiological processes, brain activity and the dream state—and we have today the knowledge, the hard facts, out of which to synthesise a new and revolutionary image of man-in-the-universe. No longer can such facts be dismissed as the product of man's incorrigible omnipotence fantasy or as residual concepts of an anachronistic Renaissance humanism, for they are demonstrably true. To assimilate these truths and this new image, to take them to heart and to mind, to live by them, as individuals and as a society, to let them influence the ways we interact with each other and with our environment, to base our values and priorities upon them, would be to consummate the hoped for 'Copernican revolution of the mind'. In man's battle for repossession of the earth and of the relinquished areas of his own self, image-change is the strategy of strategies.

Any revolution needs a manifesto, a prospectus, a programme and a carefully thought-out strategy that takes into account the realities of the situation it seeks to change. In 1973 the Center for the Study of Social Policy at the Stanford Research Institute in California produced a document which fulfils all these functions. Entitled *Changing Images of Man*, it was prepared by an interdisciplinary team of scientists and scholars for the Charles F. Kettering Foundation of Dayton, Ohio. At once lucid, comprehensive, authoritative, balanced and visionary, it must qualify as the classic of 'think tank' literature and could be to the countercultural revolution of our day what the *Manifesto* of Marx and Engels was to the Communist revolution.

In their Introduction, the authors state, 'At various times in history, man's image of himself was shaped by mythology, philosophy, and religion. In our contemporary culture, science has added a dominant formative contribution to our conception of the nature of the human being—through biology and life sciences, physics, psychology, brain research, evolutionary theory, and the growing investigation of consciousness states and parapsychological phenomena.'[20] From the data supplied by these contributions, they ask, 'Could an image of humankind emerge that might shape the future, as the currently dominant images—man as the master of nature, inhabitant of a material world, and consumer of goods—our legacy of the past, have shaped our present culture? Could such a new image provide the bridge to carry us safely over to a post-industrial age?' They not only believe that it could, but that such an image is already emergent and is manifested in: 'youth involvement in political processes; women's liberation movement, black consciousness, etc.; youth "rebellion" against societal wrongs; emerging interest in the social responsibility of business; the "generation gap" implying a changing paradigm; the anti-technological bias of many young people; experimentation with new family structures and interpersonal relationships; the emergence of communes as alternative life styles; the conservation / ecology movement; a surge of interest in Eastern religions and philosophical perspectives; a renewed interest in "fundamentalist" Christianity; labor union concerns with the quality of the work environment; an increasing interest in meditation and other spiritual disciplines; and the increasing importance of "self-realization" processes.'[21] All these disparate trends, they suggest, imply 'an emphasis on cooperation over competition, ecological interdependence over exploitation, psychological-spiritual growth over material acquisition, and an integration of intuitive knowledge processes with more rational modes'. From these social trends and reversals of priorities, together with the factual and theoretical contributions of the modern sciences, the authors maintain that it is possible to formulate a sketch of the new image and to specify some of its characteristics.

To be consistent with the new directions in science, and at the same time to be socially effective in the post-industrial future, the new image would have to:

'1. Convey a *holistic sense* of perspective or understanding of life;
2. Entail an *ecological ethic*, emphasising the total community of life-in-nature and the oneness of the human race;

215

3. Entail a *self-realization ethic*, placing the highest value on development of selfhood and declaring that an appropriate function of all social institutions is the fostering of human development;

4. Be *multi-leveled, multi-faceted*, and *integrative*, accommodating various culture and personality types;

5. Involve *balancing* and *coordination* of *satisfactions* along many dimensions rather than the maximizing of concerns along one narrowly defined dimension (e.g., economic); and

6. Be *experimental, open-ended, and evolutionary.*'[22]

This catalogue of some of the abstract characteristics of the new image of man-in-the-universe would immediately be faulted by any philosopher committed to the Western empiricist tradition, for it contravenes one of the axioms of that tradition, that descriptive and normative statements are different and unconnected, and that therefore you cannot derive an 'ought' from an 'is'. To charge the authors with philosophical naivety, however, would itself be naive, for their integrative, holistic approach necessarily implies a rejection of the descriptive/normative distinction and the problem of the arbitrariness of values that follows from it. This is not particularly original or revolutionary, except in the context of academic philosophical debate. People who are not inhibited by the scruples of empiricist philosophers (and probably such philosophers themselves when they're off duty) have no compunction about basing their values on the description of reality that hold to be true, i.e. deriving an 'ought' from an 'is'. To state that because man, nature and cosmos and their interrelations are such-and-such, man ought to behave in such-and-such ways, may not be strictly logical, but it is how human beings behave. Our goals and values, what we live, work and hope for, are determined, as Needleman says, by our cosmology and beliefs about the nature of reality. Implicit in any description of reality are prescriptions as to how man should conduct himself in relation to it. The Stanford Research Institute Report argues—and it has been the purpose of the present book to present some of the evidence supporting this argument—that modern descriptive sciences, both the life sciences and the mind sciences, combine to create an integrative paradigm of man, nature and cosmos which supersedes the divisive, mechanistic, causal, materialistic paradigm that has prevailed in our culture to date, and which, moreover, implies an ethic composed of two complementary and mutually-reinforcing principles, an 'ecological ethic' and a 'self-realization ethic'. According to this view, repossession of the earth and of the self are parallel projects, the one implying the other; a man may start with either and, provided that in working at it he retains the basic gnosis of the *cosmos*, the universal order, accomplish both.

At another time of upheaval and transition in the history of the Western world a philosopher who was greatly puzzled by the nature of man and the problem of his place and function in the universe invented a creation myth that expressed both his puzzlement and his aspirations. The time was the Renaissance, the philosopher Pico della Mirandola, and the myth was contained in his discourse *On the Dignity of Man*. God, he proposed, first made the world and all its flora and fauna, and then decided to create man because He 'desired that there should be someone to reckon up the reason for such a big work, to love its beauty and to wonder at its greatness. . . . Therefore He took up man, a work of indeterminate form; and, placing him at the midpoint of the world, He spoke to him as follows: "We have given thee, Adam, no fixed seat, no form of thy very own, no gift peculiarly thine, that thou mayest feel as thine own, have as thine own, possess as thine own the seat, the form, the gifts which thou thyself shalt desire. . . . Thou, like a judge appointed for being honourable, art the moulder and maker of thyself; thou mayest sculpt thyself into whatever shape thou dost prefer. Thou canst grow downwards into the lower natures which are brutes. Thou canst again grow upward from thy soul's reason into higher natures which are divine."[23]

This image of man as free and self-determining, as potentially both brute and divinity, this insight into the fact that his existential situation constitutes a challenge to his consciousness and his will, is as relevant to us as it was to Pico's contemporaries. What has changed since the Renaissance is the fact that today our very survival as a species on the face of the earth depends on the choice we make, on the self-image we sculpt, on the extent to which we base our lives

—personal, interpersonal, and institutional—on the rediscovered vision of the symbiotic order of man, nature and cosmos. We have the relevant knowledge, the technologies, and a plausible strategy to accomplish the 'Copernican revolution of the mind' on which not only further evolution but survival itself depends. It remains to be seen whether we also have the imagination and the will.

Notes and References

INTRODUCTION: THE NEW GNOSIS

1. Edgar Mitchell, *Psychic Exploration: A Challenge for Science* (G. P. Putnam, New York, 1974)
2. June & Nicholas Regush, *Psi: The Other World Catalogue* (G. P. Putnam, New York, 1974)
3. Elmer Green, Alyce Green & E. Dale Walters, *Alpha-Theta Biofeedback Training* (Research Department, Menninger Foundation, Topeka, Kansas)
4. Elmer & Alyce Green, *Mind Training, ESP, Hypnosis, and Voluntary Control of Internal States* (Academy of Parapsychology & Medicine, Los Altos, California)
5. Henry Morgenau, *ESP in the Framework of Modern Science* (in Smythies (ed.), *Science and ESP*, Routledge & Kegan Paul, London, 1967)
6. Thomas S. Kuhn, *The Structure of Scientific Revolutions* (University of Chicago Press, 1962)
7. Carlos Castaneda, *The Teachings of Don Juan, A Separate Reality, Journey to Ixtlan, Tales of Power* (various editions available, see Notes to Chapter Eight)
8. For information on Gnosticism on this and succeeding pages I have drawn on Hans Jonas's *The Gnostic Religion* (Beacon Press, Boston, 1958 and 1963)
9. Translation by Smith Eli Jolliffe. Quoted in Herbert Silberer, *Hidden Symbolism of Alchemy and the Occult Arts* (Dover Publications, New York, 1971)
10. From Thomas Taylor's translation of Plotinus, *The Enneads*
11. Blaise Pascal, *Pensées*, Fragment 692, translated by William Finlayson Trotter
12. Jean-Paul Sartre, *Existentialism and Humanism*
13. Quoted in Carl Rogers, *The Emerging Person: A New Revolution* (privately circulated paper)
14. Simon and Trout, *Hippies in College: from Teenyboppers to Drug Freaks* (Trans-Action No. 5, 1967)
15. Robert Houriet, *Getting Back Together* (Abacus, London, 1973)
16. Theodore Roszak, *Where the Wasteland Ends* (Doubleday, New York, 1972; Faber and Faber, London, 1973)
17. U Thant, *Challenge of a Decade: Global Development or Global Breakdown* (U.N. Centre for Economic and Social Information, New York, 1969)

PART ONE

I: THE DREAM OF REASON

1. Descartes' account of his dreams may be found in Raymond de Becker, *Understanding of Dreams* (Allen & Unwin, London, 1968)
2. René Descartes, 'The Passions of the Soul' (in N. Kemp Smith, *Descartes' Philosophical Writings*, Macmillan, London, 1952)
3. Joseph Jastrow, in Carl Murchison ed., *The Case For and Against Psychical Research* (Oxford University Press, 1927)

2: THE SLOW FUSE

1. Thomas Huxley, *Report on Spiritualism of the Committee of the London Dialectical Society* (London, 1871)
2. Frederic W. H. Myers, *Proceedings of the S.P.R.*, XV (1901)
3. For the facts and figures reported in these pages on the early work of the S.P.R. I am indebted to Alan Gauld, *The Founders of Psychical Research* (Routledge & Kegan Paul, London, 1968)
4. Ian Stevenson, *Twenty Cases Suggestive of Reincarnation* (American Society for Psychical Research, 1966)
5. Charles Richet, *Thirty Years of Psychical Research* (Macmillan, New York, 1923)
6. G. N. M. Tyrrell, *Presidential Address* (*Proceedings of the S.P.R.*, 47, 1945)
7. Frederic W. H. Myers, *Human Personality and its Survival of Bodily Death* (Longmans, Green & Co., London 1906; University Books, New York)

3: INTER-PSYCHIC COMMUNICATION

1. Manuel Córdova-Rios & F. Bruce Lamb, *Wizard of the Upper Amazon* (Athenaeum, New York, 1971). The full text of this narrative is quoted in Andrew Weil, *The Natural Mind* (Houghton Mifflin Co., Boston, 1973)
2. J. B. Rhine, *Extra-Sensory Perception* (Bruce Humphries, Boston, 1934)
3. Rosalind Heywood, *The Infinite Hive* (Chatto & Windus, London, 1964)
4. Berthold Eric Schwarz, *Parent-Child Telepathy* (Garrett Publications, New York, 1971)
5. Douglas Dean, 'Plethysmograph Recordings as ESP Responses' (*International Journal of Neuropsychiatry*, 1966)
6. Charles T. Tart, 'Physiological Correlates of Psi Cognition' (*International Journal of Parapsychology*, Vol. 5, 1963)

7. Puthoff & Targ, 'Information Transmission under Conditions of Sensory Shielding' (*Nature*, 1974)
8. Charles Honorton, *Psi Mediation and the Regulation of Sensory Input* (Maimonides Medical Center, New York)
9. Charles Honorton, *op. cit.*
10. Charles Honorton, *op. cit.*
11. Ullman, Krippner & Vaughan, *Dream Telepathy* (Turnstone Books, London, 1974)
12. Krippner & Davidson, *The Use of Convergent Operations in Bio-Information Research* (Maimonides Medical Center, New York)
13. Gardner Murphy, 'A Qualitative Study of Telepathic Phenomena' (*Journal of the A.S.P.R.*, 52, 1962)

4: THE 'PSYCHIC EYE'

1. Pieter van der Hurk & V. John Burggraf, *Psychic, The Story of Peter Hurkos* (Bobbs-Merrill Co., New York, 1961)
2. Andrija Puharich, *Beyond Telepathy* (Doubleday Anchor Books, New York, 1973)
3. Andrija Puharich, *op. cit.*
4. Lawrence LeShan, *The Medium, the Mystic and the Physicist* (Viking Press, New York, 1974)
5. Ludwig Wittgenstein, *Tractatus Logico-Philosophicus*
6. Andrija Puharich, *op. cit.*
7. Charles T. Tart, *Out of the Body Experiences* (in Mitchell (ed.), *Psychic Exploration*, Putnam, New York, 1974)
8. Charles T. Tart, *op. cit.*
9. Rex G. Stanford, *Clairvoyance* (in Mitchell (ed.), *Psychic Exploration*, Putnam, New York, 1974)
10. Glick & Kogen, 'Clairvoyance in Hypnotized Subjects: Some Positive Results' (*Journal of Parapsychology*, 35, 1971)
11. L. E. Levinson, 'Hypnosis—Key to Latent Psi Faculties' (*International Journal of Parapsychology*, 10, 1968)

5: MIND OUT OF TIME

1. H. C. Berendt, *Parapsychology in Israel* (in *Parapsychology Today: A Geographic View*, Parapsychology Foundation, New York, 1973)
2. Herbert B. Greenhouse, *Premonitions: A Leap into the Future* (Turnstone Books, London, 1972)
3. Herbert B. Greenhouse, *op. cit.*
4. C. G. Jung, *Man and His Symbols* (Aldus Books, London, 1964)
5. Douglas Dean, *Precognition and Retrocognition* (in Mitchell (ed.), *Psychic Exploration*, Putnam, New York, 1974)
6. Walter F. Prince, *Journal of the A.S.P.R.*, 17, (1923)

7. Walter F. Prince, *op. cit.*
8. Ian Stevenson, 'Precognitions of Disasters' (*Journal of the A.S.P.R.*, 64, 1970)
9. Ian Stevenson, *op. cit.*
10. Ian Stevenson, *op. cit.*
11. J. C. Barker, 'Premonitions of the Aberfan Disaster' (*Journal of the S.P.R.*, 44, 1967)
12. *Medical News-Tribune*, Jan 20, 1967. Quoted in Greenhouse, *op. cit.*
13. W. E. Cox, 'Precognition: An Analysis' (*Journal of the A.S.P.R.*, 50, 1956)
14. S. G. Soal and F. Bateman, *Modern Experiments in Telepathy* (Faber and Faber, London, 1954)
15. Helmut Schmidt, *Instrumentation in the Parapsychology Laboratory* (in Beloff (ed.), *New Directions in Parapsychology*, Elek Science, London, 1975)
16. Brier and Tyminski, 'Psi Application' (*International Journal of Parapsychology*, 34, 1970)
17. Ullman, Krippner & Honorton, 'A Second Precognitive Dream Study with Malcolm Bessent' (*Journal of the A.S.P.R.*, 66, 1972)
18. Ullman, Krippner & Honorton, *op. cit.*
19. Puthoff and Targ, *Psychic Research and Modern Physics* (in Mitchell (ed.), *Psychic Exploration*, Putnam, New York, 1974)
20. The Kipling anecdote is from William Oliver Stevens, *The Mystery of Dreams* (Allen and Unwin, London, 1950)
21. Keith Floyd, *Of Time and Mind: From Paradox to Paradigm* (in White (ed.), *Frontiers of Consciousness*, Julian Press, New York, 1974)
22. Eileen Garrett, *Adventures in the Supernormal* (Creative Age Press, New York, 1949). Quoted in LeShan, *The Medium, the Mystic and the Physicist* (Viking Press, New York, 1974)
23. Alan Vaughan, *Patterns of Prophesy* (Turnstone Books, London, 1974)
24. Robert Ornstein, *The Psychology of Consciousness* (W. H. Freeman & Co., San Francisco, 1972)
25. Puthoff and Targ, *op. cit.*
26. Puthoff and Targ, *op. cit.*

6: MIND OVER MATTER

1. Hans Bender. Communication from an informal talk to the Institute of Parascience Annual Conference, London, 1975
2. Milbourne Christopher, *Mediums, Mystics and the Occult* (Thomas Y. Crowell Co., New York, 1975)
3. John Hasted, *My Geller Notebook* (unpublished manuscript)
4. John Hasted, *op. cit.*
5. John Taylor, *Superminds* (Macmillan, London, 1975)

6. John Taylor, *op. cit.*
7. John Hasted, *op. cit.*
8. W. Grey Walter, *Observations on Man, His Frame, His Duty and His Expectations* (Cambridge University Press, 1969)
9. W. Grey Walter, *op. cit.*
10. C. Brookes-Smith and D. W. Hunt, 'Some Experiments in PK (*Journal of the S.P.R.*, 45, 1970)
11. Hans Bender, *Modern Poltergeist Research* (in Beloff (ed.), *New Directions in Parapsychology*, Elek Science, London, 1975)
12. Hans Bender, *op. cit.*
13. John Randall, *Biological Aspects of Psi* (in Beloff (ed.), *New Directions in Parapsychology*, Elek Science, London, 1975)
14. Dr Justa Smith, *Bioenergetics in Healing* (in Carlson (ed.), *The Frontiers of Science and Medicine*, Wildwood House, London, 1975)
15. J. B. Rhine and Louisa Rhine, 'The Psychokinetic Effect: 1. The First Experiment' (*Journal of Parapsychology* 7, 1943)
16. Helmut Schmidt, *Psychokinesis* (in Mitchell (ed.), *Psychic Exploration*, Putnam, New York, 1974)
17. Helmut Schmidt, *op. cit.*

PART TWO

7: PSI AND SCIENCE

1. Quoted by Bob Brier in *Methodology in Parapsychology and other Sciences* (in *Parapsychology and the Sciences*, Parapsychology Foundation, New York, 1974)
2. Henry Sidgwick, *Second Presidential Address* (*Proceedings of the S.P.R.* 1, 1882–83)
3. Hans Bender, *Modern Poltergeist Research* (see Chapter Six, Note 11)
4. Quoted by Henry Morgenau in *Methodology in Psi Research* (Parapsychology Foundation, New York, 1970)
5. Arthur Koestler, *The Roots of Coincidence* (Hutchinson, London, 1972)
6. Cyril Burt, *Psychology and Parapsychology* (in Smythies (ed.), *Science and ESP*, Routledge & Kegan Paul, London, 1967)
7. Jule Eisenbud, 'Psi and the Nature of Things' (*International Journal of Parapsychology*, 5, 1963)
8. William Roll. Contribution to an open discussion at the 1971 Parapsychology Foundation Annual Conference (in *A Century of Psychical Research*, Parapsychology Foundation, New York, 1971)
9. Werner Heisenberg, *Physics and Philosophy* (Allen and Unwin, London, 1959)
10. Cyril Burt, *op. cit.*

11. Charles Tart, *States of Consciousness and State-Specific Sciences* (in Ornstein (ed.), *The Nature of Human Consciousness*, W. H. Freeman & Co., San Francisco, 1973)
12. Charles Tart, *op. cit.*
13. Werner Heisenberg, *op. cit.*
14. Cyril Burt, *op. cit.*
15. Thomas S. Kuhn, *The Structure of Scientific Revolutions* (University of Chicago Press, 1962 and 1970)
16. Thomas S. Kuhn, *op. cit.*

8: CULTURAL CONSTRUCTS

1. Joan Halifax-Grof, 'Hex Death' (in *Parapsychology and Anthropology*, Parapsychology Foundation, New York, 1974)
2. Joan Halifax-Grof, *op. cit.*
3. Adrian Boshier, 'African Apprenticeship' (in *Parapsychology and Anthropology*, Parapsychology Foundation, New York, 1974)
4. Adrian Boshier, *op. cit.*
5. Adrian Boshier, *op. cit.*
6. Guy Playfair, *The Flying Cow* (Souvenir Press, London, 1975)
7. Lyall Watson, 'Is Primitive Medicine Really Primitive?' (in Carlson (ed.), *The Frontiers of Science and Medicine*, Wildwood House, London, 1975)
8. Guy Playfair, *op. cit.*
9. Guy Playfair, *op. cit.*
10. Guy Playfair, *op. cit.*
11. Guy Playfair, *op. cit.*
12. Carlos Castaneda, *The Teachings of Don Juan* (University of California Press, 1968; Penguin Books, London, 1970)
13. Carlos Castaneda, *op. cit.*
14. Carlos Castaneda, *Tales of Power* (Simon and Schuster, New York, 1974; Hodder and Stoughton, London, 1975)
15. Carlos Castaneda, *op. cit.*
16. Carlos Castaneda, *op. cit.*
17. Carlos Castaneda, *A Separate Reality* (Simon and Schuster, New York; The Bodley Head, London, 1971)
18. Carlos Castaneda, *op. cit.*
19. Carlos Castaneda, *op. cit.*
20. Carlos Castaneda, *op. cit.*
21. Carlos Castaneda, *op. cit.*
22. Carlos Castaneda, *op. cit.*
23. Carlos Castaneda, *op. cit.*
24. Carlos Castaneda, *The Teachings of Don Juan*
25. Carlos Castaneda, *op. cit.*

26. Carlos Castaneda, *A Separate Reality*
27. Carlos Castaneda, *Journey to Ixtlan* (Simon and Schuster, New York, 1972; The Bodley Head, London, 1973)
28. Carlos Castaneda, *The Teachings of Don Juan*
29. Carlos Castaneda, *Tales of Power*

9: THE NEW SCIENCES

1. Evan Harris Walker, *Consciousness and Quantum Theory* (in Mitchell, (ed.), *Psychic Exploration*, Putnam, New York, 1974)
2. Werner Heisenberg, *Physics and Philosophy* (Allen and Unwin, London, 1959)
3. J. A. Wheeler, *Superspace and Quantum Geometrodynamics* (Academic Press, New York, 1962)
4. Toben, Sarfatti and Wolf, *Space-Time and Beyond* (E. P. Dutton & Co., New York, 1975)
5. John B. Hasted, *My Geller Diary* (unpublished manuscript)
6. Brendan O'Regan, *The Emergence of Paraphysics* (in Mitchell (ed.), *Psychic Exploration*, Putnam, New York, 1974)
7. David Bohm, *Quantum Theory as an Indication of a New Order in Physics* (in *Foundations of Physics* 3, 1973, and quoted in O'Regan, *op. cit.*)
8. Lawrence LeShan, *The Medium, the Mystic and the Physicist* (Viking Press, New York, 1974)
9. Z. Rejdák, 'Psychotronics: The State of the Art' (in *The Parasciences: Impact of Science on Society*, UNESCO, Vol. XXIV, 1975)
10. A. Dubrov, 'Biogravitation and Psychotronics' (in *The Parasciences*)
11. A. Dubrov, *op. cit.*
12. Sir John Eccles, *The Neurophysiological Basis of Mind* (Oxford, 1953). Quoted in Koestler, *The Roots of Coincidence*, Hutchinson, London, 1972
13. A. Dubrov, *op. cit.*
14. Elmer Green. From my own notes made at the May Lectures, London, 1974 (see Holroyd, *The May Lectures*, in Carlson (ed.) *Frontiers of Science and Medicine*, Wildwood House, London, 1975)
15. Jack Schwarz. Also from my *May Lectures* notes
16. Swami Rama. Also from my *May Lectures* notes

10: PSI AND PSYCHOLOGY

1. Freud, *Psychoanalysis and Telepathy* (in Devereux (ed.), *Psychoanalysis and the Occult*, International Universities Press, New York, 1953; Souvenir Press, London, 1974)
2. Emilio Servadio, *Psychoanalysis and Parapsychology* (in Devereux (ed.), *op. cit.*, Note 1 above)

3. George Devereux, *ESP and Psychoanalytic Epistemology* (in Devereux (ed.), *op. cit.*, Note 1 above)
4. Freud, *Dreams and Telepathy* (in Devereux (ed.), *op. cit.*, Note 1 above)
5. Ervin Laszlo, *Introduction to Systems Philosophy* (Gordon and Breach, New York, 1972)
6. Ervin Laszlo, *op. cit.*
7. Quoted in Panati, *Supersenses* (Quadrangle, New York, 1974; Cape, London, 1975). A personal communication from Dr LeShan
8. L. L. Whyte, *The Unconscious Before Freud* (Tavistock Publication, London, 1962)
9. Goethe. Quoted by Whyte, *op. cit.*
10. L. L. Whyte, *op. cit.*
11. Freud, *op. cit.*, Note 1 above
12. Jung, *Memories, Dreams, Reflections*, ed. A. Jaffe, trans. R. & C. Winston (Routledge and Collins, London, 1963)
13. Jung, *op. cit.*
14. Jung, *Synchronicity: An Acausal Connecting Principle* (in Collected Works, Vol. 8, Bollingen Foundation, New York; Routledge & Kegan Paul, London, 1960)
15. Leibniz, *The Monadology*. (Quoted in Progoff, *Jung, Synchronicity and Human Destiny*, Julian Press, New York, 1973)
16. Jung, *Synchronicity*
17. Jung, *Civilization in Transition* (in Collected Works, Vol. 10)
18. Jung, *Synchronicity*
19. Henry Morgenau, *ESP in the Framework of Modern Science* (in Smythies (ed.), *Science and ESP*, Routledge & Kegan Paul, London, 1967)
20. Quoted by Roberto Assagiolo, 'The New Dimensions of Psychology' (in *Human Dimensions*, Vol. 3, Human Dimensions Institute, Buffalo, New York, 1974)

CONCLUSION: CONSCIOUSNESS EXPANSION
AND THE STRATEGY OF REPOSSESSION

1. D. H. and D. L. Meadows and Others, *The Limits to Growth* (Universe Books, New York, 1972)
2. Quoted by Herbert Weiner, 'Mystical Phenomena of our Day and the Kabbalah' (in *A Century of Psychical Research*, Parapsychology Foundation, New York, 1971)
3. B. F. Skinner, *Beyond Freedom and Dignity* (Jonathan Cape, London, 1972; Alfred Knopf Inc., New York, 1971)
4. Sam Keen, *To a Dancing God* (Harper and Row, New York, 1970)
5. Maurice Merleau-Ponty, *Phenomenology of Perception* (Routledge & Kegan Paul, London; Humanities Press, New York)

NOTES AND REFERENCES

6. Maurice Merleau-Ponty, *op. cit.*
7. Jacob Needleman, *The New Religions* (Doubleday, New York, 1970)
8. W. Pahnke, *Drugs and Mysticism*, in Aaronson and Osmond (eds.), *Psychedelics* (Doubleday, New York, 1970; Hogarth Press, London, 1971)
9. W. Pahnke, *op. cit.*
10. W. Pahnke, *op. cit.*
11. Abraham Maslow, *Toward a Psychology of Being* (Litton Educational Publishing Inc., New York, 1968)
12. Abraham Maslow, *op. cit.*
13. R. E. L. Masters and Jean Houston, *The Varieties of Psychedelic Experience* (Holt, Rinehart & Winston Inc., New York; Turnstone Books, London, 1973; Second British Edition)
14. R. E. L. Masters and Jean Houston, *op. cit.*
15. Thomas Merton. Quoted in Claudio Naranjo, *The One Quest* (The Viking Press Inc., New York, 1972; Wildwood House, London, 1972)
16. Andrew Weil, *The Natural Mind* (Houghton Mifflin Co., Boston, 1972; Jonathan Cape, London, 1973)
17. Andrew Weil, *op. cit.*
18. Andrew Weil, *op. cit.*
19. S. Koch, *Psychology and Emerging Conceptions of Knowledge as Unitary* (in Wann (ed.), *Behaviourism and Phenomenology*, University of Chicago Press, 1964)
20. O. W. Markley and Others, *Changing Images of Man* (Stanford Research Institute, California, 1973)
21. O. W. Markley and Others, *op. cit.*
22. O. W. Markley and Others, *op. cit.*
23. Pico della Mirandola, *On the Dignity of Man* (trans. Wallis, Bobbs-Merrill Co., New York, 1965)

INDEX

Index

231